# Personality Development and Soft Skills

## Preparing for Tomorrow

# Personality Development and Soft Skills

## Preparing for Tomorrow

**Shikha Kapoor**

*Professor*

Human Resource and Organisational Behaviour
Amity International Business School
Amity University
Noida (UP)

TECHSAR™

NEW DELHI

*Published and Printed by*

Techsar Pvt. Ltd.
4435-36/7, Ansari Road, Daryaganj
New Delhi–110 002 (India)
E-mail: tech_info@techsarworld.com
Website: www.techsarworld.com

ISBN: 978-93-85909-88-7



Reprint 2025

# Preface

**Personality Development and Soft Skills: Preparing for Tomorrow** is a personality development module for students stepping from academic to corporate, which aims to enhance self-effectiveness through better management of self, group and organization. It would facilitate students to gain insight into them and develop action for enhancing interpersonal and managerial effectiveness and preparing for the smart way to success.

Changes in the global environment are radical and far-reaching and the capacity to learn faster is the only source for sustaining competitive advantage. The dictum, "Know thyself, own change thyself" has become the cornerstone of managerial effectiveness. Learning implies awareness of self , your SWOT analysis, one's current position, personal strengths and limitations, and development needs. Knowing oneself is not enough. Learning about self must be translated into action for change. Consequently, change in self leads to managing the external reality. Corporate managers need to continuously upgrade their knowledge and skills in technical, environmental and leadership areas. They need to examine their values, style and typical behaviours and assess the extent to which these are facilitating them both in their professional lives and personal lives.

Personality development is such an imperative need of the hour. Today, there is as much focus on the personality of a person, just as his or her ability to perform in practical work; because with a balancing act of a pleasing personality and a simultaneous, good performance at work, therein lies the perfect candidate. Special emphasis is laid today on good personality, thereby giving rise to the exceeding popular concept of personality development; wherein study courses encompass personality development; as individual, independent study topics and as a special part of other courses as well. In any environment, one stands out if his/her personality is bright and communicative. People skills are an integral part of any personality development programme. A pleasing personality is one, that has a balance in behaviour and is moderate in his or her reactions in public, while simultaneously maintain a friendly, approachable, yet sensible approach towards people. Personality development can bring about morale and self-improvement, which both directly and indirectly, affect positively, those around you. With the fierceness in competition in the arena of business and profession, there is complete necessity to concentrate on the personality development of students before they step into the corporate world.

The book will be of great help to students at all levels and disciplines. The book will provide various techniques for attitude development, achieving concentration with self-assessment exercises, to speak smartly and managing time well, creative management, using the power of positive thoughts, goal setting to enhance capabilities. Finally, it prepares students and give tips on giving presentation, writing CV and the techniques to excel in group discussions and interviews.

The framework of the book is 3 modules consisting of Self, Group and Organisation which is again divided into 11 units.

Under Module 1: Self there are 4 units — personal effectiveness, self-development, communication, and presentation

Module 2: Group has 3 units — Group behaviour, team dynamics, and synergy

Module 3: Organisation has 4 units — Managing change, creativity in organization, business communication, and work life success.

**Ṣhikha Kapoor**

# Acknowledgements

My sincere thanks to my family for providing me the environment and constant motivation for writing this book. My gratitude to my husband Sandeep and my children Sameer and Sakshi, parents—Mr Y.D. Puri and Pushpa Puri, parent-in-laws, Late Mr B.P. Kapoor and Sneh Kapoor, friends and colleagues of various companies and management institutions.

I owe my deep sense of gratitude to Dr Ashok K. Chauhan Founder President, Amity Group of Institutions and Founder Ritnand Balved Education Foundation who has not only been instrumental for providing me an environment to accomplish my work but also for being a great motivator.

I also thank Prof (Dr) Gurinder Singh, Amity University Group Vice Chancellor, and Director General, Amity International Business School, Amity University, for his constant guidance and support.

**Shikha Kapoor**

# Contents

# CONTENT FRAMEWORK

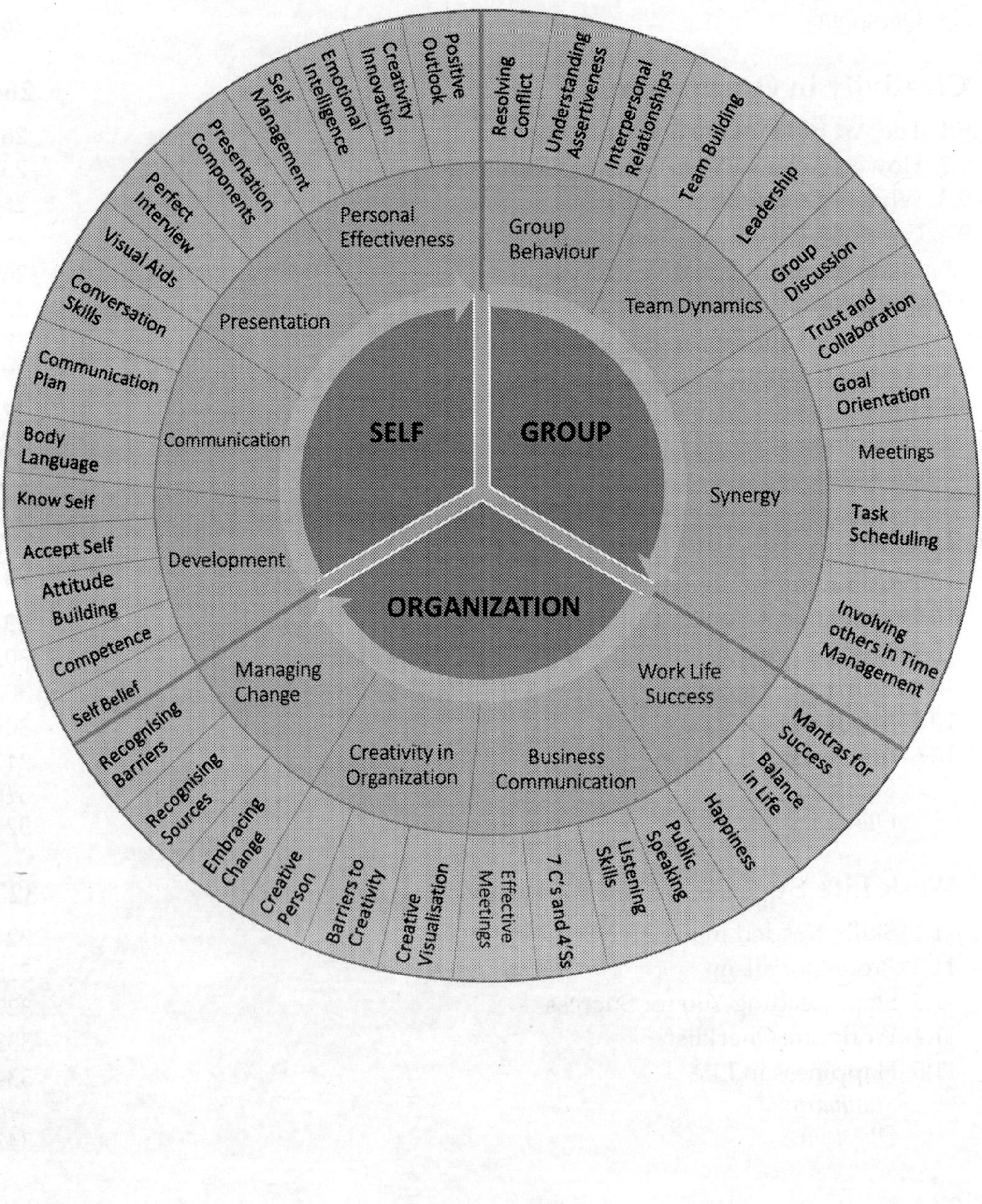

# MODULE 1
# SELF

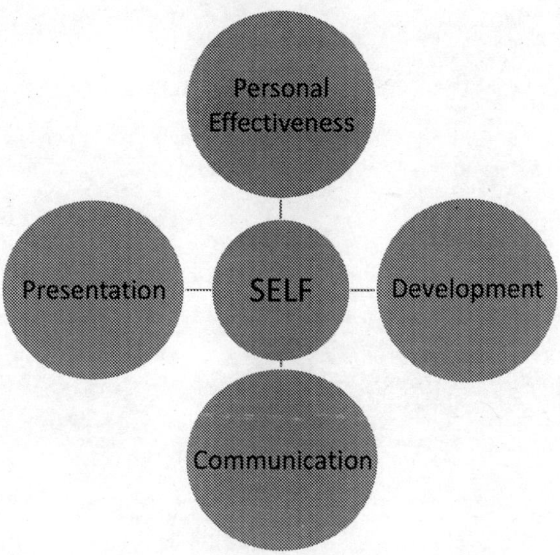

# 1 UNIT

# Personal Effectiveness

*Brains, integrity, and force may be all very well, but what you need today is charm. Go ahead and work on your economic programs if you want to, I'll develop my radio personality.*

**— Gracie Allen**

## Learning Objectives

- Self-management
- Positive Outlook
- Emotional Intelligence
- Ethical Behaviour
- Time Management
- Proactiveness
- Creativity and Innovation for Effectiveness
- Mnemonics and Mind Mapping

### The Overflowing Cup

An old ancient story of Japan says, when students wanted to get admission in a monastery they had to undergo an interview with an audience and the master. One day, a brilliant student appeared for the interview before the master. The young student started to impress the master with his knowledge and achievements.

He was offered tea by the master, instead of acknowledging it, he continued speaking about himself. Suddenly, he saw his cup of hot tea overflowing and dripping on his legs. He shouted and jumped, "Master, the cup is full and is overflowing!"

The master did not stop and continued pouring tea and replied, "So are you. Please come when you are empty and require my teachings."

Ego destroys new learning. If you fill your brain with ego, the brain will not accept any new knowledge. One should keep one's mind open to new ideas.

As Ray Kroc, founder of McDonald's once said, "When you are green, you will grow; but when you ripen, you will rot and fall."

## 1.1 WHAT IS PERSONALITY?

WORLD'S UNIQUE RESOURCE

***THE MAN***

Thinking, Conceptualising

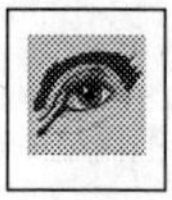

Vision, Fair play, Observance,

Listening, Judgement, Involvement

Speech, Communication, Clarity, Courtesy, Commitment

Feelings, Emotions, Sympathy, Sincerity, Respect, Loyalty, Pride

Actions, Role model, Achievement

*To be beautiful means to be yourself.*
*You don't need to be accepted by others.*
*You need to accept yourself."*

**Personality** means the effect, which an individual leaves on other people. It depicts the total picture of an individual. It constitutes two types of systems, i.e., psycho (mental) and physical, and these two systems interact with the internal and external environments.

A newborn comes to this world equipped with certain inherited capabilities for personality development. In the beginning of his life, he lacks differentiated personality. The older persons who come in his contact interpret his untutored responses in the light of their own personality reactions. Slowly, the infant begins to develop an understanding of the effects of his behaviour upon himself and other people and his personality begins to emerge.

The personality is not fixed and permanent. Heredity plays a small role in its development. It is rather the day-by-day experiences of the individual, the kind of environment in which he is developed, and the opportunities for all kinds of learning that are responsible for his personality development. There are various influences which affect the development of personality of an individual.

A personality is a form of automatic attraction which has to be charged with TRUST (INNER).

A vibrant personality has INNER MAGNETISM which is an important quality besides having outward attractiveness. It is known as PERSONAL CHARISMA. The combination of personal charisma and physical beauty is appealing. Self-discipline is needed to develop inner charm. Training and techniques are required to develop this talent.

Characteristics of PERSONALITY are:

1. Self-confidence
2. Politeness
3. Kindness
4. Humanity
5. Interest in others
6. Liveliness

Personality includes:

- Appearance
- Knowledge
- Intelligence
- Elegance
- Faithfulness
- Honesty
- Responsibility
- Administrative capacity
- Effectiveness
- Economic independence
- Ethics/temperament
- Being positive/valuable

Negative aspects of a personality:

- Unhygienic
- Attitude, which hurts
- Approach, which is not useful
- Unhealthy communication.
- Lack of integrity.
- Under/average performance.
- Egoistic
- Indiscipline
- Negative emotions.

## Values

One should evaluate and examine oneself in everyday life and **build values**. This is the first step for building a stimulating personality. Values help us to differentiate between right and wrong.

A deep conviction, a criterion, a belief, in the rightness, goodness, or desirability of means and/or end leading to stated behaviour of an individual.

Values are explicitly or implicitly desirable in an individual.

***Values are important because they allow us to live peacefully with others and enable us to achieve whatever goals we set for ourselves.***

Universal values are not learnt but are common to all. There is a similarity in everyone's reaction to being hurt, cheated, lied to, or bullied.

There are many universal values, such as non-injury, humility, and charitableness which are all based upon the same consideration of how one would like to be treated by others.

We are not born with values.

We learn them from our parents, teachers, and friends.

We also develop our values from the media, like television, movies, and the radio.

Values, set of beliefs, deep commitments mould our attitude towards people, towards situations and towards life in general. These attitudes, in turn, guide most of our actions and behaviours. Collectivity of behaviour in a society/group contributes towards emergence of "culture" in that society or creation of an environment.

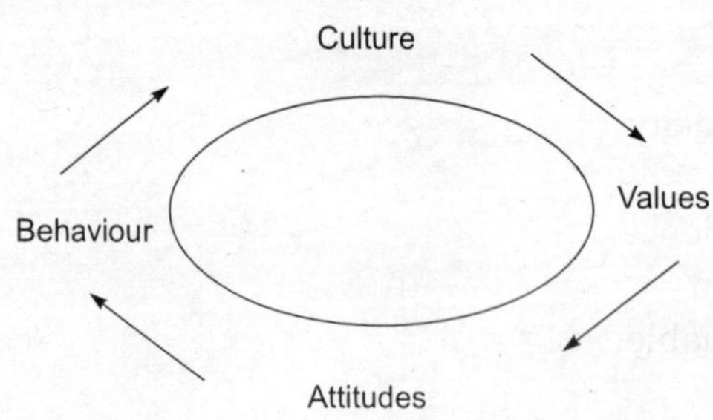

## Learning of Values

Some of the important values are respect, responsibility, love, honesty, commitment, cooperation, family, friendship, and caring for the environment.

### *Respect*

Respect means showing consideration for or admiring or showing regard for another person or thing. Respect includes treating everything and everyone with dignity.

### *Responsibility*

Responsibility means being accountable for your own words and actions.

### *Love*

Love is a deep and tender affection for, care for, adoring someone, loyalty, and unselfish kindly concern for others. Friendship also is a feeling of love and can be defined in the same terms.

### *Honesty*

To be honest means truthfulness and not to cheat, tell a lie or steal, and the way we conduct ourselves.

It is easy to say, "Everyone else does it. So why can't I?" We need to curb this thinking and recognise that this is a wrong approach.

### *Environment Awareness/Caring*

Environmental awareness is to understand that there are many things that determine the survival of the natural environment. When we make an effort to recycle, reduce, and reuse, we are environmentally aware for preserving the earth for future generations.

### *Cooperation*

Cooperation is the act of team work and collaboration to learn from each other. This enables us to synergise our abilities for a collective goal to be accomplished.

### *Compassion*

Compassion is a feeling of sympathy or pity. When we are compassionate we are sympathetic towards others — in sorrow or hardship.

*Other Characteristics Included are*

- **Punctuality**
- **Discipline**
- **Dedication**

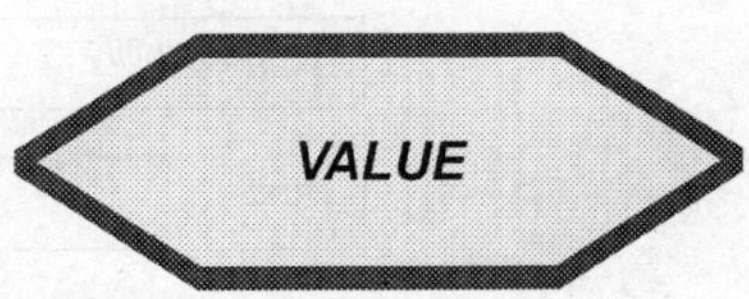


***A: Your authentic belief/commitment***
***L: What you desire to live by***
***U: Your uniqueness and understanding***
***V: What is Valuable to you***

***Identify your core values and how your action, behaviour, attitude are aligned with them***

| | |
|---|---|
| *Achievement* | **Sense of accomplishment by means of skills, practice or exertion** |
| *Adventure* | **Adventurous work which frequently involves risk taking** |
| *Aesthetics* | **Appreciating the beauty of ideas, things, etc.** |
| *Autonomy* | **Working independently without significant direction** |
| *Caring* | **Love, affection** |
| *Challenge* | **Simulates full use of your potential** |
| *Competition* | **Work as a team towards common goals** |
| *Cooperation* | **Being imaginative, innovative** |
| *Creativity* | **Pit your abilities against others** |
| *Inner harmony* | **Being at peace with oneself** |
| *Integrity* | **Sincertiy and honesty** |
| *Knowledge* | **Understanding gained through study or experience** |
| *Helping others* | **Being involved in helping others directly or in a group** |
| *Friendship* | **Develop close personal relationship** |
| *Ledership* | **Leadership influences others** |
| *Responsibility* | **Being accountable for results** |
| *Trust* | **Strong belief on right action/ thinking about others** |
| *Loyalty* | **Steadfastness and allegiance** |

## *Human Value System*

***Human value system is compared to four parts of a TREE***

***SOIL forms the Society***

***ROOTS form the values and attitudes***

***TRUNK forms the goals in life***

***BRANCHES AND LEAVES are the manifestations of all the above three things.***

***We absorb concepts from the society around us and develop the roots which form the values.***

***The effect of values are the goals and the effect of goals are the branches and leaves of a tree.***

***If we develop a strong value system, we withstand the storm like a tree with the strong roots.***

***Hence, it is essential for us to have healthy values and live by them.***

### 1.1.1 Understanding Hard and Soft Skills

Both, the hard skills and soft skills are essential for an individual. These are the skills which include the learnt skills required to perform a job. Hard skills are skills which are identified and measured by tests and exams. They are tangible skills. These skills are learnt in school from books. They are the competencies. When you write your resume you mention your schooling, degrees, training and certificates. Hard skills are the technical, mechanical, administrative or accounting, and programming skills.

Soft skills are the skills which are used for interaction. Their measurement is not easy. These are intangible skills. These are needed from time to time for networking, communication. Some of the soft skills needed are critical thinking skills, problem solving skills, self-esteem, self-control, time management, effective decision-making, leadership, skills emotional intelligence or EQ and efficient task prioritization. Soft skills rules depend on the company and the culture you work in. They are learnt by trial and error method. There are various books nowadays to give step-by-step instructions to master soft skills.

### *Hard Skills vs Soft Skills: Which are more Important?*

Different types of careers need different skills.

1. Some careers need more hard skills and less soft skills. The profession of a technical person. We can see some brilliant persons who do not work well with others.
2. Career of an accountant, lawyer need both hard and soft skills to build a successful career. Communication skills, and relationship skills are needed to deal with clients.
3. Some careers need more soft skills and less hard skills. Example is of a salesman who should know how to communicate as his job depends on his communication skills, his sales pitch, and persuasion skills.

To know how important soft skills are in your career, one has to ask oneself three questions:

1. How does my communication with others affect my performance review and the decisions for my career progression?
2. Are my communication skills liked by people in my organization?
3. Is my performance review affected by my ability to control my character at work?

If all three are yes, then soft skills are very important in advancement of your career and you should develop them.

In general, soft skills are very important in one's career than hard skills.

## Personality Development

Definitions

- It is the technique to increase the ability to influence others as well as a technique of persuasion used for personal magnetism.
- Personality development is developing and creating impact about yourself in a positive way to the targeted group and maintaining it.
- Personality is the balance between a healthy body, controlled emotions, and illuminated mind.

A developed personality attracts the surroundings and retains the contact, and interest.

### Characteristics of a Developed Personality

1. Healthy mind and body
2. Being kind
3. Unselfish
4. Good temperament
5. Obedience to values and ethics
6. Honest
7. Truthful

8. Loyal
9. Religious and spiritual

SELF-IMPROVEMENT should be slow and steady.
Wisdom should be acquired with knowledge. Wisdom involves character.

**"Knowledge and timber shouldn't be used much till they have been seasoned," says Oliver Wendell Holmes.**

One should aim to wish about life's progress to construct it and the principal urge to succeed. As a charismatic and pleasing personality leads himself/herself towards success.

For personal power one should have:

1. Healthy body and mind
2. A creative mind
3. A persuasive and convincing voice
4. Power of scrutiny and mind's eye
5. Sense of humour
6. Optimistic enthusiasm
7. Desire to excel
8. Interpersonal relations
9. A poised and confident mind

Physical appearance is the first thing which is observed in an individual. An impression is created by the neat, clean and good appearance. An impression is formed about a person what they SEE before he speaks.

*" THE FIRST IMPRESSION IS THE LAST IMPRESSION."*

## Developing a Pleasing and Influencing Personality

Features of an influencing personality are:

1. Physical
2. Social
3. Psychological
4. Philosophical

**Physical personality** depends on the external personality of an individual which is supported by his physical beauty, health and its sustenance.

**Social personality's** main factors are: societal ethics and principles, interpersonal communication skills, and the mindset.

**Psychological personality** is in relation to the personal, emotional intelligence, belief, personal opinion, which is affected by the influence by knowledge, and intelligence of a person.

**Philosophical personality** is acquired from the maturity of ideas.

**Factors for developing a strong personality in social environment:**

1. Charismatic personality.
2. Confidence in communicating
3. Adapting and adhering to social codes of ethics
4. Developing confidence of
   (a) Genuineness, honesty and trust.
   (b) Fulfilling of responsibilities
5. Other factors for impression:
   (a) Awareness about surroundings and self.
   (b) Action oriented, having in-depth knowledge for application, emotional intelligence and be smart.
   (c) Self-confidence, inventiveness, dynamic, management qualities, determination and self-control.
   (d) Adaptive to ethical values.

**Factors for developing a strong personality in operational field:**

1. Genuineness, earnestness and faith
2. Responsiveness, vigilance
3. Interpersonal communication skills
4. Responsibility, and accountability for the duties assigned
5. Pleasant appearance
6. Emotional intelligence
7. Application of knowledge in depth, logical intelligence and alertness
8. Social interaction
9. Positive thinker, logical thinking and adaptive to situations
10. Change agent and receptive to changing technologies

## 1.2 POSITIVE OUTLOOK: DEVELOP YOUR POSITIVE POWER

Personality development depends on:

1. Temperament and performance
2. Perception
3. Awareness and consciousness
4. Health and wealth

5. Intellectual capacity
6. Emotional intelligence
7. Self-confidence, will power and self-discipline
8. Duty, responsibility and accountability
9. Ethical and moral values

Attitude is one's evaluative orientation towards a person, thing, idea, etc. It is the tendency to act towards something, which becomes thereby a positive or negative value. Attitude influences an individual's perception of objects, information, colleagues and peers. Attitudes are the mental, moral and ethical dispositions adopted by individuals to others and the situations in which they find themselves.

A positive attitude is a vital asset. We must portray a positive attitude as we present ourselves as:

"The person who sends out positive thoughts
activates the world around him positively
and draws back to himself positive results."

"The longer I live, the more I realize the impact of attitude on life. Attitude, to me is more important than facts. It is more important than the past, than education, than money, than circumstances, than failures, than successes, than what other people think or say or do. It is more important than appearance, giftedness or skill. It will make or break a company ... a church ... a home. The remarkable thing is we have a choice regarding the attitude we will embrace for that day. We cannot change our past ...we cannot change the fact that people will act in a certain way. We cannot change the inevitable. The only thing we can do is play on the one string we have, and that is our attitude ...I am convinced that life is 10% what happens to me and 90% how I react to it. And so it is with you ...we are in charge of our attitudes."

— Charles Swindoll (American author)

**THINK POSITIVE**

Always ring a bell to yourself to think positive things once you get up in the morning and try to accomplish them during the day.

**MAKE OTHERS FEEL ACCEPTED**

When the NEED TO FEEL ACCEPTED is denied, the rejected person or group feels discriminated against – and becomes resentful, angry and hostile.

**MAKE OTHERS FEEL APPROVED**

Everyone has a subconscious NEED TO FEEL APPROVED. This need is so basic and so compelling that, if it is not fulfilled, its absence leaves a vacant space in the personality.

**MAKE OTHERS FEEL ADMIRED**

The gift of expressing your ADMIRATION of everyone within the range of your personality is an art and a skill which you must perfect and constantly use for being a positive power person.

**MAKE OTHERS FEEL THAT THEY ARE APPRECIATED**

One of the distinguishing (and most popular) characteristics of a positive power person is his or her ability to make others feel that they, their activities and/or their possessions are APPRECIATED.

**MAKE OTHERS FEEL IMPORTANT**

One of the most powerful motivations for all is seeking a FEELING OF IMPORTANCE.

**BE AGREEABLE . . . Agree**

Other people want agreement – not disagreement or arguments. They want to be RIGHT. They want your agreement that they are RIGHT.

**GIVE OTHERS THE ATTENTION they crave**

A few people can instinctively attract ATTENTION. But they want much more attention than they can attract.

**MAKE OTHERS FEEL NEEDED**

To make others FEEL NEEDED is the noblest use to which you can put your knowledge of psychology.

**FILL THE NEED FOR OUTSIDE HELP!**

No one is sufficient unto himself.

"The wind and the ocean quarrel. He who pays the price is the sailor in a boat."

## Develop a "can do attitude"

**DEVELOP THE YES I CAN ATTITUDE**

**Choose Positive Living**

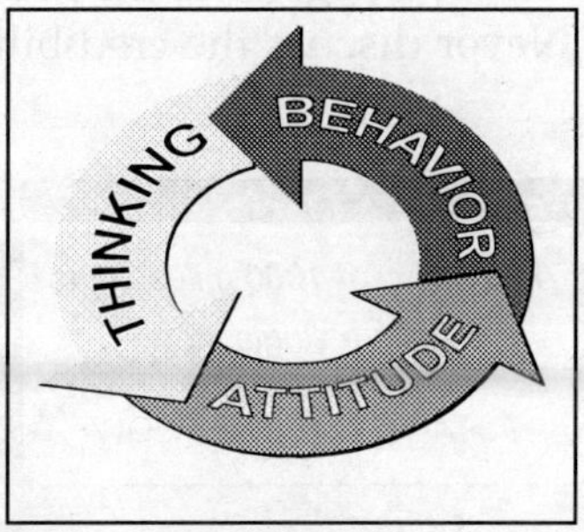


## Steps to Develop a Positive Attitude

Following are the steps to develop a positive attitude in yourself.

**Don't criticize in negative manner**

- The person becomes defensive.
- Apply sandwich approach.
- Criticize negative behaviour not the person
- Attack performance not the performer.

**Steps on positive criticism**

- When we criticize, let's criticize as a coach (of athlete)
- Be specific in criticizing, corrective and not general
- The attitude to criticism must be corrective and not punitive (not to take out your own revenges)
- If criticism is done constructively, it must be based on the facts and not on conclusions.
- Be firm but be cool.
- If criticism is given appropriately and properly, it should eliminate the need for repetition.
- When criticizing always show a benefit of correcting (advantage).
- Also show for losses for not correcting.
- Before criticizing always give the opponent an opportunity to explain.
- Your criticism is your perspective, don't over do it.
- Criticize privately and appreciate publicly.
- While criticizing don't bring personal grudges in between.
- In order to criticize constructively ask suggestions for improvement, i.e., how, when, where and who.
- If one realizes his mistake immediately then leave for positive changes.
- Close the discussion on a positive note.

While criticizing never question the integrity of the person. When integrity is on line, its better to break relationship. Never discuss the credibility issue but only the mistake issues.

## The Donkey ATTITUDE

Once there was a donkey, who was owned by a farmer . One day the donkey accidently fell into the well. The donkey cried for help. The farmer who was nearby heard his cries and tried to help him to get out of the well but was not successful, so he thought it is better to leave the donkey in the well as he had gone old and would not be useful for him any more. He thought it was better to cover him. His neighbours who heard the noise, came for the rescue of the donkey. They took a spade and started to put mud into the well. The donkey, at first was scared and he cried loudly, then he quieted down.

When loads of mud was put on the donkey, everyone was surprised to see that when each load of mud that hit the donkey's back, he would take a step up by removing the mud. Soon, to everyone's amazement; the donkey walked up and happily walked briskly off!

## Moral

Life is full of challenges, what you need to do is to shake it off and move ahead. Think and analyze the problem logically. These problems are the stepping stones. If we have the will to challenge ourselves, we can get out of the deepest of problems. NEVER GIVE UP! Shake off and take a step up.

Remember – simple rules to be happy

- ✓ Think positive
- ✓ Forgive others
- ✓ Give more
- ✓ Expect less
- ✓ Appreciate others

## WHAT IS LIFE

Life is an Adventure—Dare it.
Life is a Challenge—Meet it.
Life is Love—Enjoy it.
Life is a Struggle—Fight it.
Life is a Game—Play it.
Life is a Journey—Complete it.
Life is a Goal—Achieve it.
Life is a Puzzle—Solve it.
Life is a Sorrow—Overcome it.
Life is a Beauty—Praise it.
Life is a Duty—Perform it.
Life is a Tragedy—Face it.
Life is a Promise—Fulfil it.
Life is a Gift—Accept it.
Life is a Mystery—Unfold it.
Life is an Opportunity—Take it.
Life is a Song—Sing it.
Life is a Spirit—Realize it.

### Management Tip: Identify your unique skills

*— Harvard Business Review*

ALL OF US have at least one disruptive skill—an ability that sets us apart from others. You may have been honing yours for years, or you may be so innately good at it that you don't even notice it.

Here are three ways to identify your unique skill:

**Watch your reflexes.** You may instinctively do what you're good at without even noticing. Ask yourself: when I feel most successful or invigorated, what am I doing?

**Look for confluences.** A distinct skill may not be one thing, but an unusual intersection of ordinary proficiencies.

**Listen to compliments.** Peers, managers, direct reports, and even spouses are often good mirrors of your inherent strengths. Don't habitually dismiss compliments, but mine them to discover your unique skills.

## 1.3 EMOTIONAL INTELLIGENCE

### What is an Emotion?

*As per* Wikipedia, ***emotion***, in everyday speech, is any relatively brief conscious experience characterized by intense mental activity and a high degree of pleasure or displeasure.

**Types of Emotions**

**Happiness**: Happiness is a positive emotion. It expresses pleasure, satisfaction, good luck or fortune. Happiness increases the heart rate, blood pressure, boosts the immune system and reduces certain neuro chemicals.

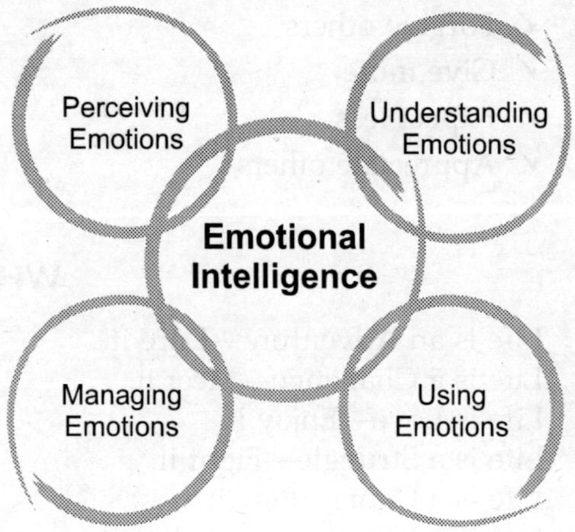


**Surprise:** An expression used when something unexpected or sudden occurs. Positive: dropped jaw, with mouth open lifted and curved eyebrows, eyes opened, wide horizontal wrinkles spanning across the forehead

**Disgust:** Disgust is a strong feeling of dislike. Negative: wrinkle your nose up, raise your cheeks, raise your upper lip, lower your brow, form lines below your lower eyelid.

**Fear:** A feeling that something dreadful or dangerous is about to happen. Negative: Eyebrows become drawn and raised, lips slightly drawn back with an open mouth, upper eyelids show wrinkles in the middle of their forehead.

**Anger:** Anger is a strong feeling of annoyance and displeasure. Negative: The brows become drawn together and lower lips set in a squarish shape, and pressed together firmly, eyes become bulgy and nostrils flare their upper and lower eyelids will tense.

## DEVELOPING EMOTIONAL INTELLIGENCE

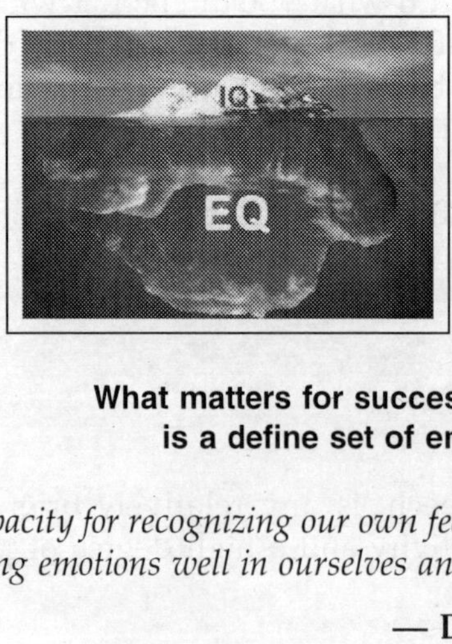


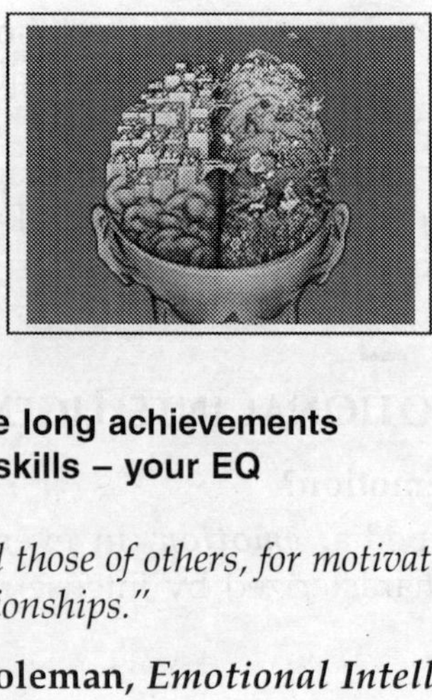

**What matters for success and life long achievements is a define set of emotional skills – your EQ**

*"It is the capacity for recognizing our own feelings and those of others, for motivating ourselves and managing emotions well in ourselves and in relationships."*

**— Daniel Goleman, *Emotional Intelligence*, 1998**

Emotional intelligence (EI) determines and influences every aspect of our working lives. It increases the competitive power and empowers to understand and effectively perform.

EI is the unique intersection of head over heart and combines emotion with intelligence.... Emotion and thinking work together, thinking is used to analyze the emotion and emotion assists thinking. So EI is used to solve the problem by using the ability to use the emotion.

The importance of emotions:

- Our margins are set up because of our emotions
- Emotions help us to connect
- Decisions are guided by state of emotions.
- Emotions play an integral part in influencing our moral judgements.

**Emotional intelligence** is a major deciding factor for relationship management and for all employees as this results in motivation, retention, self-management and managing others.

Emotional intelligence helps an individual in successfully dealing with other people, managing self, understanding one's feelings and others and responding to others in everyday life. It means dealing with emotions intelligently.

High EQ should be there in the bosses and leaders as their interaction is maximum among the people within and outside for setting the tone of the organization.

### Five domains of Emotional Intelligence

- **Awareness of self:** Observing oneself and to understand oneself.
- **Managing emotions:** Handling one's emotions and to realize the feels behind it, also a way to handle these emotions (anxieties, anger, and sadness).
- **Motivating oneself:** Channeling oneself and one's emotions; emotional will power; delaying satisfaction and harsh impulses.
- **Empathy:** Putting yourself in other's shoes – having feeling and concern about others; and helping know the feelings of people in different situations.
- **Relationship handling:** Handling emotions of others; social aptitude and social skills.

## WHY EMOTIONAL INTELLIGENCE

Extraordinary performance can be brought by ordinary people with emotional intelligence. Traditional cognitive intelligence is required to be successful at work. Ability to restrain anger and self-doubt the negative feelings and focusing confidence and congeniality the positives which is a requirement to be successful.

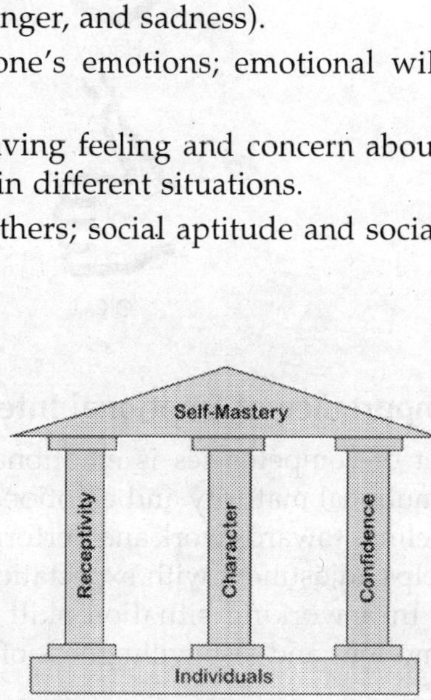

## Why Emotional Intelligence is Necessary

Helps managers handle adversity and setbacks

Teaches managers cope when change and uncertainty hit organisation

## Emotions Work with People

Emotions play a role when people are working in the same place.

## Importance of Emotional Intelligence at Work

Set of competencies is emotional intelligence. These include emotional competency, emotional maturity and emotional sensitivity which express and help to manage one's feelings towards work and performance. Understanding the moods and other's emotions helps adjustment with expectations.

In a working situation skill and knowledge is used with effective directive of emotions and also willingness of the worker is used to contribute the best in their goal achievement. In the area of work, teams have different ideas, suggestions, and opinions, The collective and effective utilization gives the best outcome.

## Suggestions Towards Emotional Intelligence

1. Following tips for emotions intelligence may help members improve their orientation and awareness towards self and hence will be proactive and help in productivity.
    1. Understand oneself and developing it
    2. Being honest
    3. Maintain truthfulness
    4. Know your worth and potential
    5. Generate awareness of knowledge and skills
    6. To focus on having positive attitude
    7. Analyse your reaction in every source
    8. Distinguish between appropriate and inappropriate reactions
    9. Open to listening to others
    10. Empathize with others' feelings
    11. Control your negative emotions
    12. Feel responsible for your actions
    13. Using self-consciously for information and feelings
    14. Positive thinking in negative situations
    15. Being action oriented, not to worry
    16. Clarity of feelings and thoughts
    17. Explanations should be clear to your subordinates and boss
    18. Improve confidence and self-control with various activities
    19. Understand others and accept people as they are
    20. Use persuasion than punishment to accomplish targets
    21. Use conflict resolution strategies
    22. Develop group synergy
    23. Be adaptable to all situations and positions
    24. Be optimistic
    25. Enjoy success and achievement
    26. Self-goal aligning with organizational goal
    27. Encourage participation
    28. Give purposeful feedback
    29. Develop organizational culture that supports learning

Leaders with empathy are able to understand their employees' needs and provide them with constructive feedback.

## EI in the Workplace

Acknowledging the emotions and developing and dealing intelligently are the main requirements at workplace. People derail because of classic emotional failings, not the lack of technical skills.

- There are adverse consequences to have low emotional intelligence. These includes:
  - ✓ Relationship problems

  - ✓ Rage in the workplace

✓ Poor decision making capability

✓ Failure to advance in career

## 1.4 ETHICAL BEHAVIOUR

From childhood we are taught by our parents what is wrong and what is right As we grow old we face it and see its complexity. Role of ethics is important in our society. We need to learn ethics as it helps in the decision making: who are we and what will be our future. Role of ethics in our society is very important as it makes our belief and standard that make everything run smoothly.

**Workplaces have changed in this 21st century. We have moved towards a global economy. Organisations should have ethical policies to maintain and progress with the workforce.**

Honesty, fairness and equity are characterized by ethical behaviour in interpersonal, professional and academic relationships and in research and scholarly activities.

Ethical behaviour is must for better performance with high morale and teamwork. The following are prerequisites for success.

- Respect
- Honour
- Integrity
- Customer focus
- Risk taking
- Passion
- Persistence

Ethics, what we already know, is the moral philosophy which determines what is right and what is wrong. A prescribed code of conduct establishes the kind of and to what extent the ethics would be practised in the organization. Why are corporates moving towards "ethically instilled workplace?

The question arises why the corporates are now more diverted towards "being ethical".

## WHY IS ETHICS IMPORTANT?

Ethics are one of the required elements for human life. The human action is totally meant by it. Without it, our actions would be random and aimless. There would be no strategy and action towards a specific target or goal because there would be no way to select a specific goal from the vast number of goals or objectives that one aims for. The pursuit of goal even with an ethical standard doesn't ensure the possibility of success. To the scale up to which a rational ethical standard is taken, which defines our ability to plan and correctly organize or characterize our objectives and efforts to accomplish our starred values, goals or objectives. Incapability or errors in our ethics will respectively affect and reduce our ability for a successful pursuit.

## ETHICAL AND UNETHICAL BEHAVIOUR

Ethical behaviour signifies the conduct that is composed and followed by the norms and standards of a society, organization or institution and is beyond criticism according to the social standards or reproach.

### Ethical Behaviour in Society

It is diverse. The behaviours considered unethical in one society can be acceptable in another and vice versa. It is totally illogical and non-specific, a society is a collection of diverse people with common beliefs. Such factors can largely affect the definition of ethical behaviour with respect to a society.

### Ethical Behaviour in the Workplace

This describes the expectation of the society or organization(s)/in the workplace by their employees which they are directed to hold while at work. They have a set of rules and regulations that the employees are expected to follow. Certainly, because an individual's representation of behaviour in the society or workplace literally describes and represents the conduct of an organization which can easily affect the relationships within an organization or in the working society where an organization is defined according to its ethical conduct, thereby generating a negative image. It may question the capability, overall performance and reputation of an organization.

### Employee's Unethical Behaviour

Corruption is a severe unethical behaviour which is not expected of an organization in any circumstances. Employees are strictly directed against such an unethical behaviour in the workplace. Unnecessary leaves, false sick reports and proxy presence are also examples of unethical behaviour. This should only happen when there is a serious necessity. Mild headaches do not count. Personal use of office supplies is unethical. Office property is the property of the organization and cannot be treated as personal property. Such conduct is even translated to theft in some organizations.

Employees are not only the ones who are expected to behave in unethical ways. To cheat during examinations is an unethical behaviour for students.

Ethical behaviours are engraved in early age. Lack of moral convictions, can easily sway one to take part in contrary behaviours.

## UNETHICAL BEHAVIOUR AT WORKPLACE

1. **Misusing company time**
   'Personal business' is not expected during office hours such as unnecessary calls, personal issues related to family, investments or any other need concerned to a specific person and his interests are unethical behaviours.
2. **Abusive behaviour**
3. **Lying to employees**

## 1.5 TIME MANAGEMENT

"To choose time is to save time."

*"Come what come may, Time and the hour runs through the roughest day"*

**— William Shakespeare**

*"Dont thou love life? Then do not sunder time, for that's the stuff life's made of."*

**— Benjamin Frankin**

Time in minutes is now considered a major resource along with 3Ms of money.

Efficiency is in doing a job properly, whereas effectiveness is doing a job properly at a correct time, at a proper place and achieving the desired results.

All successful men have a few common characteristics, for example, they act at the earliest and do not postpone carrying out their activities.

**Procrastination:** Term used for people who make tomorrow as their watchword as long as they do not have to work now.

*"It is not enough to be busy. The question is what are you busy about. "*

**— Henry David Thoreau**

***On Time***

*Little drops of water and little drops of sand make the mighty ocean and the pleasant land.*
*So the little minutes, humble through they be, make the mighty ages of eternity.*

**— Julia Fletcher Carney**

Seven important things necessary to plan your time:

**Step 1: Set an aim.** It should be clear, firm and achievable. Time management is really not working faster, but doing the right thing at the right time and at the right place.

**Step 2: Set your objectives.** Divide the main aim into achievable and identifiable short-term objectives.

**Step 3: Work out key result areas (KRAs).** It helps to separate the vital from trivial and trash.

**Step 4: Planning of time.** Every moment spent on planning saves three in the execution. A proper plan helps in accomplishing the task in less time. Important matters must be given prime time, when concentration is maximum. The routine work can be done when one is relatively tired.

**Step 5: Time blocks.** Divide work and time in such a manner that you can handle both easily.

**Step 6: Recording of time.** Record the time spent on wasteful activities like attending telephone calls, showing courtesies to visitors, etc.

**Step 7: Take stock of time.** At the end make a score of the tasks completed, analyze the reasons for the jobs which could not be completed and rearrange the priorities to fit them into the next day's list of jobs to be done with anticipated time required against all-important tasks. Habit of listing your tasks on a piece of paper or in your desktop computer can help ensure their timely completion.

**Work out timings backward:**

Train leaves – 6 P.M.

Reach railway station – 5.30 P.M.

Leave hospital for railway station – 4.45 P.M.

Reach hospital to meet friend – 3.45 P.M. and so an

Never ignore adding time cushion. Hence, by immaculate planning, a manager can assign work which will stretch subordinate's capabilities and bring out the best in them—specially during his prolonged absence.

*"Like the waves make way towards the pebbled shore, so do our minutes hasten to their end."*

**— William Shakespeare**

As a guideline, one must complete every day's work, the same day. This goal must be achieved unless there is an important reason for not doing so. It is a secret of efficient time management.

## Relaxation

*"To be effective, the executive must be fresh and energetic. He must therefore learn to relax adequately and wisely."*

**— Peter. F. Drucker**

### *Relaxation Rejuvenates*

Work should be done at the right time and at right place in the right manner. If you have too many jobs at hand, best is to note them down on a piece of paper and lay down the relative priority, based on their importance. Just as you can take one step at a time, speak one word at a time, you can only do one job at one time.

Most successful men maintain some sort of diaries wherein they note down any worthwhile thought generated or work that is required to be done.

Allocate sufficient time for its successful completion.

## Steps in the Time Management

1. Establish roles, priorities, and objectives
2. Time awareness
3. Eliminate unnecessary, unimportant, and inappropriate actions
4. Freeing time through delegation
5. Eliminate or reduce time consuming actions
6. Plan and schedule use of time
7. Unblocking action

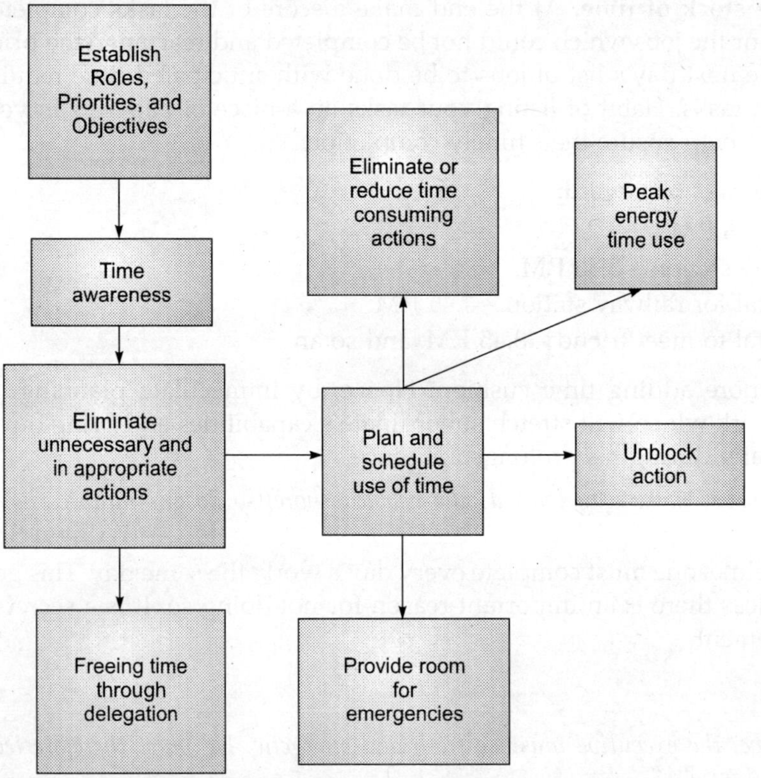


## Planning and Scheduling Framework

- Life goals
- Mission (where do we want to go?)
- Your situation now

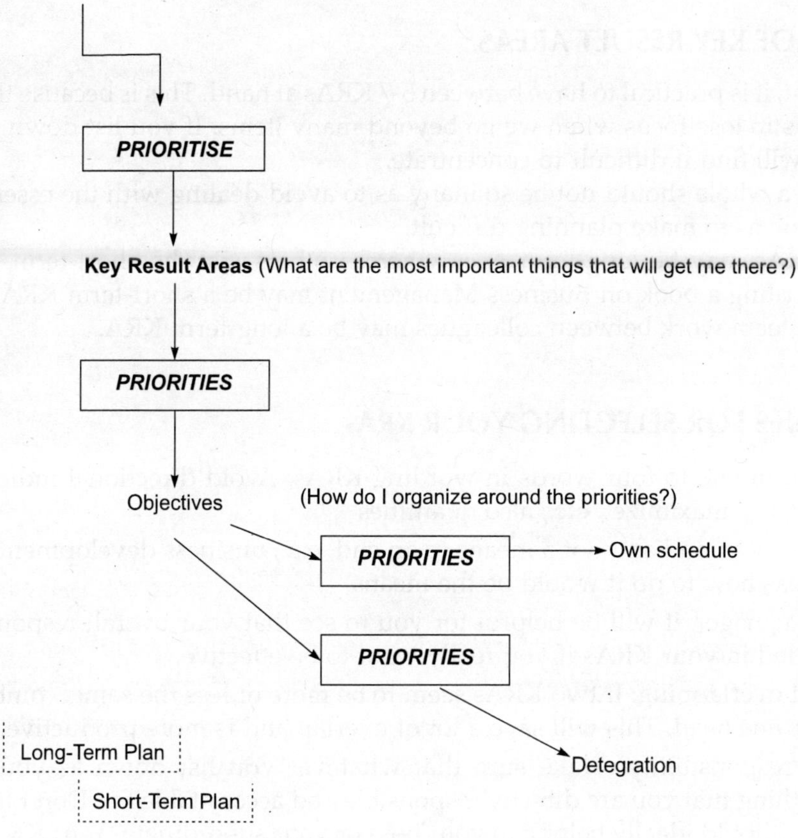


## WHAT ARE KEY RESULT AREAS (KRAs) BASED ON

Identifying KRAs or focus areas in which desired impact/favourable change is to be created for overall success, requires an awareness of:

- Life time goals
- Our roles
- The needs/expectations/unsolved problems of other systems/sub-systems interdependent with our own
- Situational analysis of environment
- Internal strengths, weaknesses
- External opportunities, threats
- Our own expectations and the expressive impulses of our innermost being.

## NUMBER OF KEY RESULT AREAS

At any point, it is practical to have between 5-7 KRAs at hand. This is because the human mind begins to lose focus when we go beyond many items. If you list down too many areas, you will find it difficult to concentrate.

KRAs as a whole should not be so many as to avoid dealing with the essence of the job, or so few as to make planning difficult.

Some KRAs may be long-term ones whereas others may be short-term ones. For example, writing a book on Business Management may be a short-term KRA, whereas developing team work between colleagues may be a long-term KRA.

## GUIDELINES FOR SELECTING YOUR KRAs

1. Use from one to four words in wording KRAs. Avoid directional indicators like 'increase', 'maximize', etc., also quantities.
2. A KRA is an end and not a means to an end, e.g., business development is a KRA whereas how to do it would be the means.
3. As a manager, it will be helpful for you to see that your overall responsibility is included in your KRAs if you really want to be effective.
4. Avoid overlapping: If two KRAs seem to be more or less the same, combine them under one head. This will save a lot of overlap and is more productive.
5. Your responsibility: Make sure that whatever you list down as your KRA is something that you are directly responsible and accountable for. Don't take KRAs which should ideally belong to your boss or your subordinate. Your KRAs should be those in which you are directly involved.

## EXAMPLES OF KRAs

- Quality
- Personal development
- Staff oraganisation
- Customer satisfaction
- Special projects
- Business development
- Costs
- Delivery security
- Timeliness
- Subordinate development
- Maintenance
- Planning

## OBJECTIVES

Having identified our KRAs, the next step is to spell out objectives in relation to each KRA. (There can be more than one objective under one KRA.)

### What is an Objective?

An objective is a statement of a desired result to be achieved within a specified period of time. An objective tells us in concrete measurable terms what we want to achieve and whether we are moving closer towards our goal.

The keyword to remember while setting objectives is SMART!

S – Specific. It indicates 'what' must be done keeping in mind the desired result.
M – Measurable. How will you know that the objective has been achieved? Set up a standard of performance that is quantifiable.
A – Attainable. You realistically achieve it.
R – Relevant. Should be related to your role/priorities.
T – Time-bound. By what time should it have been achieved.

All objectives that you set must be mutually consistent (to avoid conflicts); and written down (for easy reminders and review).

Correctly stated (or SMART) objectives help us:

- to plan our activities effectively;
- to measure performance against the plan;
- to inform others about what we are trying; and
- to enhance communication.

## WHERE DO OBJECTIVES COME FROM?

In an organization, a manager has to consider the objectives of the organization, his department or boss's objectives, his own as well as those of his colleagues and subordinates.

1. Objectives that come from the top:
    - The objectives of the organisation
    - Things the boss wants you to do, arising out of the corporate plan.
2. Statutory objectives:
    - Objectives arising out of external law or internal company objectives.
    - Legal requirements, routine (e.g., account closing, safety audit).
3. Improvements to the ongoing work:
    - Objectives arising out of desire to achieve a higher standard of the existing work.
    - Can I do more?
    - Can I do better?
    - Can I do differently?

4. Things which a manager alone can see:
   - New ideas, development, research.
   - New possibilities on your own initiative.
5. Manager's own development:
   - What do I need to learn/do to improve my personality
   - Do I need to develop my subordinates better?
   - Do I need to be more friendly and informal?
6. Staff Development:
   - How to develop my staff better?
   - What are their development needs?
   - What are the skills that they need to develop?

Example of an Objective
KRA: Quality
Objective
To reduce the rejection rate of item xyz from 6% to 1% by 31st Dec 2018

**The book of life**

"As skill in self-determination improves, self-knowledge increases. Self-observation and self-knowledge lead to a clear comprehension about the causes and consequences of one's actions.

This makes us aware of which action is the right one for us. Ultimately, perceptive insight itself results in the right action at the right moment."

**J. Krishnamurthy**

## Time Log

Maintain a time-log as it is the best way of utilizing your time effectively.

Maintain a time-log for at least 10 days. Each day is divided into half hour blocks and a record made of the activities for each half hour. Another way of maintaining a time log is task wise, i.e., mention how much time it took to do a particular task.

At the end of each day, you can look at each activity and rate how useful your work was. Serveral days of such data-gathering and analysis give a clear picture of your time utilization. Merely estimating on recall often is grossly inaccurate and a time-log is by far the most efficient way of gaining time-awareness. Use the following rating while analyzing how usefully you have spent your time at the end of each day in relation to your objectives:

I = Important
D = Doubtful
U = Useless

At the end of seven days, look at your analysis. It will give you valuable clues about how you are spending your time.

**Some broad headings for activities could be:**

**On the job:**

1. Telephoning
2. Dictating
3. Reading
4. Writing
5. Travelling
6. Meeting
7. Entertaining
8. Researching
9. Dealing with people

**Personal Work:**

1. Sleeping
2. Eating
3. Dressing
4. Commuting

**Family:**

1. Wife/husband
2. Children
3. Parents
4. Relatives

**Personal Growth:**

1. Reading
2. Meditation
3. Learning

**Benefits of Time Log**

- Gives you concrete data on your time expenditure.
- By jotting down how you are spending your time, you automatically become more aware.
- It is confidential and is not to be shown to anyone else.

**Time Log**

| Date | Time | | Activity/task | Time spent (min) | Rating |
|---|---|---|---|---|---|
| | From | To | | | |
| 5.11.91 | 7 | 7.30 | Dressing up | 30 | I |
| | 7.30 | 8.15 | Breakfast | 45 | D |
| | 8.15 | 9.15 | Commuting | 60 | I |
| | 9.15 | 10.15 | Project report | 60 | I |
| | 10.30 | 10.45 | Tea | 15 | D |
| | 10.45 | 11.45 | Meeting | 30 | U |
| | . | . | . | . | . |
| . | . | . | . | . | . |
| | . | . | . | . | . |
| . | . | . | . | . | |

Total time spent on items I = 5 hr

D = 7 hr

U = 4 hr

**Time Log**

| Category Summary | |
|---|---|
| A. | PLANNING, PREPARATION AND UPDATING |
| A1 | Planning ahead |
| A2 | Preparation for interviews/visits, etc. |
| A3 | Keeping your knowledge up to date. |
| B. | CUSTOMER INTERVIEWS (IN BRANCH) |
| B1 | Lending interviews – personal and commercial |
| B2 | Other interviews with customers arranged to increase business, etc. |
| B3 | Non-lending/non-business development interviews |
| C. | CUSTOMER CONTACT – INFORMAL (IN BRANCH) |
| C1 | Working at an enquiry desk |
| C2 | Meeting customers informally in the banking hall/casual meetings |
| C3 | Working at a customer point |
| D. | STAFF CONTACT |
| D1 | Checking/advising on the work of others |
| D2 | Briefing staff about changes in working routines/products, etc. |
| D3 | Training staff/discussing progress/coaching others |

| | |
|---|---|
| E. | OFFICE – ROUTINES AND PROCEDURES |
| E1 | Dealing with correspondence/telephone calls, etc. |
| E2 | Attending to faults, problems, priorities, administration, etc. |
| E3 | Interpreting/issuing HO advices/procedures |
| F. | ATTENDING MEETINGS |
| F1 | Meetings with Area Manager or equivalent |
| F2 | Attending non-business professional meetings |
| F3 | Meetings with other departments (e.g., marketing, personnel) |
| G. | WORKING OUTSIDE THE BRANCH |
| G1 | Seeing customers at their premises |
| G2 | Visiting existing/prospective business clients |
| G3 | Meeting/lunching with professional contacts |
| G4 | Visits/talks/films shows outside the branch |
| H. | OTHER CATEGORIES |
| H1 | |
| H2 | |
| H3 | |

**Analysis of Time Log**

At the end of seven days, transfer the data generated to this page.
Total hours available to you/week ..................... waking hour
No. of hours spent on important activities/week ........................
No. of hours spent on doubtful activities/week .........................
No. of hours spent on useless activities/week ..........................
Are you satisfied with the way you are spending you time?

Yes ☐ Excellent! You are a rare person indeed! You really do not need to know anything more about time management. Gift the manual to someone else.

No ☐ Join the gang! You have taken the first and most important step towards better time management, namely, identified what you are really doing with your time, your most important resource. This is the first step towards getting back in control of your life and priorities.

## Exercise-1 Time Analysis Work Sheet

Having established the priorities in your life and what is it that you would really like to achieve in your personal and professional life. We now need to look at what we are actually doing with the time at hand.

The following
*Time-Analysis Work-Sheet*
is very useful for this purpose

## Time Analysis Worksheet

1. Spending too much time?
   (What are the activities on which I am spending too much time and which are not really so important?)

1. ....................................................................................................
2. ....................................................................................................
3. ....................................................................................................
4. ....................................................................................................

2. Where do I need to spend more time? (What are the things that I need to concentrate more on and on which I am not spending enough time now?)

1. ....................................................................................................
2. ....................................................................................................
3. ....................................................................................................
4. ....................................................................................................

3. What need not be done by me? (What are the things that I am doing and spending my time on which need not be done by me or need not to be done at all?)

1. ....................................................................................................
2. ....................................................................................................
3. ....................................................................................................
4. ....................................................................................................

4. What are the things that can be delegated? (What are the things that I am doing that can be done far more economically and may be better by my subordinates, thereby releasing more time for me?)

1. ....................................................................................................
2. ....................................................................................................
3. ....................................................................................................
4. ....................................................................................................

5. Most important time savings? (Which are the areas/items where I can save time?)

1. ....................................................................................................
2. ....................................................................................................
3. ....................................................................................................
4. ....................................................................................................

6. Overusing others' time? (What are the ways in which I can avoid overusing others' time so that they, in turn, can use their time more productively?)

1. ..........................................................................................................
2. ..........................................................................................................
3. ..........................................................................................................
4. ..........................................................................................................

7. Effective time saving? (What are the practical ways in which I can make effective time-savings and improve my time-utilization?)

1. ..........................................................................................................
2. ..........................................................................................................
3. ..........................................................................................................
..........................................................................................................

## DESK/PAPER MANAGEMENT

*"Next to the dog,*
*The waste paper basket*
*Is man's best friend."*

A neat, orderly and clean working environment does wonders, not only for more organized and well planned way of working, but also for a more comfortable and stress-free life. Misplaced documents, files that can't be found at the right time, desk space cluttered with files/paper/notes, etc., are some of the occupational hazards of a manager's working life. Working under these circumstances is exhaustive as well as unproductive.

### Your Desk

Your desk should be clean, neat and devoid of all paper/files except the ones you are working on at the moment. The only things that are really required on your desk is your pen, your diary and the telephone. The rest should be either in the drawers or neatly filed.

Information in the office comes in many forms such as:

- Scribbled memos from colleagues
- Messages left by staff
- Your own reminders
- Books/journals
- Telephone message
- Computer printouts
- Reports
- Pending letters.

It is important to plan and develop efficient system for better paper handling.

## TIPS FOR BETTER PAPER HANDLING

1. Handle each piece of paper only once.
2. Sort into priority A, B, C.
3. Scan and make notes if required. Take action and file in relevant files.
4. Delegate C priority paperwork to secretary.
5. Throw away junk mail.
6. Get your secretary to sort out mail, handle routine letters and put up only important ones to you.
7. Has your secretary screen all publications/articles and forward those only which are relevant.
8. Organize a good filing system with index and keep a list of files with you.
9. Use the wastepaper basket generously for useless information.
10. Answer correspondence briefly.
11. Arrange filing cabinets within easy reach.
12. Keep different files for projects on hand.
13. Edit your information needs to only that which is very important and relevant.
14. Eliminate paperwork by use of the personal computer.

## 1.6 PROACTIVITY: A TOOL FOR ENRICHING SELF-AWARENESS

Proactive behaviour is one of the techniques for enhancing one's self-awareness.

*For example, when a child starts walking, the mother keeps the child in constant supervision so that he/she does not fall. If the child falls she is over-protective, she consoles the child, also beats the floor in front of the child on which the child has fallen down. The child gets the impression that the floor is responsible for his fall. As per the study the mother is not spoiling the child but is over-protecting the child. The child should learn from his mistakes. This will help him to face the hurdles boldly.*

What we learn from this is that we should own up our mistakes rather than blame others for our misfortunes. That is the essence of proactivity, which is its most important dimension.

Responsibility = "Response-ability"

Proactive people:

Behaviour in the product of one's decision based on values
Personal leaders
Take the initiative and the solutions to problems
Successfully handle direct, indirect and no-control problems

## PROACTIVE MODEL

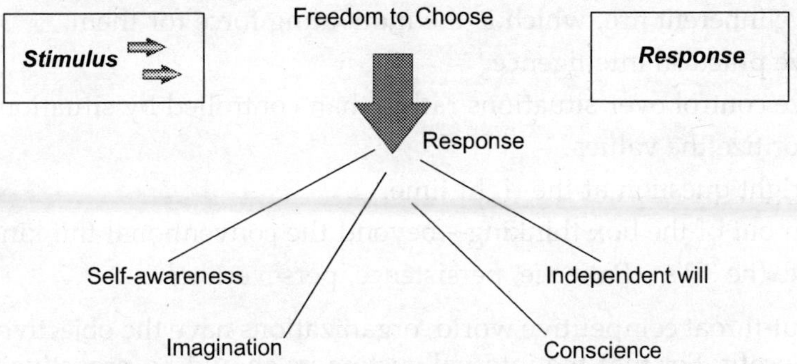


| Reactive Language | Proactive Language |
|---|---|
| There's nothing I can do | Let's look at our alternatives |
| That's just the way I am | I can choose a different approach |
| He makes me so mad | I control my own feelings |
| They won't allow that | I can create an effective presentation |
| I have to do that | I will choose an appropriate response |
| I can't | I choose |
| IU must | I prefer |
| If only | I will |

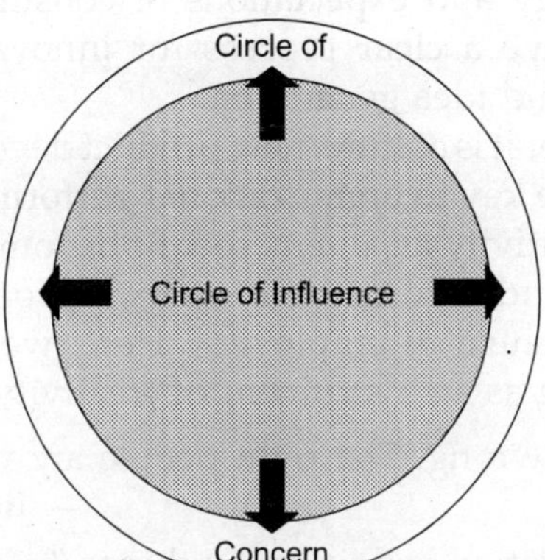


Proactive Focus

Positive energy enlarges circle of influence

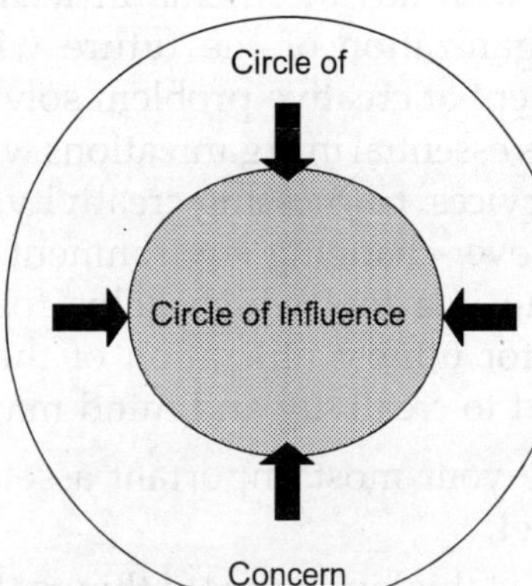


Reactive Focus

Negative energy reduces circle of influence

*Source: The Seven Habits of Highly Effective People* by Stephen R Covey.

**Seven characteristics of proactive people are:**

- They have inherent fire, which is the motivating force for them.
- They have practical intelligence.
- They have control over situations rather than controlled by situations.
- They prioritize the values.
- Ask the right question at the right time.
- Believe in out of the box thinking—beyond the conventional thinking.
- They have the 3P's – Patience, persistence, perseverance.

In today's cut-throat competitive world, organizations have the objective of customer service with a profit. For that the internal customers should be proactive and own up their responsibilities without blaming others and serve the external customers. This is applicable to any organization. If employees accept their responsibility for the work assigned to them with enthusiasm, interest, commitment and creativity, the organization they own or lead will have a unique perception in the mind of external and internal customers.

## 1.7 CREATIVITY AND INNOVATION FOR EFFECTIVENESS

### Mind Mapping

In today's highly competitive marketplace, one of the key ingredients of a company's survival is its ability to generate new ideas. Organizations are constantly adapting to keep pace with advancements in technology and expectations of consumers. The successful organization of the future will have a clear process for innovation and employees adept at creative problem solving and idea generation.

Creativity is essential in organizations whether it is culture, new product development, innovative services. Harnessing creativity is the key to organizational performance and success in an ever-changing environment. Creativity as an emergent phenomenon and mind mapping is a tool which helps foster and facilitate the creative process in an organization for utmost utilization of the potential of employees. Here, we focus on aspects related to creativity and mind mapping as an instrument of creativity.

"People are your most important assets" is wrong. The right people are your most important asset.

— Jim Collins

"Creativity is thinking up new things. Innovation is doing new things."

— Theodore Levitt

Ford (1996) stated that all creative ideas originate from human mind; therefore the importance of mind in generating creative ideas should be understood and emphasized.

Creative thinking is essential for organizations; creativity involves generation of new ideas.

Creativity can be used as a successful application of the problem-solving process.

Solving process model has been developed by Michael Mumford. The framework includes the following processes:

1. Problem identification and construction
2. Information search
3. Generation, evaluation and selection of ideas
4. Implementation, planning and monitoring

According to Michael Michalko, the writer of *Cracking Creativity*, "a mind map is 'the whole-brain alternative' to linear thinking. It reaches out in all directions and catches thoughts from any angle."

Mind mapping is an introduction to how the creative process works and also helps in understanding the ideas which are generated by using creative thinking techniques effectively.

Creative people, besides having above average intelligence, have the ability to visualize, imagine, and make mental transformations. A creative person sees modifications, new combinations, or new applications. In doing so left and right both sides of the brain are used to increase the memory and brain power.

**Left side of the brain**

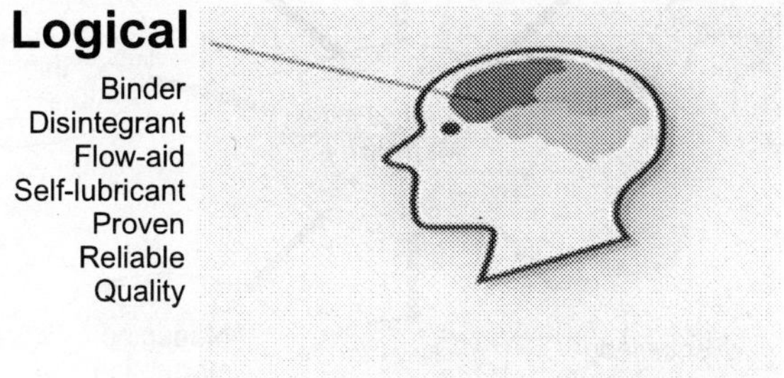


**Right side of the brain**

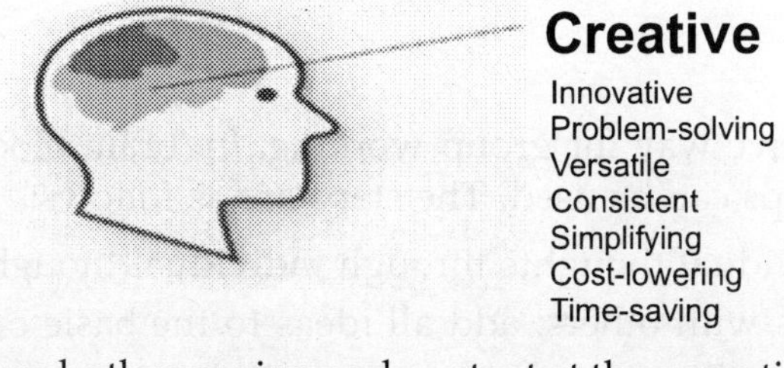


Visual diagrams convey both meaning and context at the same time so they are powerful communication tools, they show how different elements and ideas relate to each other. They help demonstrate creative thinking and problem solving.

**Value of Mind Mapping**

Mind maps are used in business for organizing ideas, planning projects, preparing and delivering presentations, decision making, problem solving, knowledge management, note taking in meetings, workshops, creative thinking, strategic planning, group brainstorming, life management/goal setting, training and education, business process mapping, event planning, research, SWOT analysis, performance improvement, etc. Innovation and creativity in management development programmes are essential for unleashing the creative potential of managers.

Mind mapping helps increase the sales of the company through better product design, better market planning, and better communication with the market. Expenses can be lowered by faster decisions to operate projects more efficiently. It can also provide better solutions and higher profit margins through gathering and process information providing better solutions to problems.

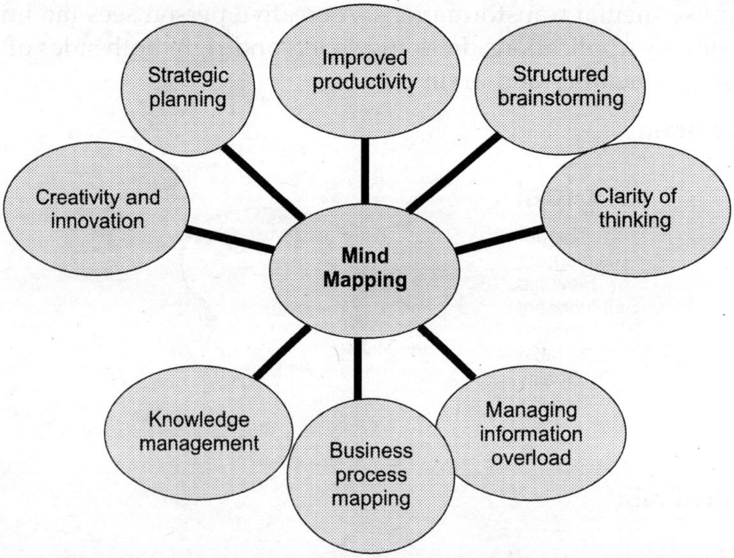


**Group Mind Mapping**

Mind maps are an effective way for group working. In 'brain blooming' which is like brainstorming, mind maps can be used. The steps are as follows:

1. Capture your individual thoughts through individual thoughts.
2. Blend the thoughts with others, add all ideas to the basic ordering ideas (BOIs) and catch all the input.
3. Group thinking can be illustrated through group mapping.

## MNEMONICS

Mnemonics is a learning technique which helps in retention in the human memory. The information is transformed in the brain in such a manner that it helps in retentions. It

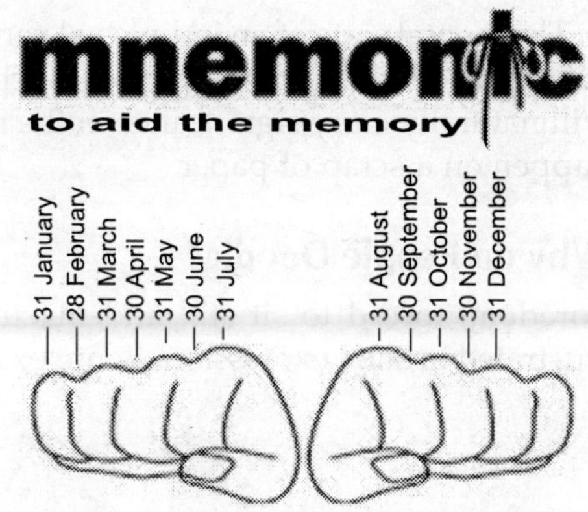


is usually used as short poems, acronyms, or memorable phrases, but it can also be used in visual or kinesthetic forms. The human mind easily remembers spatial, personal, surprising, physical, sexual, humorous, or otherwise "relatable" information so it can be used in music, names, words, expressions rather than more abstract or impersonal forms of information. It can also be used by constructing pictures.

Effectiveness of mnemonics varies from young children to the elderly. This type of learning strategies needs time and resources by educators to develop creative and effective devices. This learning techniques is helpful for long-term memory. It also helps as an instructional technique to help students improve their memory of important information.

The method enhances memory of complex words or ideas and promotes better retention of the material to be learnt.

Keyword — A keyword is a familiar word that sounds similar to the word or idea being taught. The teacher creates an illustration that links the prior and new information in the student's memory. Example: The scientific term for common frogs is ranidae. A helpful keyword for ranidae might be rain and a teacher could show a picture of frogs hopping in the rain.

## DOODLINGS AND THE SECRETS BEHIND IT

**Doodles** are simple, unclear drawings or abstracts made when a person is not concentrating on one thing and is occupied elsewhere. One can see doodling in school notebooks, or when you are having a long conversation on a telephone and a pen or paper is availabale to you. When a students is daydreaming or losing interest during class, he usually doodles.

Popular kinds are cartoons of teachers or comic characters, invented fictional beings, landscapes, geometric shapes and patterns, textures, banners with legends, and animations made by drawing a scene sequence in various pages of a book or notebook.

The mental state of an individual can be revealed by doodling. Most shapes are circle, sun, and square. Some properties, such as aggression, repetition, fluidity or neatness – will naturally carry significance in the interpretation. It is an unconscious work and can happen on a scrap of paper.

## Why do People Doodle?

Boredom, forced to sit still and inactive for any period of time creates an outlet for frustrated artistic expression. Some examples of doodling:

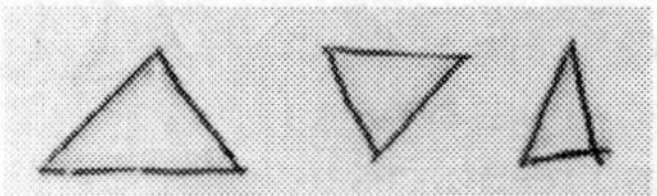

Triangle bold arrows - Suggest an aggressive personality, highly competitive

**Geometric Shapes:** Regular patterns from geometric shapes tend to indicate an organised and efficient mind. Triangles are a geometrically stable shape but also suggest direction and sense of purpose.

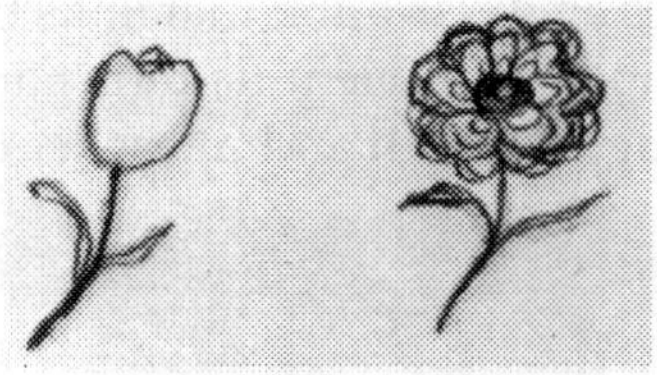

Flowers: are imagination - love of beauty and a search for love.

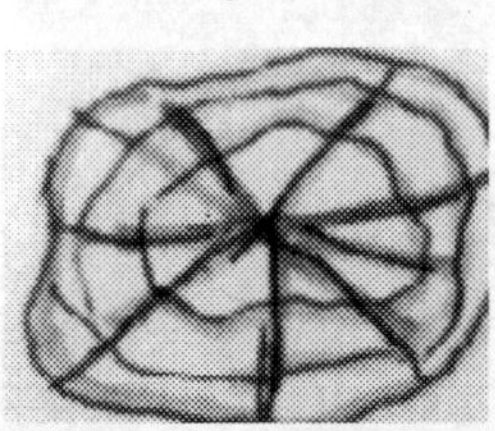

Webs: an intricate web shows a desire to accumulate friends, money and status.

Writing your own name over and over again means egotism.

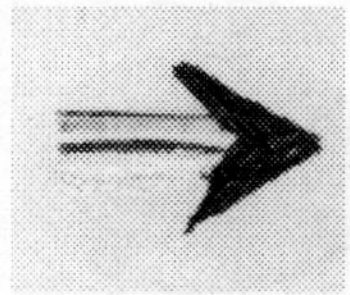

Bold arrows: very determined, great drive, direct

Arrows represent direction and ambition. Drawn aggressively, they represent a desire for action. Drawn in careful outline, they indicate a desire for progression or advancement, especially if pointing upwards.

## MEANING OF COLOURS

Colour often has a degree of innate meaning due to visual associations: red, orange and yellow are warm colours, while green, blue, blue-grey and violet are cool.

**Red:** It represents power.

**Blue, black and grey:** Conventional colours, indicating stability and strength. Dark blue indicates security. Grey is sometimes called 'the colour of sorrow'.

**Purple:** Purple represents royalty.

**Brown:** It indicates a conservative personality, even repression.

**Green:** Suggests well-balanced individuals.

**Hearts:** Hearts are drawn by people in love.

**Dots:** Dots are often regarded as a sign of great unease and a disordered personality.

**Faces:** Interpretation partly depends on whether the face represents the self or someone else. A beautiful face can also indicate a sociable 'people person'.

**Eyes:** They are sometimes regarded as showing a wish to be desirable.

## 1.8 PERSONAL EFFECTIVENESS

Personal effectiveness means making the most at all personal resources at our disposal, i.e., our personal talents, energy and time relative to what's most important to us.

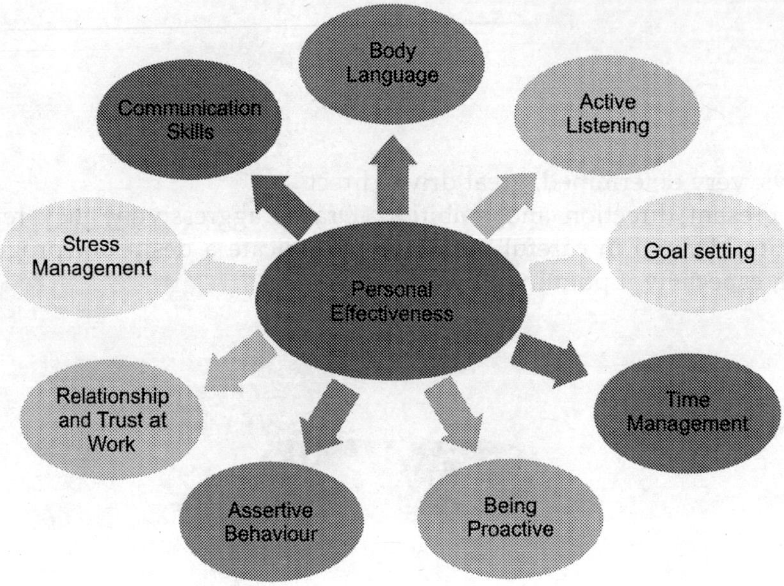


## 7 Habits of Highly Effective People by Steven Covey

1. Be proactive
2. Begin with the end in mind
3. Put first thing first
4. Think win-win
5. Seek first to understand, than to be understood
6. Synergize
7. Sharpen the saw

Learn a set of principles and personal management skills that will change how you view your life and enable you to grow in confidence and effectiveness.

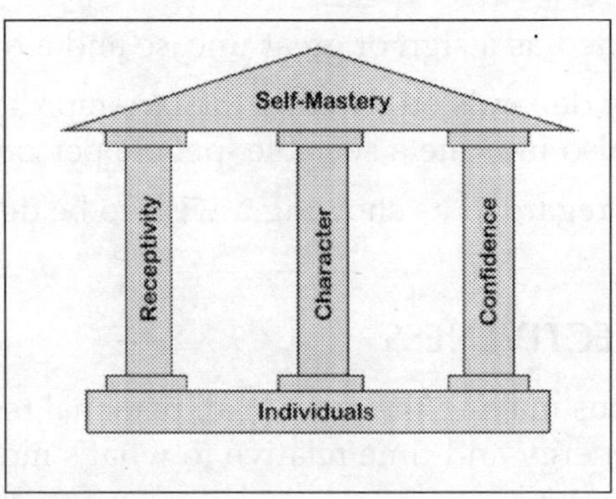

## Exercise-2

## PICTURE PERCEPTION TEST

**How do you perceive the picture?**

**What can be the significance of the picture?**

**What do you understand by this picture?**

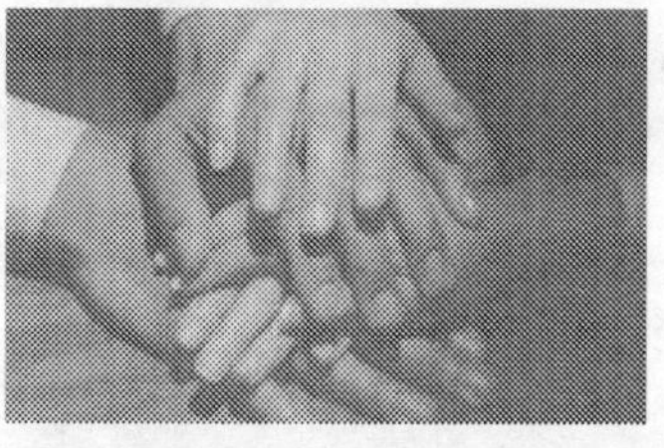

## CASE STUDY

## The Fence and the Nail

There was once a boy of a very difficult character. He was very abusive in the class and used to beat the classmates. His father was fed up with is misbehaviour. He then gave him a bag of nails to be put one by one in the garden fence when he did something bad or abused some one.

The first day the boy drived 50 nails in the garden fence.

During the days he learnt how to control himself and was fed up with the activity. He started conrolling his behaviour. The boy thought that it was easier to learn control himself than to hammer nails in the fence.

At last, the boy controlled himself and did not drive any nail in the garden fence. He told his father that he did not need to hammer any nail.

His father then instructed him to take out the nails from the garden fence every day.

This helped in controlling his temper and not losing his patience.

After days of removing nails from the fence the son came to the father.

The father brought his son in front of the fence and told him:

"My son, you behaved well, but look how many holes you left in the fence".

The relationship breaks when you have an argument with someone and tell him bad words, you leave him with wounds like these. "Sorry," hardly makes a difference, the wound will stay. A wound caused by words hurts just as bad as a physical wound.

***Answer the following:***

1. What is the significance of the story?
2. Justify the approach of the father to change the behaviour of his child.
3. Suggest a title to the story.
4. What are the other approaches you can use to change the personality of an individual?

## SUMMARY

- **Personality** means the effect, which an individual leaves on other people. It depicts the total picture of an individual. A personality has to be charged with inner faith.
- Values are important because they allow us to live more peacefully with others and enable us to achieve whatever goals we set for ourselves. There are certain values that most people believe to be particularly important. Some of them are respect, responsibility, love, honesty, commitment, cooperation, family, friendship, and caring for the environment.
- Personality development is developing of a personality to create a strong positive impression about self with the targeted group and maintain for a long run.
- Personality development depends on temperament and performance, perceptions and values, awareness and consciousness, health, wealth, intellectual capacity, self-confidence, emotional intelligence will power and self-discipline, duty, responsibility and accountability, ethical and moral values.

- Develop your positive power by making others feel accepted, approved, admired, appreciated, important, needed.
- Develop a "CAN DO ATTITUDE".

## QUESTIONS

**I. Explain in Brief.**

1. List the characteristics of personality.
2. Why are values important for building a personality?
3. Write down five core values.
4. What do you mean by personality development?
5. Write down four aspects of an influencing and pleasing personality.

**II. Answer the following questions.**

1. Define and describe personality.
2. What are values? How does it help in developing your personality?
3. What are the major requirements towards the development of a fine personality?
4. Mention five main factors each for developing a strong personality in social environment and in working fields.
5. What is self-development and what are its major factors?
6. Write down three positive attitude quotes.

## ASSIGNMENTS

- Check Exercises 1 & 2 of chapter 2 and on p. 87.

## PROJECT

- Read the autobiographies of five successful persons and write down their personality traits which have made them successful.
- Talk to your peers and elders and prepare a questionnaire to assess their attitude and motivation in life.
- Plan and write down your own personality traits.

**DID YOU KNOW?**

## SLEEPING STYLE ALSO DEPICTS A PERSONALITY OF AN INDIVIDUAL

This posture indicates that you are a confident person. You will see success in whatever you undertake, owing to your unrelentless endeavour. People who sleep on their right side with their right arm stretching over their head and lying on the right side are said to be blessed with power and fortune.

Contrary to the previous one (curling up), you are gentle, polite, sincere, and loving. Well, nothing is perfect. Build up your self-confidence and learn to accept mistakes or imperfections. Happiness will then come your way!

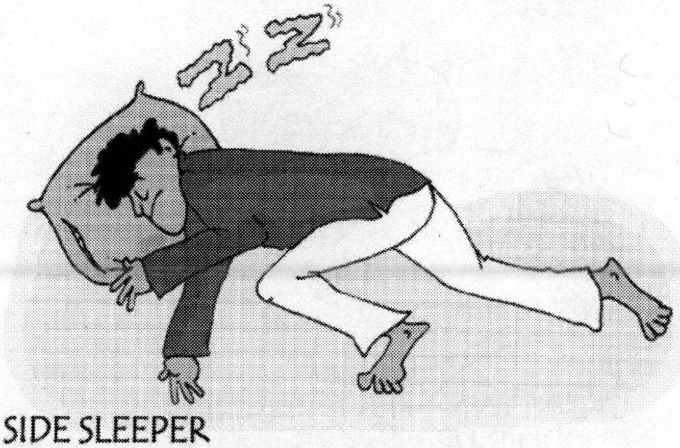

## SIDE SLEEPER WITH ONE KNEE BENDED:

You are inclined to be fussy, always whining and complaining. Nervousness is probably your second name. You tense up easily and get overly excited over small matters. Life isn't such a big deal. Learn to relax.

## SIDE SLEEPER CURLING UP:

Selfish, jealous and vindictive are words that describe you. People around you got to be careful not to step on your toes as you are easily irritated!

## UNKNOWN CUDDLED UP:

You feel lonely and depressed because you are obsessed with your past failures and setbacks. You are hesitant and indecisive, giving others an impression that love has been missing in your life.

## HOME ALONE

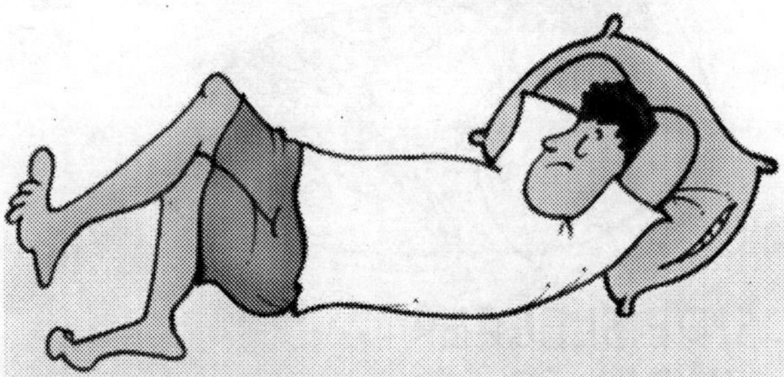

## BACK SLEEPER WITH LEGS CROSSED

Anyone who sleeps cross-legged is said to be self-obsessed and finds difficulty in accepting changes. Solitude is your priority. Yet, your redeeming quality is your threshold for tolerance.

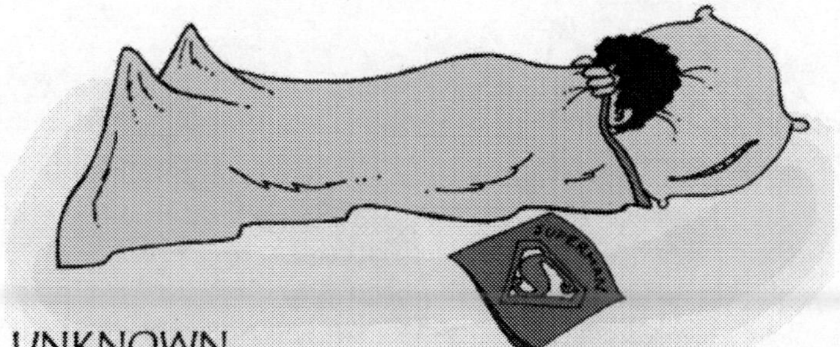

## UNKNOWN<br>COVERING FROM HEAD TO TOE:

You may appear real macho in public, but deep down inside you are shy and weak. You tend to keep loads of secrets. If you encounter any problem, you will rather keep it to yourself and agonise over it than ask for help. No wonder you grimace in your sleep!

## TUMMY SLEEPER SLEEPING ON THE STOMACH

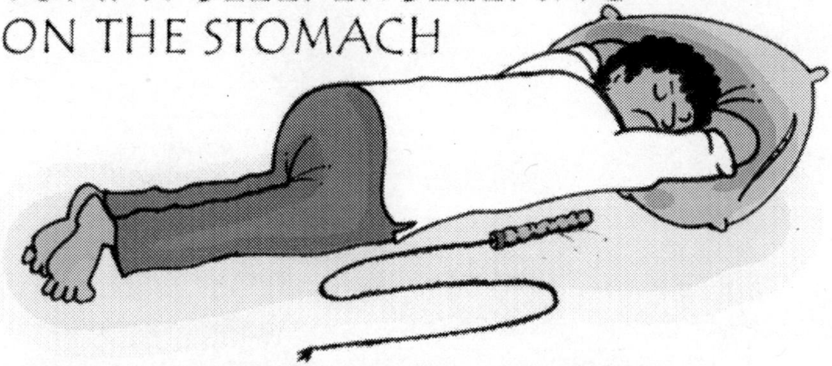

If you sleep face down all night, you are likely to be narrow minded. You are probably self-centred and always force people to comply with your own needs. You are also likely to be reckless and desultory. Time to change your sleep posture.

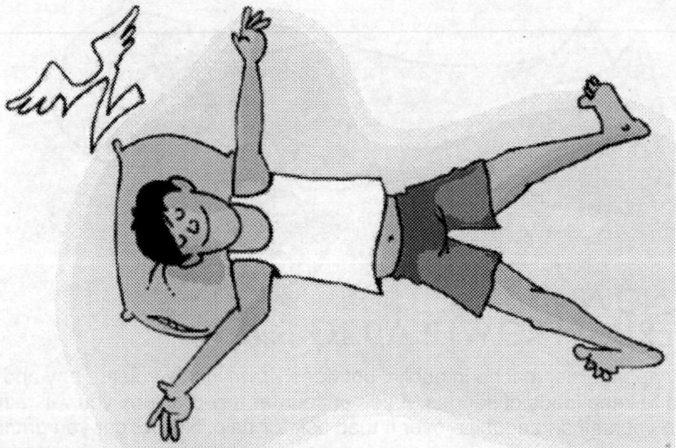

## BACK SLEEPER WITH ARMS AND LEGS SPREAD OUT:

What a liberty loving-soul! Well, this posture reveals your true identity. Comfort-lover and beauty-worshipper, you are also a real spendthrift (but luckily you earn just as much). Your other undesirable trait is that you are a bit nosy and seem to enjoy gossiping. Well, who did you mention in your tales lately?

# 2 UNIT

# Development

*Change and growth take place when a person has risked himself and dares to become involved with experimenting with his own life.*

**— Herbert Otto**

## Learning Objectives

- Know and Accept Yourself
- Living Your Attitude
- Developing Personal Competence
- Develop Personal Resistance
- Create a Positive Self-Belief System
- Increasing Attention Span

### Believe in Yourself

An elderly Chinese woman had two large pots, each hung on the ends of a pole, which she carried across her neck. One of the pots had a crack in it while the other pot was perfect and always delivered full portion of water. At the end of the long walk from the stream to the house, the cracked pot arrived only half full. For a full two years this went on daily, with the woman bringing home only one and a half pots of water. Of course, the perfect pot was proud of its accomplishment. But the poor cracked pot was ashamed of its own imperfection, and miserable that it could only do half of what it had been made to do. After 2 years of what it perceived to be a bitter failure, it spoke to the woman one day by the stream. The old woman smiled, "Did you notice that there are flowers on your side of the path, but not on the other pot's side? That's because I have always known about your flaw, so I planted flower seeds on your side of the path, and every day while we walk back, you water them. For two years I have been able to pick these beautiful flowers to decorate the table. Without you being just the way you are, there would not be this beauty to grace the house."

**Moral of the Story:**

Each of us has our own unique flaw…

But it's the cracks and flaws we each have that make our lives together so very interesting and rewarding.

You've just got to take each person for what he is and look for the good in him.

## 2.1 KNOW THYSELF, OWN CHANGE THYSELF

*"A pessimist sees the difficulty in every opportunity; an optimist sees the opportunity in every difficulty."*

**— Sir Winston Churchill**

Changes in the global environment are radical and far-reaching and the capacity to learn faster is the only source for sustaining competitive advantage.

The dictum, "Know thyself, own change thyself" has become the cornerstone of managerial effectiveness. Learning implies awareness of the job, one's current position, personal strengths and limitations, and development needs. Knowing oneself is not enough. Learning about self must be translated into action for change.

Consequently, change in self leads to managing the external reality.

Managers need to continuously upgrade their knowledge and skills in technical, environmental and leadership areas. They need to examine their values, style and typical behaviours and assess the extent to which they facilitate them both in their professional lives and personal lives.

**Many people have the aptitude and also the desire to be successful in their jobs and yet they do not get going.**

**WHY?**

**Perhaps, they think, since they can master the job, there is no need to master themselves.**

### Self-Scanning Exercise-1

### ACCENTUATE THE POSITIVE

### Objective

To break self-imposed barriers that don't allow people to "like themselves"; to enhance one's self-image by sharing comments and personal qualities.

### Procedure

Most of us have been brought up to believe that it is not "right" to say nice things about one's self or for that matter, about others. This exercise attempts to change that attitude by sharing personal qualities with each other. In this exercise, each person provides his or her partner with the response to one, two, or all four of the following suggested dimensions:

1. Two personality qualities I like in myself.
2. One talent or skill I like in myself.
3. Identify your two strengths in your present role
4. My hobby
5. One exciting event/thing that you look forward in the near future for yourself.

**Exercise-2**

## SELF-ASSESSMENT

Date –
Name –
Industry/Institution
Please rate yourself in the five-point grade

**A – Above 90% B – 75-90% C – 65-80% D – 50-65% E – Below 50%**

**PERSONALITY TRAITS**

| | A | B | C | D | E |
|---|---|---|---|---|---|
| Self-confidence | | | | | |
| Confidence in communicating with others | | | | | |
| Fluency in language | | | | | |
| Comprehension of ideas | | | | | |
| Freedom of expression | | | | | |
| Managing your time | | | | | |
| Decision making in different situations | | | | | |
| Leadership traits | | | | | |
| Knowledge about surroundings | | | | | |
| Coping with circumstances | | | | | |
| Positive thinker | | | | | |
| Creativity of ideas | | | | | |
| Sense of self-worth | | | | | |
| | | | | | |

## 2.1.1 The Mirror Reflection Technique

What matters most is how you see yourself.

Once in a day we wonder how to change our lives for the best. At least once in a day we are judgmental about another, but never during the day do we analyze ourselves. The irony is that we all want to rectify the world but not ourselves as individuals. We go around seeking answers from various learned people and after reaching a dead come back more dissatisfied. We all know that the answer to various questions lie within ourselves, but does one know how to tap into the indefinite knowledge and power in the mind?

Look into the mirror and you will see reflection of your face. But the mirror that reflects your face also reflects what is going on in your mind. If you look happy it is reflected in the mirror, you look sad that too is shown, but what is actually weaving our destiny, moulding our everyday life, it is our thoughts. Our outer world is the projection of what we think the whole day long. Whether it is anger or love, we will invite situations corresponding to our mental state as the vibrations we send out will be felt by one and all…

One must experiment with life then only we build our faith. Many people base this mirror reflection pressing conditions, like for instance, trying to get rid of a smoking addiction, but forget that if one's inner core is built of positivity and strength none of the issues would work their negatives. Tap into this mind. Introspect. Ask yourself, as you look into that mirror, what you are all about, where you wish to reach. Be self critical, and when you know your weaknesses, blast them out of your mind by replacing them with the positive ones. After affirmations like 'I am, strong' or 'I am happy and peaceful' or 'I am perfect' have done wonders to the psyche of one and many. It's all about convincing your own mind that you are all that you wish to be, the mirror is your tool showing you how far you have reached. Train your mind by feeding it with positives and live the life you dreamt of. Turn around your life, as till now we have all been busy trying to change other lives.

**To rectify the world and put it on the proper path, we have to first rectify ourselves and our conduct.**

## 2.1.2 The Power of Self-Talk

***What is Self-Talk?***

It is the words that we say to ourselves. The positive self-talk gives us encouragement and self-worth. The negative self-talk makes us feel small and incapable or unworthy.

If you feel you don't deserve something or have no worth or no body respects you, you probably have some negative self-talk and it is time to take action.

You can change your self-talk by telling yourself that you are worthy and you deserve it.

## *Some Negative Self-Talk*

- I am not that smart.
- I am not respected by others.
- I have short stature.
- I am not OK.
- I don't have the looks.
- I am so unlucky.
- People consider me to be a useless person.
- No one loves me.
- I am old.
- I am helpless.
- What is there in life.

**Psychologist tell that**

That more than 90% insults and emotional wounds are created by self without any bad intention on others' part; and, the rest 10% emotional wounds, which others inflict, are intentional.

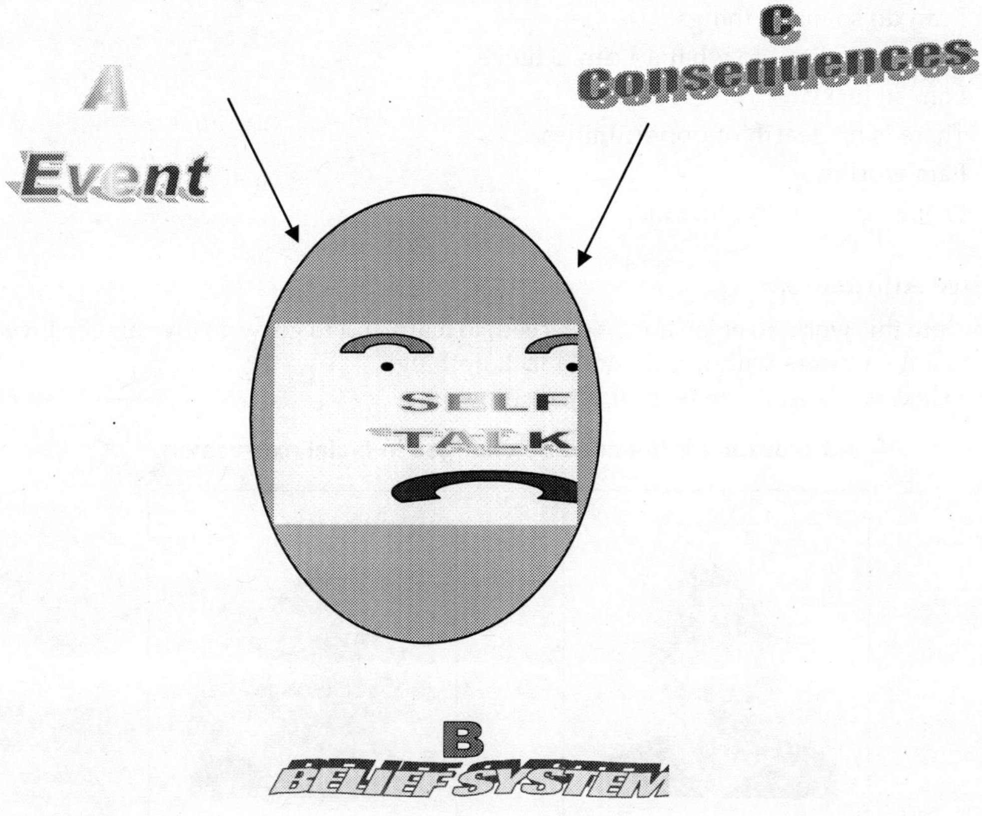

### *How to Correct Negative Self-Talk?*

### Try to Distinguish between Rational and Irrational Talks

Rational means "verifiable" or "realistic" or "sensible". Something for which any proof or evidence exists.

Rational thinking is the skill of questioning, challenging and attacking the sentences which we tell ourselves.

How to check your self-talk?

- ➢ Check
- ➢ Challenge
- ➢ Correct

### Some Positive Self-Talk

- I am wonderful.
- I am happy.
- I am loveable.
- I am young.
- I can do so many things.
- There is no limit to what a I can achieve.
- I am so lucky.
- There is no dearth of opportunities.
- I am worthy.
- People love and respect me.

### Positive Affirmations

I came into this world to enjoy and to succeed, to learn and to grow, to love and be loved.
I have all the powers within me – and I lack nothing!
I say so because I am the master of my destiny!

**Attitudes are influenced by changes in facial expression**

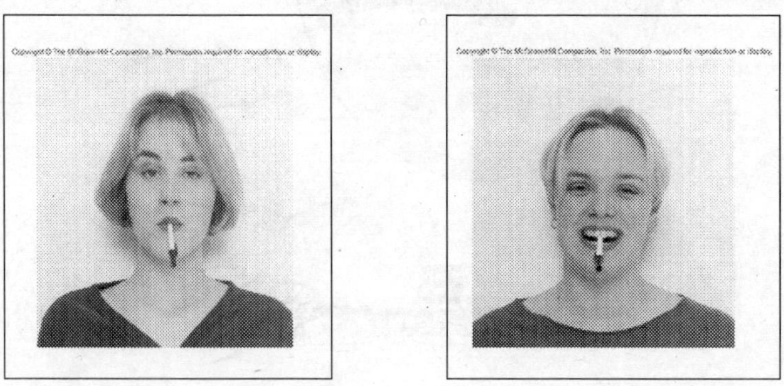

### 2.1.3 Technique of Giving Self-Introduction

#### *Self-Introduction*

Self-introduction tells people about yourself and the way it is given depicts your personality. It should be given, what we want others to know about yourself and your business. It should be given in such a way that your words attract the attention of the audience. It is the first impression, so the first impression should be made the last impression. Giving self-introduction is an art so it warrants some careful attention.

*An Effective Self-Introduction*

- Short and sweet is the key
- Be aware of the setting
- Embrace understatements
- Focus on the other person
- Have a call-to-action
- Finish strong
- Use the person's name
- Be well prepared (do your home work well)
- Compliment and thank the audience

*How to Give Self-Introduction*

Self-introduction makes the first impression on the other person. There are some points that should be considered while giving self-introduction.

1. **The impact should be the focus point.**

   The impact should be brief, organized, and assertive. The focused impact leaves a good impression. Keep it to one to two minutes maximum.

2. **Take turns for the impact.**

   More than one introduction has to be developed as there should be several different ways to introduce yourself, if same people are present frequently. Develop yourself for the situations in which you have to present yourself — an introduction for each.

3. **Make introduction audience relevance.**

   Give introduction depending on the listener(s) interest and select an aspect of your business that will be relevant.

4. **Believe in yourself.**

   Believe in yourself when creating your introduction. Do not oversell yourself or your services, as it would not sound convincing, and it reflects you and your integrity.

5. **Put your influence behind it.**

   Deliver your introduction with honesty, humility, without hesitation, without confusion, without being submissive. Use sentences that strengthen it.

6. **Smile and sound happy about what you say.**

   Happiness attracts attention. Being happy with yourself and your work will attract attention of others.

7. **Look at your listener(s).**

   Eye contact should be there with the listener as it shows confidence and gives attention to the listener. Making eye contact is the best way to show yourself in the brief time you have.

8. **Know when to use it and when not.**

   Select the right time to introduce yourself. Great introduction falls flat, if given at the wrong time and can leave a lastingly bad impression.

9. **Know when and how to stop.**

   The introduction should be crisp and hard-hitting. Adding more and more information dilutes the impact. A compact one gives an impression of certainty and strength, so keep it brief.

10. **Give space for a response.**

    Listen and then talk. Let the listener ask the questions so that he can know you better and let him/her to ask for your card, for more information, for clarification. Make him comfortable. Come to a stop and wait for him/her to speak. In some professions, the wait is as important as words you use.

## MEANING OF NAME AND ITS EFFECTIVENESS

### Importance of Name

Name is the most important in addressing or giving self-introduction. It depicts a personality of a person. A name is a label for person, that is used to distinguish one from another. "We all own one precious thing no one can take away from us that is our name."

### *Components of Name*

Name is made of 3 components:

- First name
- Middle name
- Last name

Eg: Subhas Chandra Bose

**Three types of names a person can have:**

- **Formal name:** known to everyone
- **Common name:** which describes a characteristic of the person
- **Secret name:** which is a name known only by the name bearer and the one who gives him the name.
- Named after a beloved person

- Named to give respect to an important person in the family or society.
- Named for an excellence or quality that our parents hoped we would symbolize.
- Named to recall an event that occurred when born.
- Named after sound of the name liked by our parent.

*Examples*

**MIRA**

Means "prosperous" in Sanskrit. This was the name of an Indian princess who devoted her life to the God Krishna.

**PREETI**

Means "love" in Sanskrit.

**RAMESH**

This is one of the names of Vishnu.

Try to know the meaning of your name and incorporate it with your personality and this should be the first sentence of your SELF-INTRODUCTION.

**Introduction**

For example, the name Shikha signifies top of everything. In self-introduction it should be said, I try to remain at top by my hard work and sincerity and devotion and I am consistent in achieving it.

## 2.2 BUILDING SELF-CONFIDENCE

**How to overcome lack of confidence, nervousness and shyness and how to build confidence.**

- Self-confidence is not to be confused with conceit and arrogance – rather arrogant
- People lack confidence.
- With confidence life becomes exciting, and colourful.

### Symptoms of Lack of Confidence

(a) At parties and picnics you are asked to sing. You are a good singer but you could not even stand and came up with excuses.

(b) You are expected to speak on your subject and the tongue gets glued up with upper jaw. You start shaking and fumbling.

(c) School and college time –why you could not ask questions to clear your doubts.

(d) As the time of air fight approaches –you start feeling butterflies in your stomach.

(e) You want to propose a girl for marriage and you end up by saying "let us have a cup of tea".

(f) Norman Davis, a great speaker, first time could not speak more than "I conceive, I conceive, I conceive" — a lady sitting in the front row, "I conceived once and delivered a baby." Norman Davis took it as a challenge and became a great orator.

Lack of confidence results in inferiority complex and imaginary fears and phobias. For such people procession on fears starts right from morning, i.e., of losing of job, fire, open spaces, height, health, heart attack, etc. and how to overcome these fears?

Why some people keep on worrying for nothing and move about carrying weight on their minds of futile fear and phobias? Why some people live with inferiority complex and lack of will power? Why some people mishandle opportunities and job interviews due to nervousness and shyness? Let us discuss various approaches to overcome symptoms of lack of confidence.

## HOW TO BUILD CONFIDENCE: THREE APPROACHES

Confident people tackle their problems smartly keeping smile on their face and handle opportunities for their advantage.

1. **Action Plan**
   (a) Acquisition of number of skills—never be held back by timidity or self-depreciation. Do-death of the fear is certain.
   (b) Enroll in a public speaking course—ability to speak is a short-cut method to gain confidence.
   Master these three points to become a good conversationalist and a speaker.
   - Be at home with yourself (feel free mentally and physically)
   - Be at home with your subject
   - Be at home with your audience
   (c) Now you will be given bigger responsibilities, don't refuse the opportunity.
2. **Psychological Approach – God has sent us in this world with special spark. Recognise it and develop it.**
   (a) Never condemn yourself.
   (b) Untoward childhood experiences and adverse things.
   (c) Love other (look to the good points of the people) and love yourself. With love one can influence people and rule others (Hitler's example)
3. **Auto suggestion approach** – I am improving my relations with everybody. I will do to others as I expected from them.
   (a) I am growing more and more confident every day.
   (b) My English vocabulary is improving every day.
   I am becoming a better speaker and developing good qualities.

## Self- Focus by SWOT Analysis

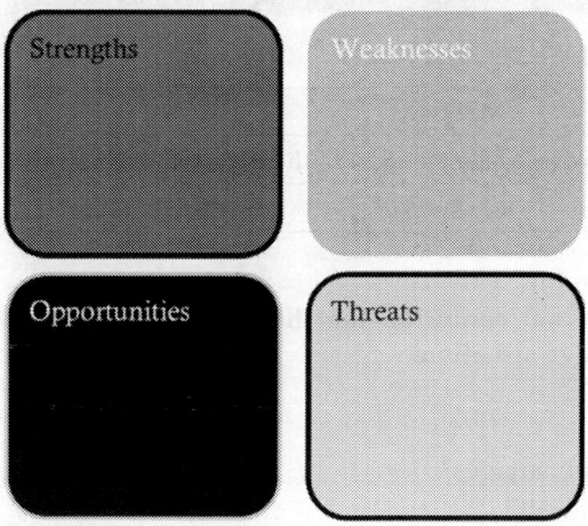


SWOT matrix is the best management model and each of the four quadrants, in turn, are to analyze where you are now, where you want to be, and then make an action plan to get there.

SWOT is a planning tool to understand the strengths, weaknesses, opportunities, and threats. It involves specifying the objective of the business or project or individual and identifying the internal and external factors that are supportive or unfavourable for achieving that objective.

SWOT analysis generates information that is helpful in matching an organization or group's goals, programmes, and a capacity to the social environment in which it operates

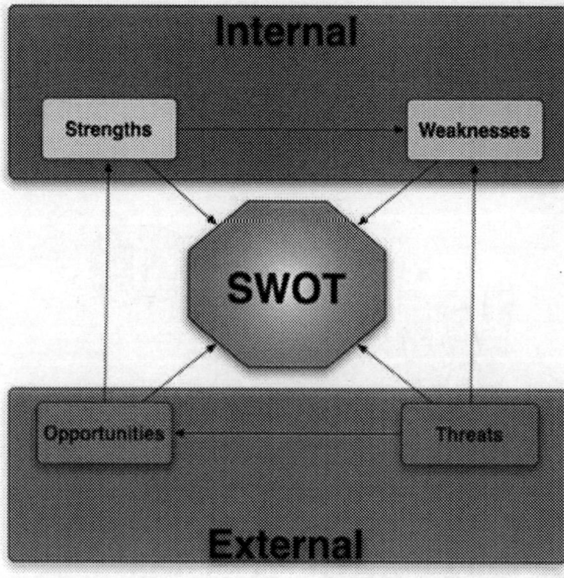


| | Strengths | Weaknesses |
|---|---|---|
| Oppurtunities | Offensive: Make the most of these | Defensive: Watch competition closely |
| Threats | Adjust: Restore strengths | Survive: Turn around |

**SWOT is the acronym for**

**S–Strength is an internal condition that has the potential of improving the self/ institution's competitive situation.**

*Strengths:*

- What are your advantages?
- What do you do well?
- What relevant resources do you have?
- What do other people see as your strengths?
  - Make a list of your characteristics. Some of these will hopefully be strengths!
  - Looking at your strengths, think about them in relation to your competitors.

**W–Weakness in contrast is also an internal condition that leaves the institution's strategically vulnerable.**

- What do you have to improve?
- What people do not like about you?
- What should be avoided?

- See yourself internally and externally – do other people perceive about you, do they list down your faults? Be realistic to the unpleasant truths as soon as possible.

**O–Opportunity is an environmental condition that offers significant prospects for improving the institution's position relative to the competition.**

- ➢ What are the good opportunities at present favouring you?
- ➢ What are the motivating facts you are aware of?

Useful opportunities are strengths that can help you reach your goals.

**T–Threat is an environmental condition that offers significant prospects for undermining the institution's competitive position.**

- ➢ What difficulties are you facing?
- ➢ Who are your competitors?
- ➢ What are the changes in your specification that are essential for your job, products or services?
- ➢ Is changing technology threatening your position?
- ➢ Is your weaknesses threatening your business?

  This analysis will often be enlightening – in what need to be done in putting problems into perspective and eliminating them.

## Steps in Listing the SWOT MATRIX

- ➢ **Step 1 – In the here and now...**

  List all strengths and weaknesses and be realistic
- ➢ **Step 2 – What might be...**

  List all opportunities as they are the potential future strengths. Then list all threats they are potential future weaknesses.
- ➢ **Step 3 – Plan of action...**

  Review your SWOT matrix and create an action plan to address each of the four areas.

In summary:

- Strengths need to be maintained, enhanced
- Weaknesses need to be remedied and converted into strengths
- Opportunities should be the priority and utilized to the optimum
- Threats need to be conquered and minimized.

SWOT matrix is used for strategic planning towards achieving your goals, Use it and reap the benefits.

**SELF-ANALYSIS (How is self-analysis done and judged in a negative and positive way)**

1. **Initiative**

| POSITIVE | NEGATIVE |
|---|---|
| Enters in a calculated manner | - Makes a feeble entry |
| and at the acceptable moment | - Becomes unnecessarily aggressive. |
| - Holds the audience by being, | - Does not wait for the correct persuasive and convincing opportunity to make his point and misses his original point or argument along the way |
| - Concludes each argument at the right time and manner | - Very hesitant about his point of view. |
| | - Attempts to be forceful in his point of view Easily loses his confidence. |

2. **Knowledge**

| | |
|---|---|
| - Has in depth understanding and knowledge about the subject | - Shows shallow understanding |
| | - Gives wrong facts. |
| | - Bombards with data and confuses the issues at hand. |

3. **Value addition to the group**

| | |
|---|---|
| - Consistently gives | - Takes the discussion on a tangent quality to the discussion by adding irrelevant points. |
| - Makes original points that steer the group | Harps on small points and the topic - into discussion other angles to miss the critical issues. |
| Agrees/disagrees without explanation | - Uncooperative towards the groups efforts |

4. **Participation**

| | |
|---|---|
| - Comes in often | - Shows interest or involvement in spurts. |
| - Is sustained in his participation | - Disinterested towards group's efforts. |
| - Shows interest in the group's activities | - Speaks only to do his duty |

**5. Thinking/Reasoning**

| | |
|---|---|
| - Logical and rational | - Displays irrational arguments |
| - Consistent | - Does not listen to reason |
| | - Is easily swayed by others' arguments. |
| | - Unwilling to modify his point of view. |
| | - Shows inconsistency in his reasoning |

**6. Communication Skills**

| | |
|---|---|
| - Communicates ideas fluently and effectively | - Poor listening skills |
| - Listens attentively | - Poor linguistic skills |
| | - Is unable to coherently express |

**7. Personal Skills**

| | |
|---|---|
| - Relaxes | - Shows disrespect |
| - Confident | - Tense and fidgety |
| - Pleasant | - Impolite |
| - Courteous | - Makes no effort to deal with others in the group (stays cold and aloof). |

**8. Group Skills**

| | |
|---|---|
| - Displays leadership by steering and group. | - Mistakes aggressiveness for leadership |
| - Builds up the confidence of the group. | - Is perceived as disruptive by the group. |
| - Is able to hold attention consistently | - Group indifferent to him. |

What can you read from the above? Some will say good and some evil. You can choose either 'good' or to see 'evil '. It's a conscious choice and it completely shapes what you see.

The point here is that you choose how you want your life to be.

## FOR PEAK PERFORMANCE

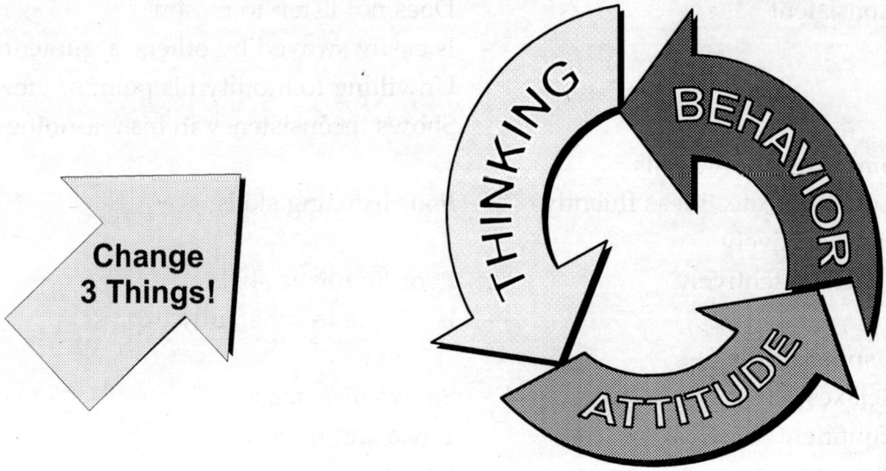


The difference between ordinary and extraordinary is a little EXTRA

## 2.3 ATTITUDE BUILDING

### Components of Attitude

- **Perception**: The conscious mental awareness and interpretation on sensory stimulus.
- **Values**: They are our paradigms which we use to distinguish between the 'good' and 'bad', or 'desirable' and 'undesirable'.
- **Beliefs**: A descriptive thought that a person holds about something

- **Experience**: The effect upon the judgment or feeling produced by an event whether witnessed or participated in.
- **Emotions**: Psychological and physical responses of our body to the sensory stimuli.
- "Emotions are the medium for the exchange and expression of feelings."
- **Tendencies**: Our predisposition or mental frames to respond in specific ways to specific situations or attitude objects.

**"Living Your Attitude"**

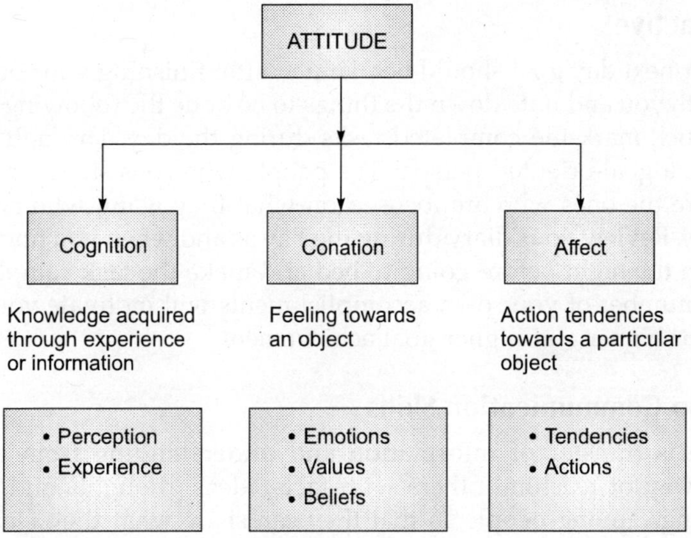


## Principles for Developing a Positive Attitude

### Step-1: Do Your Own Introspection

Talk to yourself and decide to be a positive thinking person. Do your own introspection. Do your SWOT analysis, i.e., identify your strengths, weaknesses, opportunities and threats so that you are in a much better position to take your control? Try and make all efforts to overcome your weaknesses and try to convert them into strengths by thinking in a positive way. Spend time improving yourself. The more you increase this introspection time; more opportunities will open for you. **Change focus from negative to positive.**

### Step-2: Believe in Youself and Continuous Improvement

Self-confidence raises belief in oneself. Increase your knowledge base and do your groundwork properly before starting any new activity so that you are confident. Your confidence level will decide your success rate. Believe in yourself and your potential and you will always pull through all the difficulties.

## Step-3: Broaden Your Knowledge

Knowledge is power. It is the engine of growth for individuals as well as for organizations. Try to increase your knowledge by reading newspapers, magazines, journals, surfing net, attending seminars/workshops, listening to TV programmes, interacting with great personalities. Influence others through personal charisma. In today's high tech world, expertise has become an increasingly powerful source of influence. Have your own USP (unique selling point)

## Step-4: Be Proactive

Plan ahead, your next day goal should be planned after finishing your day's work. Use a small diary with you and note down the things to be done the following day. Prioritize your tasks and tick mark the completed tasks during the day. Through this approach you will become a goal-oriented person. The people who consistently get through the most in a day are the ones who are focused on what they want, who have fixed their goals for that day. Review your diary during the day as and when you find it convenient. Review finally in the night before going to bed and make the task completed as done.

The growing number of your own accomplishments will motivate you and enhance you capability for higher and higher goal achievement.

## Step-5: Develop Communication Skills

Communication is transfer of information and understanding from one person to another. It is a way of reaching others with facts, ideas, thoughts and values. It is a bridge of meanings among people so that they can share what they feel and know. A good communicator establishes rapport with his listener instantaneously. People are willing to listen and work as per his command. You must demonstrate a high level of confidence and clarity of thought so as to impress others. For effective communication you have to take care of your body language and dress. Establish eye contact with your listeners so as to know their reactions and make them interactive.

## Step-6: Show Empathy

Show kindness and respect when interacting. Everyone whom you encounter should be valued, and treated with courtesy. Acknowledge others' feelings and their perspectives. To whomsoever you meet show your warmth and concern. Your concern for them will help you also in the sense that your feelings and emotions get recharged. You feel good from the response you get from such concerns may be about their health, children, career, growth, family matters, etc., depending on your intimacy level with the individuals. Truthfulness and a genuine concern always create a good understanding between two individuals.

## Step-7: Stay Healthy

A healthy body has a healthy mind. Take care of your health. Have some routine for physical exercises, morning/evening walk. Start your day at the earliest to have plenty of fresh air and water to remove the toxins from your body. Physical exercises, Yoga reduce your stress and generate feel good sense motivating you to have greater achievements. A good health is a must for any growth and have positive approach in life.

Ignoring health is just ignoring yourself and inviting trouble in the future that is going to create hurdles in your smooth working.

## Step-8: Have a Social Support

Social support is a must to reduce stress. Choose friends wisely. Like elevator buttons, they will either take you up or down.

A person is greatly affected by the company he keeps. In fact the lifestyle of your friends gives an indication of your own lifestyle. Your friend's attitude towards life is equally important for you. Mixing with positive people will uplift your spirit. There are different groups and social and professional organizations. Be a part of it to improve yourself emotionally and professionally. Positive affirmations set themselves in your subconscious mind and guide you to greater accomplishments.

Believe in charity whenever and wherever an opportunity arises. Be generous to share your riches that you can afford. It is in giving that you take as it comes back to you in multiples.

What you get will help you make a living. What you give to the needy will give you life.

## Step-9: Motivate Others

Helping others in their need generates a positive thought process in you and thereby opens new frontiers for growth. Be a listener and a counsellor. Whenever you motivate others to help them to better in life, you are also, in turn, getting motivated yourself to do better in life. Whenever you find an opportunity of encouraging people in their hour of need, crisis you must help them to come out of their troubles or do better in life. But you must develop trust first before you can motivate anybody else. It is impossible to motivate people who don't trust you. Your words of motivation may become guiding stars in their pursuit of excellence.

## Step-10: Plan Your Finances

Plan your savings and investments keeping in view your future requirements. A proper planning will always help you in your need of hour. If your finances are well organized, you will be able to perform many demanding tasks.

## Step-11: Set Goals

Think of expectations as a sort of a self-fulfilling prophesy. Expectations of how someone is likely to act cause that person to fulfill the expectations. People who expect more get more. Start with small wishes building up your confidence and gradually raise your expectations over time. Think only the best, work only for the best and except only the best. You ask for the best and you will get the best in life.

Take hold of the wheel and guide yourself forward to the destination of your choosing by setting SMART goals for yourself. SMART stands for:

S – Specific
M – Measurable
A – Attainable
R – Realistic
T – Time oriented

Life goals can be short term and long term. Short-term goals can be of one year or less duration and long terms goals can be of more than one year duration.

### *Short Term*

Arranging family functions, increasing knowledge base, attending training programmes, reading books, planning investments, leisure travel, celebrations, picnics, finding new friends, etc.

### *Long Term*

Some of the examples may be purchasing a house/car, marriage of kith and kin, finding new opportunities of growth and progress, career progress, children education, planning for health/insurance/travel/abroad/investments, marriage, setting to new place.

## Step-12 Develop Your Hobbies

Hobbies enrich you in terms of broader vision besides rejuvenating you. Enjoy the little things happening to you. It generates creativity of mind and motivates you achieve new heights of growth in your life. It charges your batteries and helps you to refocus on your goals.

## Step-13 Learn from Mistakes and Pick up the Positives from Others

If you learn from your own mistakes only then you will be wasting much of your life in committing the mistakes and rectifying them later on. It is better you learn from the mistakes of others and save your time of repeating these mistakes and subsequently suffering from the same. All mistakes are to be paid for in terms of money, efforts, growth, etc., so why not avoid in the first instance as far as possible through taking proactive steps. Seeing the best in others will make you understand them in a better way. Your relationship with them also will be positive and rewarding.

## Step-14: Grab Opportunities

Do not wait for opportunity to come your way. Actively search for opportunities and grab them when you see them. Future is not what happens to you, but what you make of it. Whenever and wherever you get an opportunity you must consider it. Think many times before deciding to leave an opportunity. Opportunity is never lost but someone else takes it and opens doors for his growth. Opportunity is a blessing in disguise knocking at your door for opening the door to growth.

## Step-15: Initiate Now

Sorrow will keep you focused on the past. Worry focuses around the present. Faith, action and determination build the future. If you decide to stop your negative thinking in a week, you will spend the whole week counting down and enjoying the same as much as possible. Instead, quit now your negative thinking. By putting it off, you will only prolong the quitting process.

William James of Harvard University said, "If you are going to change your life, you need to start immediately," So your time starts JUST NOW.

### *A Few Points to Remember*

1. To create your own thoughts, feelings and actions.
2. Situations do not affect us. It is the view we take of the situation which affects us.
3. There are always different possibilities of looking at situations. You have the power to change your perception. Remember that perceptual alternatives open to you. You can tap the potential of the progressive power of positive perception.
4. Action ....... Choosing the active line, creating, doing, achieving through choice.
   Reaction ........ Prisoner of habit, passive, reacting, blaming, helpless.
5. Thoughts, beliefs, perceptions
   ↓
   Emotions, feelings
   ↓
   Actions
6. You are beyond all conclusions about yourself. A growing process never concludes.
7. Everything in life will strengthen me. Everything will nourish me.

## Road of Life

On the road, it is never the question of whose mistake, but it is the question of whose life!

The responsibility of 'not hitting' and 'not being hit', both are yours and yours alone.

On the road, if you want to be alive YOU make the adjustments.

Blaming makes no sense.

Similarly, in the road called life, in dealing with the traffic called relationship, it is not the question of whose mistake, but is the question of whose life.

In relationship too, if you want happiness YOU have to make adjustments.

Here too, blaming makes no sense.

## A FEW MORE IDEAS

* Keep yourself up-to-date in both your profession and in management techniques generally. Always read trace papers, go to exhibitions, read quality newspapers and watch current affairs programmes on TV. Try to spot trends. Be aware and alert for opportunities.
* Learn to read tasks regularly. Much of the really effective learning goes on by reflecting on experience gained: reviewing the good things so that they can be repeated and reviewing the bad things so that they can be avoided. It is true that experience is the best teacher but only when it is reviewed systematically.

## SELF-DEVELOPMENT

Self-development is an approach that emphasizes the importance of life-long learning. It recognizes that we all have a great potential for learning and for changing what we do. It differs from traditional, instructor-centred approaches by giving the primary responsibility for learning to learners themselves: they are shown how to use a variety of methods to diagnose their needs and then create an action plan for implementing change.

### Learning Cycle

Self-development focuses on the above-mentioned cyclical process of learning, which encourages us to build the ability to take responsibility and be proactive – initiating action, rather than being reactive in the way we work. Being proactive assists us in gaining more awareness of our power to respond to any situation by recognizing our own role in influencing its outcome. Self-development enables us to recognize, and to own, our responsibility in influencing outcomes by taking risks and doing things differently.

Heraclitus, 500 BC said that, "Everything flows and every thing is constantly changing. You cannot step twice in the same river, for other waters are consistently flowing on."

Self-development is a holistic approach, because it involves our whole selves. Our inner selves (which look at our own belief, values and motivation), outer selves (which relate to other people).

### Main Factors for Self-development

1. Self-control and self-conscious
2. Mature and self-discipline and inculcating will power to stand against bad times.
3. Responsible and accountable to duties assigned.
4. Love and appreciation
5. Sensible with emotions.
6. Be a good listener
7. Don't accept failures, but reason and rectify the mistakes done.
8. Ability to do, determination to achieve and pleasure to help.
9. Lateral thinking, out of the box thinking
10. Encourage happiness in surroundings
11. Help the needy
12. Positive attitude
13. Knowledge management, develop positive intelligence
14. Time management
15. Hobbies to utilize oneself effectively.
16. Confidence and determination should be a strategy to get the things done.

## GROWING THE HOLISTIC ACTION PLAN FOR SELF-IMPROVEMENT

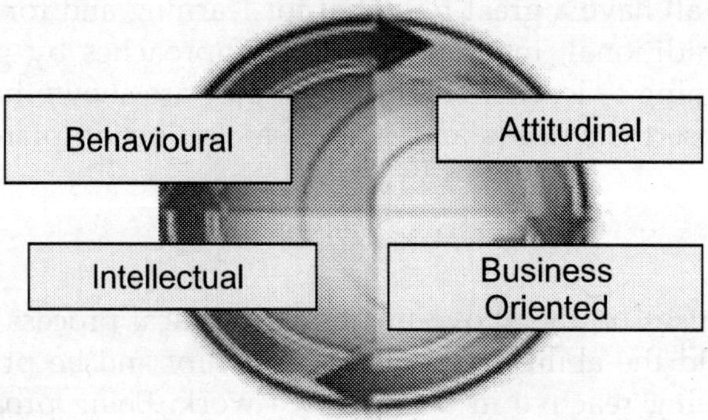


**BEHAVIOURAL**
Planning and organizing
Prioritizing and focusing
Team spirit
Leadership
Business etiquettes
Empathy
Motivation

**ATTITUDINAL**
Goal/result orientation
Initiative and drive
Self-confidence
Self-orientation
Positive mindset
Passion for excellence

**INTELLECTUAL**
Knowledge about surroundings
Content knowledge
Best practices in own field of expertise

**BUSINESS ORIENTED**
Business communication
Sensitivity towards others
Negotiating skills
Quality of service

Self-development is a holistic approach, because it involves our whole process.

Self-development is an approach that emphasizes the importance of life-long learning. It helps to recognize that we all have a great potential for learning and for changing what we do.

Mike Peddler and Tom Boydell remind us that this approach involves both our outer selves and our inner selves. The outer selves relate to other people. Our inner selves looks at our own motivation, values and beliefs.

## THE INTERACTION BETWEEN OUR INNER AND OUTER SELVES

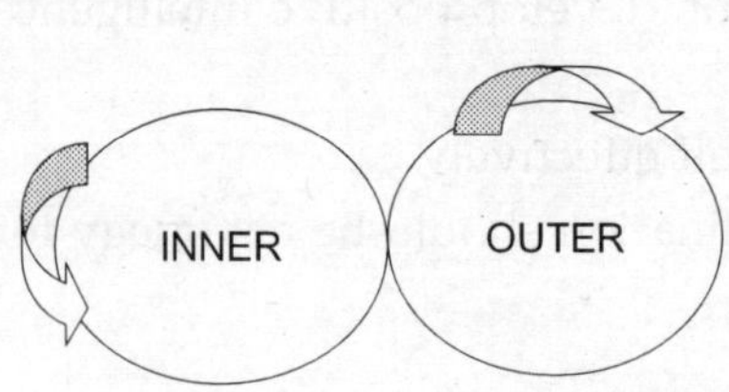

**Step 1**

The inner self starts with our desire to learn, be clear about what you want to learn, understand a new way of working, master a computer package, find better ways of working in team. There may be a list of things you want to do. Sort them in some order. The most important ingredient is a desire to do things differently, until you have that attitude, self-development cannot start.

**Step 2**

Think about yourself, where is the dissatisfaction and what you want to do about it. Initial workshops on self-development will help you in self-diagnosis in a number of ways and clarify what you want to do. This may involve assessing your pattern of learning in addition to focusing on what you want to learn. This may help you to clarify your learning preferences and learning blockages.

Encourage self-development belief in yourself, i.e.:
I can make a difference in my works.
I can develop myself to do and be more that I am at present.

**Step 3**

Set realistic goals for self-development and describe how you would like to be different.

**Step 4**

Move from your inner to your outer self and take risks related to the goals you have set. Take feedback from others on your performance at work or on work you have never done before. The risk should challenge you to go beyond your experience to try something new and learn from it.

This step will help you to prove to yourself that you are able to change. This is an intention to initiate your own development. Once you have taken a small risk, it feels easier to commit yourself to making other changes in the future.

**Step 5**

Design your learning process according to your goals, find appropriate resources and support to enable you to achieve those goals.

**Step 6**

Share your goals with others and take help from your colleagues, friends, people with particular skills and resources, member of a professional associate and partners and family. Other participants on your self-development programme may be particularly useful in providing mutual support and challenge.

**Step 7**

Preserve your learning programme. Sometimes it will be difficult to stick to it. Focus on your inner self and think why these changes are important for your long-term development. This may help you to put short-term pressures, which might interrupt your development.

### Step 8

Assess yourself against your goals. What you have learnt from your successes and failures? What has happened that you did not expect, and how has that affected you ?

Return to your outer self and get feedback from others to assess your progress. This information should be taken to decide whether you are on the right track or whether you have to revise your goals.

Celebrate success with those who have helped you and then return to Step 1 to begin your next development plan.

Self-development is a life long process. It is a way of planning and working that becomes so challenging and exciting that you want to integrate it into your life on a continuous basis.

### The Dilemma

To laugh is to risk appearing as a fool.
To weep is to risk appear sentimental.
To reach out for another is to risk involvement.
To expose feelings is to risk rejection.
To pace hour dreams before the crowd is to risk ridicule.
To love is to risk not being loved in return
To go forward in the face of overwhelming odds is to risk failure.

But risks must be taken because the greatest hazard in life is to risk nothing.

The person who risks nothings does nothing, has nothing, and is nothing. He may avoid suffering and sorrow, but he cannot learn, feel, change, grow or love; only a person who risks is free.

## DEVELOP YOUR PERSONAL COMPETENCE FOR SUCCESS

Self-enhancement, personal competence and personal skills are the traits which aim at changing oneself and the world. In an organizational setup productivity, profitability and performance help in organizational competence.

Personal competence aims at defining the quality of effective person based on his/her personality traits and skills which directly reflects the potential of an individual. These skills are significant for developing human relationships. These help to develop and build integrity, ethics and most importantly the **"self"**. Personal competence is a set of "individualist traits which enables an individual to manage themselves independently and capably " One has to recognize his/her own strengths, emotions, strengths, worth, knowledge, capabilities, impulse, honesty, integrity, flexibility and many more to lead a successful life.

### Personal Competence is "how we manage ourselves"

Personal effectiveness is an underlying technique and approach required to eradicate personal failures. One should know how to handle himself in a given situation and anticipate future developments within the self. This behaviour is called "**personal competence**".

*"The rules for work are changing. We're being judged by a new yardstick: not just how smart we are, or by our training and expertise, but also by how well we handle ourselves and each other".*

**— Daniel Goleman**

Success in any challenging role is expansion of personal relationships which an individual widens over a period of time in his or her professional as well as personal life.

Life long learnings set a stage of enhancement of personal knowledge. Psychosocial abilities help to overcome personal and social problems that we face everyday.

**Personal Competence is**

**Self-Regulation:** Managing your internal states, impulses and resources
**Self-Control:** Keeping distruptive emotions and impulses in check
**Trustworthiness:** Maintaining standards of honesty and integrity
**Conscientiousness:** Taking responsibility for personal performance
**Adaptability:** Flexibility in handling change
**Innovation:** Being comfortable with novel ideas, approaches and new information

## Dimensions of Personal Competence

### *Self-Awareness*

*"Knowing others is wisdom, knowing yourself is enlightenment."*

### *Self-Confidence*

Self-confidence is a strong wisdom of your self worth and capabilities.

### *Self-Regulation*

It is organizing one's desires, instincts, emotions and circumstances. It is an internal transaction modulating thoughts and behaviour of an individual.

### *Trustworthiness*

It is defined as safeguarding one's honesty and integrity. The trait displays faithfulness, reliability, dependability – a person who handles responsibility well, a person with whom you can unburden your heart who can be given credit to his worthiness as he or she constantly helps others, a person who is trusted with commitments and has no fears of failures.

### *Conscientiousness*

It means taking responsibility for one's personal performance. There are abilities like neatness, carefulness, delicacy, meticulousness and precision in this component.

### *Adaptability*

It is the personal mannerism where an individual has flexibility in handling changes and situations by understanding them. It has some specific and rare characteristics like softness, bendiness, quietness and grace in its acceptance of different environments.

### *Creativity and Innovation*

Both these concepts blend together in an individual who is highly imaginative and possesses original ideas inspired by his/her ideas to think out of the box. Creativity involves thinking, passion, awareness and producing. It is making miracles into reality.

### *Emotional Intelligence*

It is a set of skills which is required to dedicate and sustain effectual work relationship. The five significant skills are self-awareness, empathy, self-regulation, motivatiopn and social skills. Goleman revealed, "Emotional competencies were found to be twice as important in contributing to excellence as pure intellect and expertise."

### *Self-Motivation*

Self-motivation is a set of complex emotional inclinations that channels and facilitates one to reach goals. It inspires an individual to be energetic, enthusiastic, keen, passionate, delighted, eager about the things they are aspiring for life.

### *Self-Control*

It is a process of organizing the self in many ways. This involves behaviour, action and the thought. It can linger into other aspects like respect, will power and an ability of individuals to put forth their will above their body or not be in charge of their self.

### *Commitment*

Commitment binds the self, both intellectually and emotionally, to access the loyalty to work. It is an act of committing, keeping promises and trust, it is devotion towards personal and professional obligations.

### *Self-Knowledge*

It is getting acquainted with intellectual wisdom which is the result of constant learning and using knowledge strategically to meet situations.

**Becoming competent is a transformation in the thinking process, attitude, reflection and perception.**

## 2.4 DEVELOP PERSONAL RESILIENCE

A flexible container when imposed by external force changes its shape temporarily, but springs back to its previous shape shortly thereafter. It is resilient. According to laws of physics, resilience is the ability to demonstrate the quality of elasticity. Some individuals have the innate capacity to bounce back from adversity, others develop it through confidence, self-efficacy, flexibility and optimism. In today's stressful and rapidly changing world resilience is a must.

Highly resilient people don't fight against disruptive changes because they adjust to new situation quickly. They accept change and deal with it. Resilient people's flexibility and adaptability lets them adjust their responses to achieve positive outcomes in new situation. Resilience enables a person to handle stress, to listen, to handle pressure of work and to accept feedback from others without "losing one's cool". They take initiative, are surrounded by supportive and encouraging network of family and friends and are also flexible. They are clear about their vision in life. This gives a clarity and meaning to their life. They take locus of control and are not bothered to things not covering in the locus of control.

In a workplace, change is constant, work is relentless, turbulence is normal. Stresses are there in the form of work overload, time indigestion, globalization, work-life imbalance, deceased safety, need to adjust to intrusion, less social affiliation, lack of control, a need to adjust to intrusion, less social affiliation, innovation. Resilient individuals have the psychological and biological strength to successfully master the change.

A split mind, burnout, workplace imbalance, depression in relationships, failures, are some of the few instances when resilience is most needed. Resilience is the learned behaviour.

## Ten Ways to Build Resilience

1. Bridge connections
2. Do not view crises as impossible problems
3. Accept change
4. Move to ten ways to build resilience
5. Take decisive actions
6. Keep things in perspective
7. Maintain a hopeful outlook
8. Find the road to self-discovery
9. Have a positive view of yourself
10. Take care of yourself

The key to success: Apart from learning from experience of other people, identify ways that are likely to work well for you as part of your own personal strategy for fostering resilence.

## Characteristics of a Resilient Individual

- A sense of hope and trust in the world
- The ability to tolerate pain and distressing emotions

- Interpreting experiences in a new light
- A meaningful system of support
- A sense of mastery and control over one's destiny
- A good self-image and self-expert
- Self-reflection and insight
- A wide range of interest and a sense of humour

## 2.5 CREATE A POSITIVE BELIEF SYSTEM

*"No one can make you feel inferior without your consent."*

**— Eleanor Roosevelt**

*Whatever the mind can conceive and believe, it can achieve."*

**— Napoleon Hill**

The roadblock towards success in not to believe in yourself. We usually often tend to fail to notice our strengths and see our limitations as a focal point. We usually try to diminish our negative attitudes which have accumulated during the years. When should we focus on our strengths and improve our positive belief system rather sticking to our negatives. We should try to convert our negatives to positives. An optimistic and positive attitude is formed by a positive belief system. We will keep well mentally and physically also when we have a positive belief system. This will lead to positiveness both at home and at work.

It has been said that success is 80 per cent attitude and 20 per cent aptitude. In other words, our natural talents are not as important as what we do with them.

## BELIEVE IN YOURSELF AND MAKE IT HAPPEN

**Instruction:** The following reminders can be pasted on you mirror, refrigerator or desk or be given to friends who may need a little uplifting.

### Things to Remember

- Success is an attitude.
- Whatever mind can conceive and believe, you can achieve.
- Dream great and work to make them come true.
- You are unique and special.
- Never affirm self-limitations.
- To accomplish great things, you must believe, dream, plan and then act.
- Yes you can!
- Believing is magic.
- You can always better your previous best.

- You don't know what you can do until you try.
- There is no failure except "not trying".
- Defeat may test you: it need not stop you.
- If at first you don't succeed, try another approach.
- For every obstacle, there is a solution.
- Nothing in the world can take the place of persistence.

**COURAGE**

the quality of mind or spirit that enables a person to face difficulty, danger, pain, without fear, and bravery.

**"Self-esteem means believing in yourself"**

## Keys to Remember

| | | |
|---|---|---|
| 1. WHAT CAN YOU CONTROL? | …………………….. | YOU. Not others. |
| 2. WHAT CAN YOU DO NOW? | …………………….. | THINK OF STRENGTHS AND POSITIVES. |
| 3. WHAT DO YOU WANT TO DO? | …………………….. | FOCUS YOUR THINKING. |
| 4. WHAT DO YOU NEED TO DO? | …………………….. | PRIORITIZE and FOCUS YOUR ENERGY NOW. |

"The way your act will eventually be determined by the way you think, feel and believe."

## 2.6 HOW TO INCREASE YOUR ATTENTION SPAN

### Schedule Yourself

#### ✓ *Set a Routine*

Routine is a must for everyone. Routine habit should be inculcated in oneself the right from the initial years, he or she will be able to effectively meet the challenges thrown up by life.

### ✓ *Have a Fixed Place to Study*

A proper study table affects the concentration. If one sits at a desk, on a straight back chair, one is more likely to be able to concentrate than when rolling around on a sofa. Lying down on the bed while reading will most probably make you sleepy or you will fall asleep. So it is best to sit at a table or a small desk.

### ✓ *Make a Proper Time Table*

Organise time better so that he/she can get his/her work done and enough free time to do non-academic activities. Make a time table for studying and recreation and stick to it.

### ✓ *Study for a Minimum of One Hour at a Time*

It takes the mind at least 8 – 10 minutes to clear out other distractions when we sit down to study. So once you get into the mood set it for the next 50 minutes or so. Let there be no disturbances in these sittings. Otherwise, the focus will be lost. Some like to study in the morning, and some late in the night.

### ✓ *Take Rest after an Hour*

Take rest for 5-10 minutes after an hour to freshen up the brain.

### ✓ *Set a Goal*

It is very important that you decide how much one should accomplish in one hour. One should try to achieve these targets and brag about it.

### ✓ *Reduce Distractions*

If you feel that TV viewing is distracting, avoid late night TV or other forms of entertainment. You can even stop talking to a friend on the phone for long.

### ✓ *Eat Light Meals*

Eat light food along with juices and milk shakes. Intake of heavy food is bound to make you the feel lethargic and lazy. Eat at regular intervals, not at one go. Take a good brain tonic like milk, fruits, cheese and similar energizers.

### ✓ *Be Orderly*

In order to avoid clutter at the last moment, organize the study material well in advance. For example, sharpen the pencil and fill the ink pens much before the exam. Take head bath regularly in order to have an alert mind. Let the clothes be ironed properly. These are small things that matter in creating an ambience.

### ✓ *Cultivate an Intense Desire to Excel*

You have to impart a drive in you, a drive to excel and come out in flying colours. Therefore, you have to be focused. Take keen interest in whatever you are studying, not just for the exam but also for the exam of life.

### ✓ *Have Faith in Yourself*

Never allow yourself to indulge in self-doubt or worries. Be confident on your abilities. Avoid last minute exam-time preparation.

## APPENDIX

### Exercise-1 Overcoming Fear

1. Write down the greatest fear that you have overcome.

_______________________________________________

_______________________________________________

_______________________________________________

_______________________________________________

_______________________________________________

_______________________________________________

_______________________________________________

2. Write a brief statement about how you overcome your fear. What did you do, how did you do it and what feelings did you have afterward?

_______________________________________________

_______________________________________________

_______________________________________________

_______________________________________________

_______________________________________________

_______________________________________________

_______________________________________________

### Exercise-2 Who are You? Your Personality Strengths

Take time to think about your positive, personal characteristics that make you WHO YOU ARE TODAY. Everyone has positive qualities, but often, we do not take time to identify them.

**Instructions**

Circle those words that best describe how you see yourself today: your personality, character, intellect and outlook on life, be as objective and realistic as possible.

| | | |
|---|---|---|
| Accepting | Enterprising | Persuasive |
| Achieving | Entertaining | Poised |
| Active | Enthusiastic | Precise |
| Adventurous | Expressive | Productive |
| Affectionate | Fair-minded | Professional |
| Ambitious | Friendly | Quick |
| Articulate | Gentle | Rational |
| Attractive | Genuine | Realistic |
| Caring | Good-natured | Receptive |
| Charismatic | Helpful | Responsive |
| Charming | Humorous | Self-aware |
| Cheerful | Happy | Self-confident |
| Committed | Imaginative | Sensitive |
| Compassionate | Independent | Serious |
| Confident | Insightful | Sincere |
| Congenial | Intelligent | Sociable |
| Conscientious | Intuitive | Spontaneous |
| Considerate | Knowledgeable | Steady |
| Co-operative | Logical | Strong |
| Creative | Likeable | Sympathetic |
| Dedicated | Open-minded | Talented |
| Dependable | Optimistic | Tolerant |
| Determined | Objective | Trusting |
| Distinctive | Orderly | Truthful |
| Dynamics | Original | Unique |
| Efficient | Outgoing | Unpretentious |
| Empathetic | Patient | Warm. |
| Encouraging | Perceptive | |
| Energetic | Persistent | |

## Exercise-3: Your Interest

**Instructions**

1. List 20 THINGS your enjoy doing. These may include hobbies, amusement, social activities, sports, classes, etc.

1. ____________________
2. ____________________
3. ____________________
4. ____________________
5. ____________________
6. ____________________
7. ____________________
8. ____________________
9. ____________________
10. ____________________
11. ____________________
12. ____________________
13. ____________________
14. ____________________
15. ____________________
16. ____________________
17. ____________________
18. ____________________
19. ____________________
20. ____________________

2. Ask yourself the following:
   - How often do you do those activities?
   - Are there significant patterns? For example, are the activities enjoyed along or with others?
   - What skills do you use most often: physical, analytical, creative or verbal?

## Qualities of Professionals

| | |
|---|---|
| Dependability | The ability to be assigned a task and see it through despite all the foreseen and unforeseen pitfalls. |
| Enterprising | The ability to put in one's 100%. |
| Flexibility | The ability not to take on a rigid stance in case a situation demands a review or change in the course of action. |
| Integrity | The ability to ensure adherence to an ethical course of action. |
| Knowledgeable | To be well informed abut the content of the job at hand. |
| Interactivity | To be able to create and maintain good rapport with one and all. |

| | |
|---|---|
| Tolerate | To be able to view and accept and reject others perceptions in an objective manner. |
| Eagerness | The enthusiasm to learn. Assimilate and act creativity in a manner which benefits the organization optimally. |

## Exercise-4 Assess Your Self-Esteem

The following self-inventory shall enable you to assess your self-esteem. The statements are typically true of persons with good self-esteem.

Rate your responses to these statements as to how true each statement is for you. Use the following keys.

1 = I never do
2 = I occasionally do
3 = I usually do
4 = I always do.

- ❒ I accept myself just as I am.
- ❒ My opinion of myself is more important than other's opinion of me.
- ❒ I forgive myself for my mistakes.
- ❒ I am not afraid of failure or defeat.
- ❒ I do not compare myself unfavourable with others.
- ❒ I am as important as anyone else.
- ❒ I accept full responsibility for may problems.
- ❒ I feel worthwhile even when I do things imperfectly.
- ❒ I do not accept blame for other's painful feelings.
- ❒ I do not look down on anyone.
- ❒ I accept nothing as true without reasonable verification.
- ❒ I do not try to impress others.
- ❒ I willingly accept life as it is, no matter how I want it to be.
- ❒ I control my emotions.
- ❒ My accomplishments have no bearing over my worth as a person.

**SCORE:** Add all the numbers to arrive at your score. The result will be percentile indication which areas need some work. Those statements that you have marked with the lowest numbers are the areas in which there is room for improvement.

## How to Make Changes in Our Self-Esteem

Sound self-esteem is the basis for all self-improvement. Our potential is limitless, our abilities inexhaustible, and the possibilities for creative and constructive changes are endless. But we won't experience satisfactory progress towards our goals or make any lasting improvement unless we believe in ourselves that our lives will improve permanently when we believe. So improving our self-esteem inwardly is vital for improving our lives.

We can do so by constantly thinking positively of ourselves through affirmations.

**Try some of the following ways:**

- ✓ Put affirmations to work just when you notice your putting yourself down.
- ✓ Counter-attack with these positive self-statements to cancel our effects of those that are negative.
- ✓ Repeat them when you are riding the bus, during the lunch hour or coffee-break, while waiting for an appointment, when doing housework or any other task which does not demand your full attention.
- ✓ Keep repeating affirmations.
- ✓ Write some of these affirmations down on paper at intervals during the day.
- ✓ After you work on positive self-statements for a certain length of time, they become assimilated into your belief system and you no longer have to think of them this way. They get internalized into your persona.

## Visualization

Visualization is the process of using our imagination to create realistic mental picture of behaviour we would like to adopt and then regularly focusing our attention on these pictures until we manifest them. Visualization is a useful fool to help make the changes. It is used by orators, athletes, and even doctors, to speed and improve healing. In the cognitive behavioural area of psychology, it is used successfully to help people reduce stress and stress-related problems, to stop smoking and to eliminate other self-defeating behaviour by creating desirable mental blueprints for our future. Use the following tips:

- Decide what behaviour you want to change and then create a mental pattern of exactly how you want to act in a particular situation.
- Find the quietest place where you are least likely to be internal body as deeply as possible. Lie down or sit in a comfortable position. Take several slow, deep breaths, relaxing more with each breath.
- When you are comfortable, imagine yourself performing the new behaviour exactly as you want. Embellish your mental picture with every detail you can think of, making it vivid and as real as if it were actually happening.
- When you have finished, relax a few moments longer, holding on the emotions and sensations as long as you can. Repeat these tips two or three times each day, until you feel so comfortable with your new behaviour.

This way you create a new character, not stick to the same old one which made you unhappy. You might feel uncomfortable with this different new behaviour. But any behaviour that is repeated often enough eventually becomes comfortable. After a certain amount of practice you shall become comfortable. After that when the time arrives for your real-world performance, it shall happen easily and naturally.

In a nutshell, the more clearly we identify the changes we will to make the quicker we will make them in reality. Also, we often fail to achieve realistic goals because with the help of affirmation and visualization we gradually convince ourselves to have what we want. This way we unleash the energy in us, and open ourselves up to ways to get it or to make it happen.

| Nurse's Attitude | Mother's Attitude |
|---|---|
| Leadership | Ownership |
| Correcting others | Continuous self-correction |
| Learning | Unlearning |
| Compulsive teacher | Acute listener |
| Infinite efforts and zero alertness | Infinite alertness and zero efforts |
| Self-esteem, security or physiological needs | Self-actualized |
| Crisis management | Opportunity management |
| Acts when problem is a sprout, a bud or a flower (reactive or preventive) | Acts when the problem is in seed stage (proactive) |
| Believes that necessity is the mother of inventions | Believes in inventing |
| Talks more than she knows | Knows more than she talks |
| Curses the darkness | Lights one candle |
| Addicted to result | Addicted to process |
| Work is duty | Work is dharma |
| Job enrichment | Mind enrichment |
| Ego driven | Pride driven |
| Five per cent of potential profits | Ninety-five per cent of potential profits. |

## Accepting Responsibility for Oneself

For successful living one needs to accept responsibility for oneself. Excuses for giving up one's responsibility can be summarized as below.

1. Powers I keep - This is the power which will help me to develop and grow and also to help others to do the same.
2. Make feel - This is the power that others are given for making me feel bad or hurting me, e.g., `you make me feel...........'.
3. Fate - This is the power I give away which helps me to believe that my fate is determined by my horoscope or certain things are going to be done has determined it.
4. Subconscious - This is the power which I give away by doing things suddenly and later have no control over it.
5. You owe me - This is my power that fastens me up because others do not change, I am not OK.
6. Gene theory - This is the power that makes my thinking not being activated because I think I can't change because I am made this way.

## Exercise–5 Steps to Use the Power Gram

1. Reflect for a moment on your life and how you accept responsibility for yourself. Think of your total energy and how much you keep and how much you give away. Then take an average of the last few months and draw it on the graph.
2. Look at what you drew. Think about it. Are you satisfied? Are you and others growing from this type of behaviour?
3. What contracts would you make for change.

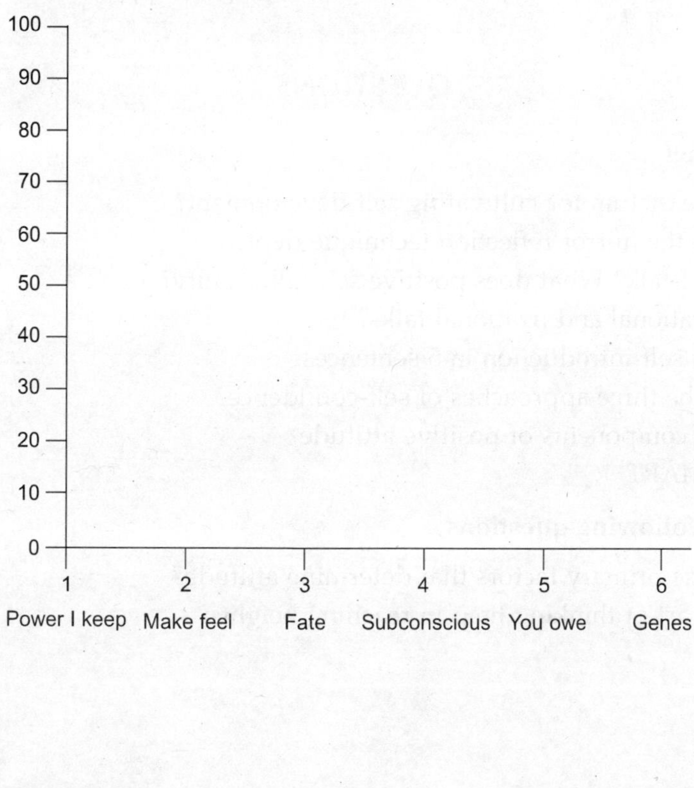

## SUMMARY

- To rectify the world and put it on the proper path, we have to first rectify ourselves and our conduct.
- The positive self-talk gives us encouragement and self-worth. The negative self-talk makes us feel small and incapable or unworthy.
- While giving self introduction, focus the impact, rotate the focus, make it relevant to your audience, believe in yourself, put your full weight behind it, smile and sound happy about what you do, look at your listener(s), know how to deliver, know how to stop, leave space for a response. Confident people tackle their problems smartly keeping smile on their face and handle opportunities for their advantage.
- Attitude should be adopted to reach the "apex". It is an essential and a stepping stone towards success. Attitude building is a constant process orientation but this requires regular trust. A person will develop a positive attitude if he is a positive thinker. The components of attitude are perception, values, beliefs, experience, and emotions.
- Principles for developing a positive attitude: Do your own introspection, believe in yourself and do continuous improvement, broaden your knowledge, be proactive, develop communication skills, show empathy, stay healthy, have a social support, motivate others, plan your finances, set goals, develop your hobbies, learn from mistakes and pick up the positives from others, grab opportunities, initiate now.

## QUESTIONS

**I. Explain in brief**

1. What is the dictum for cultivating self-development?
2. What does the mirror reflection technique depict?
3. What is self-talk? What does positive self-talk signify?
4. What are rational and irrational talks?
5. Write your self-introduction in 5 sentences.
6. What are the three approaches of self-confidence?
7. Name five components of positive attitude.
8. Expand SMART

**II. Answer the following questions**

1. Describe the primary factors that determine attitude?
2. How does art of thinking help in reaching heights?

3. Prepare your action plan for self-improvement, taking into consideration the 360 degree approach to self-development.
4. Do all the exercises for self-development given in the chapter and evaluate yourself for self-development.

## GROUP ACTIVITY

### SURVIVAL

#### A Simulation Game

Radhika and Praneet have just survived the crash of a small plane. Both the pilot and co-pilot were killed in the crash. It is mid-December, and they are in Kashmir, India. The daily temperature is 5 degree, and the night time temperature is below zero. There is snow on the ground, the countryside is wooded with several small streams in the area. The nearest town is 10 km away. They are formally dressed as they had to attend a business meeting. They managed to salvage the following items:

A first aid box
A small rope
Newspapers (one per person)
Cigarette lighter (without fluid)
Extra shirt and pants for each survivor
An axe
A sectional air map made of plastic
One quart of 100-proof whiskey
A compass
Family-size chocolate bars (one per person)

Your task as a group is to list the above 10 items in order of importance for your survival. List the uses for each. You MUST come to agreement as a group.

# UNIT 3

# Communication

**Learning Objectives**

- Need for Communication for Self-Development
- Scope and Objective of Communication
- Process of Communication
- To Understand Principles and Other Technicalities of Conversation
- Delivery of Effective Oral Communication
- Panchshila of Good Talk
- Non-Verbal Aspects of Communication
- Understanding Body Language

## 3.1 DEVELOP COMMUNICATION COMPETENCE (COMMUNICATION PLAN)

### The Story of the Beekeepers and their Bees

This is a story of two beekeepers, who had a beehive each.

The beekeepers worked for a company called Honey Bee. The company was doing well and customers were satisfied with the honey and they loved it and wanted more. The beekeeper was told by the company to produce more honey. Different approaches were designed to improve the performance of their hives. The approach of the first beekeeper was to how many flowers are visited by the bee to measure the performance of the bee. A measurement system was devised to count the visits of the bee. Feedback to each bee was provided on his individual performance in the mid term, but the goal of the hive to produce more honey was not spelt to increase honey sales. Special awards were designed.

The bee performance management approach was introduced by the second beekeeper also. This approach communicated to each bee the goal of the hive—to produce more honey. The performance indicator was the amount of nectar each bee brought back to the hive and the amount of honey the hive produced. The overall performance of each bee was charted in the hive's bulletin board for all the bees to see. Incentive programs were rewarded to each bee in the hive based on the hive's production of honey.

At the end of the season, the approaches of the beekeepers were evaluated.

**Questions**

1. Which beekeeper's approach was effective and why?
2. Why there is a need of proper communication in an organization?
3. Plan a communication strategy for effectiveness of better productivity of honey in the organization.
4. Give another title to the story.

## Communicating: Vital Aspect of Management

***The art of being able to structure and transmit a message in a way that another can easily understand and/or accept.***

### 3.1.1 Role of Communication in Developing Self

Communication is the ability to share information which can be understood by others and convey feelings. Communication can be in the form of gestures, facial expressions, signs, vocalization (including pitch and tone), in addition to speech and written communication. Communication conveys actions. A smiling, nodding face indicates that the listener is interested.

Communication is a cooperative, and mutual event undertaken by active participants. Listeners are alive, reacting, thinking. An audience is not a dormant set of faces… an audience feels and reacts. Communication is a goal-directed dialogue. Your audience may not answer back verbally, but react back with facial expressions, body movements, and sounds of assent or disagreement. If you believe that you are talking to your audience, you will be far more effective and engaging.

When two people begin to communicate, they agree to join actively in a goal-directed behaviour. Their purpose is to explore ideas and share perspectives. Perhaps you have noticed that you really begin to understand your ideas after you struggle to explain them to another person.

Persuasion is a special type of communication. It is a communication with a goal, it is a process.

A professional persuader, whether a car salesperson, missionary, professor, or IRS agent, begins by deciding where the listener is (his knowledge, his experience, and his attitudes) and where he wants the listener to be, what the listener will know, experience and believe because of the persuasive communication. The persuader must undergo a process of enhanced knowledge about the listener and because of the consensus-seeking nature of business communication, become a bit more enlightened himself.

**Knowledge:** Persuasive messages can be designed to change people's knowledge of a topic. To suggest that persuasion is the transmission, reception, and adoption of information may strike some as unique.

**Feelings:** People's attitudes and feelings can be either roadblocks and obstacles that inhibit their ability and desire to change, or catalysts that make that change happen faster.

Professional persuaders realize that change is difficult for all of us. It is said that "The only person on earth that likes change is a wet baby."

We all resist change, particularly change that comes to us from outside forces (government, spouse, boss, even weather). To persuade somebody, you must convert the emotional obstacles into motivational attitudes.

**Behaviour (Doing):** Frequently, the object of your persuasive communication is to get others to change their way of doing things, to get them to join in a process, attend an event, or perform a task in the best possible way.

Which do you think you should do first: Change a person's way of doing a task or get him to change his attitude towards doing it?

### 3.1.2 Scope of Communication

- External communication promotes goodwill with the public
- Internal communication helps in planning, organising, motivating and coordinating.
- Written and oral communication are used to transmit the message.
- More communication technologies have emerged.
- Subject of communication is very wide and comprehensive.
- It has unlimited dimensions and is interdisciplinary.
- Involves both the receiver and the sender

Communication is the continuous process of exchange facts, ideas, feelings, attitudes, opinions, figures and interaction with other.

### 3.1.3 Objectives of Communication

The objectives of communication include:

1. Information
2. Order
3. Persuasion
4. Warning
5. Motivation

6. Advice
7. Suggestion
8. Education
9. Raising morale

### 1. *Information*

- Passing or receiving information can be done either through spoken or written language or by signs or signals.
- Information to plan and organize and execute its job satisfactorily and the source should be reliable, accurate, complete, and recent.

### 2. *Order*

- Order is a directive to a subordinate to do something in a particular way.
- Order moves downwards, it can be written or oral, general or specific and should be clear and complete, capable of being executed, given in a friendly tone.

### 3. *Persuasive*

- It is an effort to influence the attitudes, feelings or benefits of others.

### 4. *Warning*

- Warning means forceful communication, as it demands immediate action.

### 5. *Motivation*

- The determination which leads one to persist to reach greater heights,
- It is personal or professional and drives from internal or external source.
- The individual determines his level of motivation.

### 6. *Advice*

- Effective advice is both man oriented and work oriented. It promotes understanding, and can become a two-way channel of communication.

### 7. *Suggestion*

- Suggestions can be voluntary and can submitted through suggestion boxes.

### 8. *Education*

- It involves both teachings and learning with a purpose to widen knowledge as well to improve skills. It is carried on at three levels: 1) management, 2) employees' level, and 3) outside public.

### 9. *Raising Morale*

- High morale acts as a kind of lubricant among people, improves togetherness and compels to work in cooperation with one another in the best interest of the organization.

## 3.1.4 Communication Process Model

Communication process model is the art of encoding a message to communicate the intended message of the clients/customers.

Verbal communication is communication of thoughts through words, ideas, opinions, directions, dissatisfaction, objections, your emotions and pleasures.

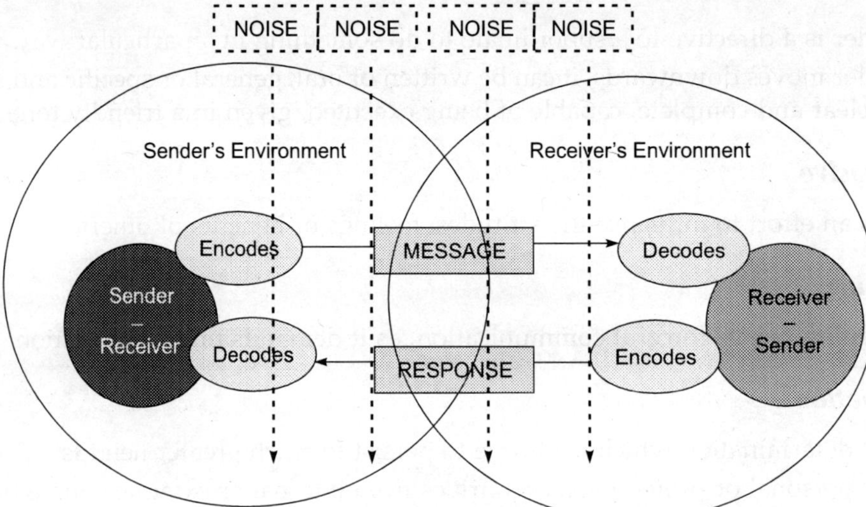


### *Sender*

Encoder is a person or group who wants to convey a message to another *(Source – encoder)*,

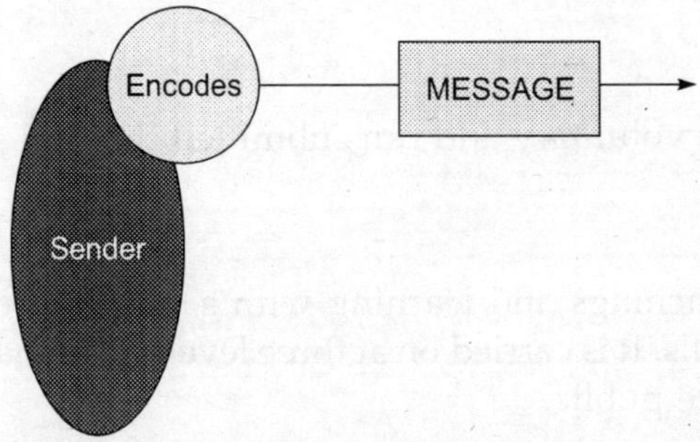


**Encoding:** Using specific signs or symbols (codes) i.e., language and words to use to transmit the message. The tone of voice and gesture to be used.

### *Message*

Messages can be transmitted in written or oral form or by body language that accompanies the words

Face-to-face communication is more effective than telephoning or writing a message.

Recording a message to communicate can be done for larger audience.

Written communication is longer explanation but it is authentic and can be used by the court of law.

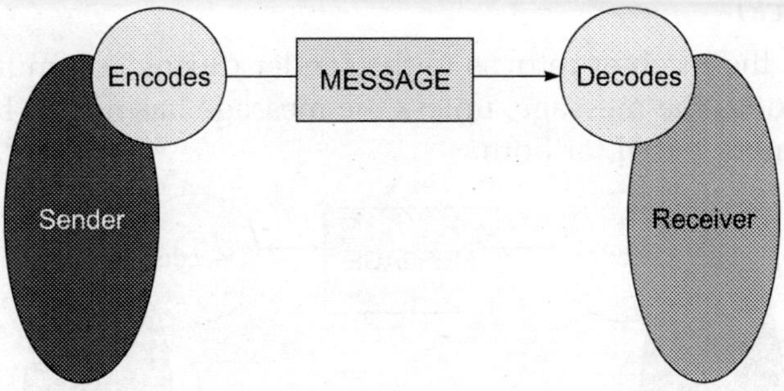


### *Channel*

Channel is the medium used to convey the message and it is the target of the receiver's sense. It should be appropriate for the message and it should help make the message more clear

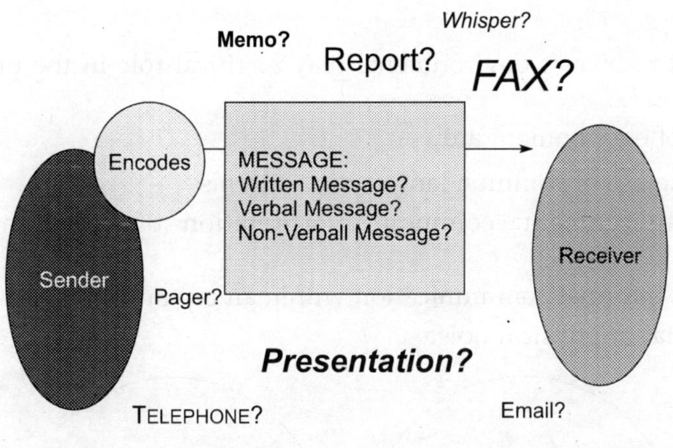


### *Receiver*

Receiver listens, observes, and attends (decoder), and perceives what the sender intended (interpretation).

Communication is effective if the meaning of the decoding message matches the intent of the sender and is ineffective if it is misinterpreted by the receiver. Ineffectiveness occurs when the message sent is according to the sender's intent, depends largely on their similarities in knowledge and experience and socio-cultural background

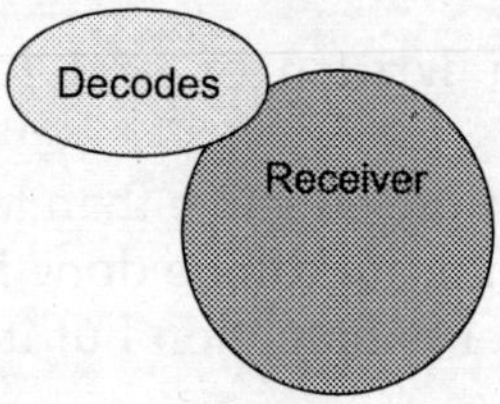


### *Response (Feedback)*

Is the message that the receiver returns to the sender during communication.

The receiver decodes the message, unless the message has not, in fact, been received and can be verbal, non-verbal, or both.

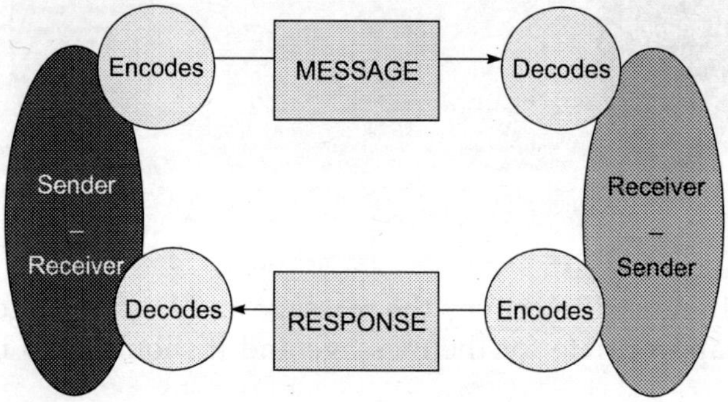


### Environment

The sender's and receiver's environments play a critical role in the understanding of the message.

The elements of environment are:

1. Symbols: the use of common language and terms
2. Cultural environment: common interpretation of verbal and non-verbal communication
3. Formal and informal communication within an organization
4. Noise: mental or physical noise

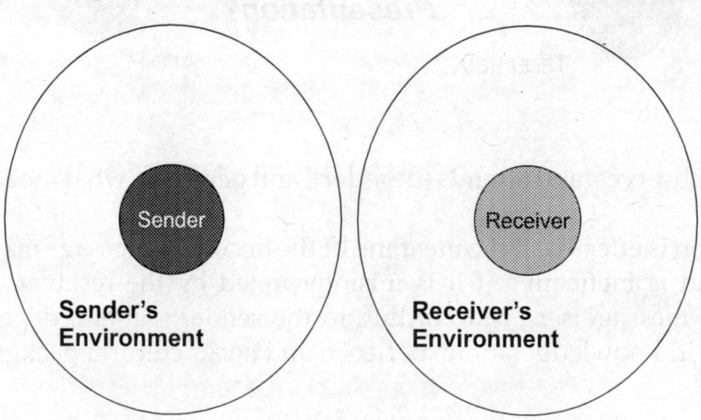

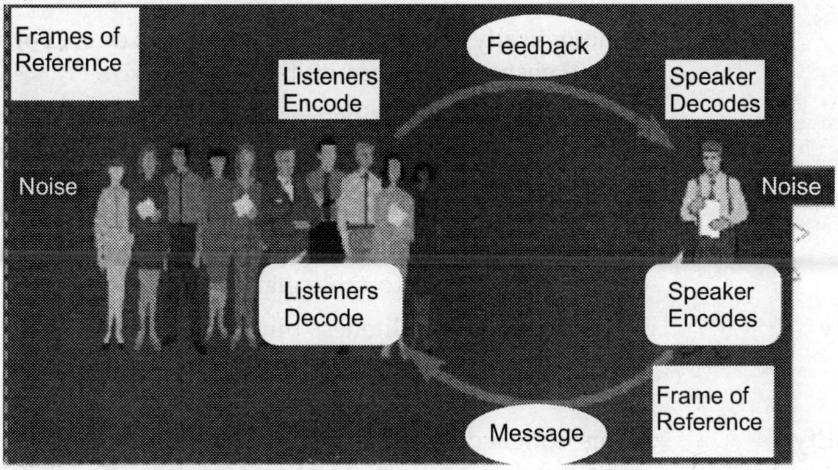


## 3.2 CONVERSATION SKILLS

The principles of conversational skills are clarity, brevity, simplicity, courtesy, originality pleasantness of tone, flexibility of tongue, etc.

To understand these principles and other technicalities of conversation we must master the below-mentioned principles.

**Clarity** : Clearness in speech is essential if our conversation is to be useful. Conveying of exact idea is possible only through clear speech. Vague expression does not yield results.
Precise manner of expression is needed—not laxy thinking or incomplete sentences.
A clear speaker is able to achieve a sense of harmony with his listeners, inspire confidence with his logical sequence of thought.

**Brevity** : To be brief is a sign of accuracy of thought. An editor is supposed to eliminate such substances, so that what the reader gets is clear, comprehensive yet concise piece of writing.
Truthful speaker is usually known for his brevity.

**Simplicity** : Simplicity is the essence of all great arts. It is not necessary nor is it an attribute to pepper out conversation with long words and complicated construction. This is not a mark of a scholar.

**Courtesy** : "Grace of God is in courtesy".
Bluntness, misused as frankness, is negation of courtesy.
Courtesy costs nothing. But it pays its dividends.
Reasoned and well chosen words of a sincere talker make for a pleasant relationship between him and others.

Energetically gesticulating speaker is also devoid of courtesy. Some gestures are permissible.

**Tact** : A tact may be described as a combination of intellectual quickness with lively sympathy. Somebody may be reminded of some unfortunate topic which may make recall some of his/her hard times. All these situations require tact. We must be quick to understand the feelings of injured one's hurt expression, uncomfortable glance and change the subject.

**Sincerity** : Say things with politeness but with dignity.
Do not say ideas which are not your own. Don't utter positive untruths.

**Originality** : This is most difficult to achieve. It requires intensive thought and practice and power of imagination. You must remain in the company of cultured speakers and acquaint yourself with good literature.

**Pleasantness of Tone** : A voice full of life is always engaging and draws attention of listeners and one is always attracted to it.

**Flexibility of Tongue** : Complete control of the voice, i.e., no gasping for breath, no talking between the teeth, no swallowing of words, no talking through the nose, etc.

1. Communications are not always rational. Words can be used to conceal as well as convey ideas.
2. Without effective communication, one cannot succeed in maintaining good relations with others, thereby reducing one's chances of success in life.

**Remember:** Good management depends, to a large extent, on good communication.

## Oral Communication

Oral communication is interaction in which spoken words are used which is an integral part of the modern business world.

"The ability to communicate effectively through speaking as well as in writing is highly valued, and demanded, in business."

Oral communication in an organization includes staff meetings, personal discussions, presentations, telephonic discourse, and informal conversation. Face-to-face meetings, telephone calls, speeches, teleconferences, or videoconferences are done outside.

Oral communication builds up human relationship. Without it any organization will become just lifeless.

It includes:

- Face-to-face conversation
- Conversation over the telephone
- Radio broadcast, interviews
- Group discussion, meetings
- Conferences, seminars, speeches, etc.

For managers conversation management skills are essential, and this depends on the areas such as client/customer presentations, employee interviews, and conducting meetings. Effective oral communication should be clear, relevant, thoughtful in proper phrase, tone, concise, and informative. For ensuring business health and growth conversations that bear the above qualities should be an important tool. Goodwill needed for the overall business needs employess to team together with no communication gap. Unclear, inaccurate, or inconsiderate business communication affects the overall business.

The speaker should consider his or her vocal pitch, rate, and volume. The delivery of effective oral presentations requires changes in the vocal pitch to avoid monotony. The pause to allow the listener to reflect upon specific elements of the overall message and an appropriate volume is essential to the success of a presentation. Extraneous words or sounds—such as "um," "you know, "or "okay"—between words or sentences should be avoided in a presentation.

## 80% of Working Day Involves Communication

| | Used | Taught/Addressed |
|---|---|---|
| Listening | 45% | Least |
| Speaking | 30% | |

Reading 16% ⟩ Most
Writing 9%

Listening:
45% of communication
25% efficiency

**When giving instructions you need to consider your**

- Material
- Audience
- Learning styles
- Language
- Audience expectations
- Audience willingness to participate

THINKING CLEARLY is the prime requisite for effective communication.

**Giving instructions requires you to plan**

- How you will present information
- The sequence

- The language you will use.
- The depth of detail.
- It also requires you to listen carefully and observe non-verbal communication.

**Planning guidelines for delivering**

- Use words you understand
- Use simple, not complex language
- Explain words that might be misunderstood
- Give examples
- Be specific
- Watch, listen and understand your audience
- Think before you speak

### 3.2.1 Power Speak Your Way to Success

Language makes a big change. Rediscover yourself with your own speech and step towards success. Build your vocabulary and try to hear your voice by speaking aloud. So, the first step towards success is reading aloud and try to record it if possible. This will help you hear your voice and think of better modulations. Then focus on your speech and style and pronunciation. There should be enthusiasm and vigour in your speech.

**Presentation with style.** Be positive, and promote a positive attitude. Do mirror practice so that you can check your expressions. Smile while you speak, it will take you to miles.

**Modulate your voice.** Pitch, tone and volume are the most important factors in voice modulation. Start with soft notes. Be and feel happy, calm and composed.

**Talk intelligently.** Be clear, and brief with your conversation. Speak the truth and be tactful but know realities too and act sensibly. Convince your listener with persuation.

**Smile while you speak.** Speak your mind from the depth of your heart.

**Have a sound vocabulary.** Mind your words and language while speaking. Speak words which are meaningful, related to the topic. Work on pronunciations.

**Be enthusiastic.** Be dynamic and lively with your presentation. This chases away the nervousness and is effective in persuasion.

**Have confidence.** Confidence with your speech makes people listen and get attracted towards the listener. It evokes curiosity, love, understanding, excitement, etc.

### 3.2.2 Voice Modulation

**Voice is a powerful tool. "Speech is silver, silence is gold."** There are different types of voice. It depends on the situation in which a person speaks. A charming person has a pleasant voice, a dynamic person has a vibrant voice and a confident person an assured voice. Different types of voice include:

1. **Monotonous voice**
   - It indicates that the individual lacks vigour, enthusiasm and zeal.
2. **Speed slow, low pitched**
   - If the speed is slow and the pitch is low it signals the worst kind.
   - Due to certain psychological reasons the interactant barely has the stamina to continue speaking.
3. **High pitched**
   - Enthusiasm, on the contrary, is backed by a high pitched voice in which sufficient emphasis is laid on the words.
   - The excitement is connoted by the use of a high pitch and voice modulation.
4. **High pitched, long drawn-out speech**
   - In this case co-participant is not likely to believe all that is being said by the speaker to him.
   - More conviction in speech is needed if the sender wants the recipients to believe in his statements.
5. **Ascending tone**
   - Astonishment at the happening or the interaction is indicated by the tone, which is ascending in nature.
6. **Abrupt tone**
   - The interactant wants to indicate by the abruptness in the speech that he has had enough and would like to cut short the interaction.
   - If this is coupled with anger, words used are going to be terse and the tone, sonorous.
   - The loudness in the tone is indicative of the fact that it is time for the co-interactant to take cognizance of the utterances made by the sender.

### Three Things in Your Voice to keep Audience Interested

1. Be enthusiastic
2. Exaggerate voice inflections
3. Do not speak in a monotone.

## THE PANCHSHILA OF GOOD TALK

It may be about a new process, a product, a project or an idea that we want to explain effectively in a short period of time. Steps for success in talk are discussed below.

1. **DEFINE THE PURPOSE:** We should be able to state in one sentence what we wish to accomplish.
2. **PREPARATION:**
    - Analyze the audience
    - Plan your time
    - Anticipate questions
    - Take a look at the room/place
    - See if the facts/material are ready.
3. **PROBLEMS:** Answer the question why one should listen?
4. **POSSIBILITIES:** Try to think of all choices
5. **PROPOSAL:** What you say should satisfy the other person(s).

## How to Begin a Talk

- Set up a good relationship with the audience. Be friendly and look friendly.
- Grab the attention of your audience with an incident of your own experience.
- Arouse curiosity
- Present arresting facts or catchy statements
- Ask a question

## How to End Your Talk

- When you have said what you wanted to say stop
- Go back to the story with which you started
- A summary is helpful
- Have a strong finish
- Don't leave the speakers stand while saying the last few words.

## How to Structure Your Talk

- Read a lot, fill you mind with the latest and the best.
- Picture your audience. Get your thoughts together.
- Make yourself interesting
    1. Use examples/jokes/quotes
    2. Go from things to idea

- **A good talk should have four parts**
    - Introduction
    - An indication of the structure
    - The body of your talk
    - Conclusion

- *Analyze the reaction of your audience*
- Ponder on where you can improve

## NON-VERBAL COMMUNICATION

Communication without words (anything someone does to which someone else assigns meaning). It can be structured or unstructured, i.e., more or less according to explicit norms. Hand signals, shrugs, head movements, facial expressions are used which is often subconscious. It can be used for expressing love, showing aggression, anger, supporting or accepting qualities.

Non-verbal behaviour is commonly called body language.

### Misleading Approaches

1. Symbolism (all body communication is symbolic expression, Jungians).
2. Power (bodily communication is always more powerful).
3. Controllability (we can control all the messages we send).
4. You can read people like a book.

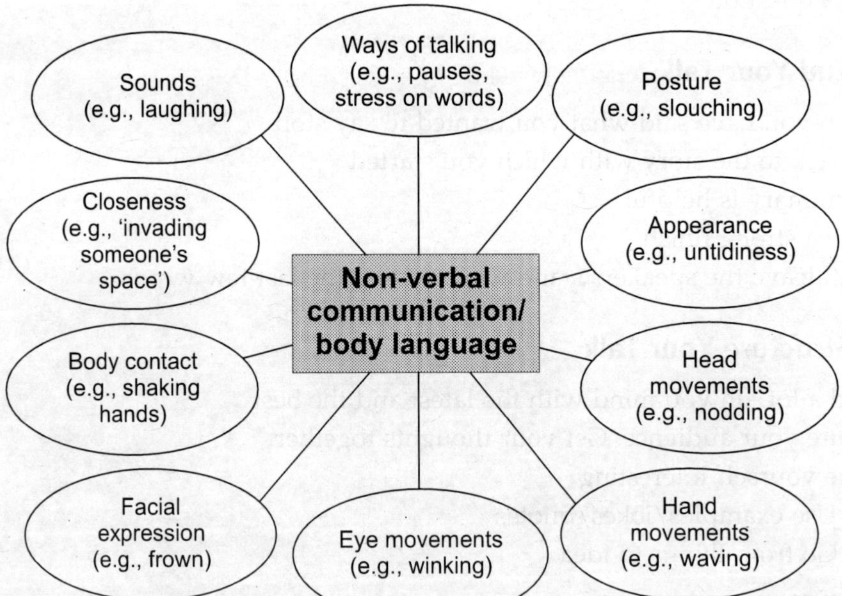


**Non-verbal communication (NVC)** includes facial expressions, tones of voice, gestures, eye contact, and spatial arrangements, patterns of touch, expressive movement, cultural differences, and other "non-verbal" acts. NVC is important in understanding human behaviour and the non-verbal "channels" it is more powerful than what people say.

Cross-culturally people from different countries having different languages, values, emotional expressions, norms, rituals, rules, expecsstations, family background, and life experiences communicate through body language.

## 3.3 BODY LANGUAGE

*"THE BODY SAYS WHAT WORDS CANNOT".*

Body language plays an important role in oral communication. It helps in analysis of the motion of the "intelligent' body in the context in which it is represented. Body language depicts our inner self and conveys more than our tongue.

Body language is by using body movements or gestures instead of, or in addition to, sounds, verbal language or other communications. Every human being communicates through verbal and non-verbal languages. Exchange of words refers to verbal communication while non-verbal communication refers to all external stimuli other than spoken or written words and includes:

1. Body gestures
2. Postures
3. Facial expressions
4. Personal appearance
5. Eye contact
6. Modulations in voice
7. Use of space and distancing.

### Dimensions of Body Language

**Communication Skills**

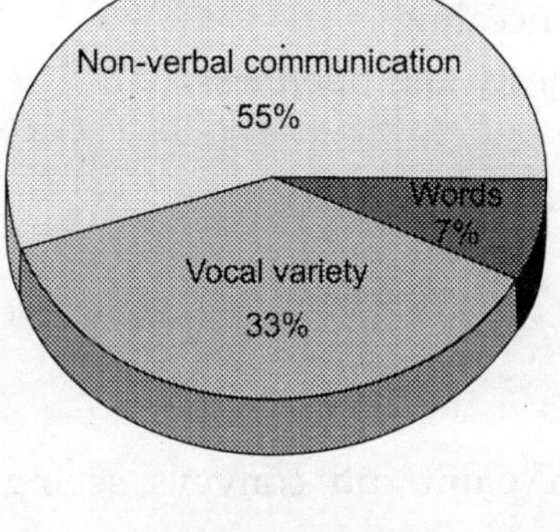

- In face-to-face interaction 93% meaning is transferred through non-verbal communication.
- 55% is body and face gestures.
- 38% is volume, pitch and inflection.
- 7% is through words.

By non-verbal signals emotions of a person can be depicted. If a person is tense he will sit or stand rigidly, with hands clasped together, legs crossed, and muscles tense.. If a person is happy his facial gestures will show bright eyes, bulging (smiling) cheeks.

**Personal Appearance:** The first impression is the impression everyone is concerned with. A person has his own aura which radiates a message to the outer world. One's appearance may put others into a resistant or even a hostile attitude or induce in them a receptive mood.

**Posture:** Every person stands, sits and walks in his own style. Posture refers to the way a person walks, sits and stands. An individual personality is known by his movement of the body, the position of hands and legs and other parts of the body. These reveal whether he is vibrant, alive and dynamic, nervous and jittery, confident and self-assured, etc. Walking or gait of the person conveys his confidence, nervousness, and energetic behaviour. The sitting posture may display unhappiness or inattentiveness.

**Gestures:** A gesture is a communication tool which uses signs, signals or cues in relation with, or apart from, words. An idea, an emotion, or state of mind can be expressed in verbal or non-verbal body movements. Gestures are the 'visible' bodily actions by which a word or a language is represented. A communication is also effective with a well timed gesture. Similarly, a key-chain, or clasping one's hand tightly, playing with a handkerchief, twisting your hair, hinders the effectiveness of communication of a speaker. All oral communications should be accompanied by proper gestures for better understanding. And also add a greater value for a powerful impact.

**Palm Gestures**

- Closed palms convey concealing
- Open palms convey honesty and openness
- Hand shake conveys:
  - *Aggressiveness*
  - *Assertiveness*
  - *Passiveness*

**Hand and Arm Gestures**

- Thumb and finger rub\palm rub conveys seeing some benefit
- Clenching hands convey controlling, flight or attack
- Steeping hands convey maturity
- Gripping arms and wrist conveys hesitance, fear

**Head Tilt**

- Head up conveys arrogance
- Head straight conveys straightforwardness
- Head down conveys inferiority, dejection or deviousness
- Hands behind the head conveys arrogance

**Cross Positions**

- All cross positions are barriers
- Arm cross or leg cross conveys defensiveness, resistance, or aloofness
- Leg cross for women is a sign of decorum
- American cross is a sign of openness

**Hand to Face Gestures**

- Mouth guard, nose rub, ear rub, eye run all convey some form of, deviousness, lying, or being unsure.

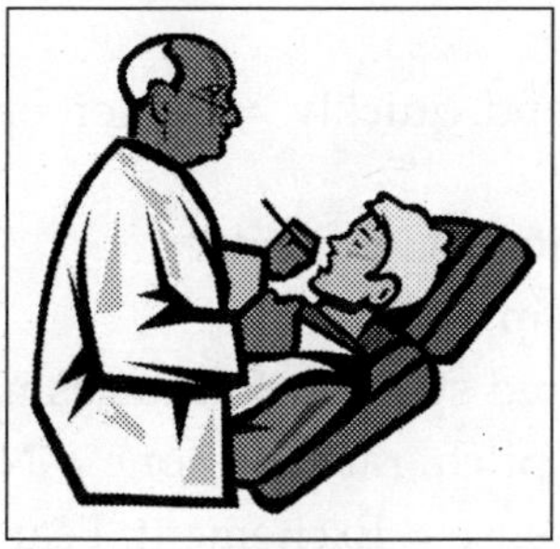

**Facial Expressions:** "Face is the mirror of life." Our identity is by our face. Face helps to express our moods, attitudes, opinions and also how we relate to others. A face expresses the emotions of a person and it is mightier than the word. A smile is the best facial expression which helps to unite and is an effective signal of acceptance. Our face is very expressive, the features on the face depict various meanings. A smile conveys friendliness, a frown shows discontent, raising eyebrows shows surprise or disbelief, tightening the jaw muscles shows aggression. Bright eyes may show enthusiastic whereas wooden expressions conveys depression. Anxious people generally have horizontal creases on forehead, raised eyebrows.

**Eye Contact:** Eyes are very expressive in dealing with emotions and moods. The eyes can show disinterest, a terror, anger, love.

Dilated pupils convey receiving, contracted pupils convey, fear, anger, withdrawal.

- Business gaze is fixed around the region of eyes and forehead.
- Special gaze flits all over, or fixes to regions that are personal.

Chin stroking may convey:

- Evaluation
- Boredom

**Space and Distancing:** Proxemics is the study of people's appreciation and use of space. This varies from culture to culture, and individual to individual. The amount of space a person needs also determines the personality of a person. One can observe this by the amount of space a person requires for sitting. A shy person may occupy less space while sitting. An egoistic person may use the space of the chair by extending his arms, this depicts the lust for power.

**Modulation of Voice:** Tone of voice reflects the strength in which a person communicates a point. Clear controlled voice depicts the confidence while speaking which is expected from students in interviews, presentations, trainers, lecturers. Toned voice gains the confidence of others too. A significant number of voice qualities are universal across all human cultures.

**(a) Interpretation of Voice**

- Speaking at full volume and quickly = Anger or lack of interest in the other person's views.
- Clear controlled steady voice = Confidence
- The softer pitch = Friendship
- Vibrant, energetic, modulated speech= Enthusiasm.
- Lowered volume, reduced pitch, rate and tone = Negative attitude. Nervousness
- To speak unclearly or nonsense = Excitement. Fear
- Hesitating = Less confidence
- Crying, moaning and sighing = Silent grief. Bad tempered nature
- Murmur and boo = Disapproval

**(b) Reading Mind through Laugh**

Human laughter can be read with the sounds they make.

'Ha-Ha' is laughter that comes from the heart and shows pure joy and self-fulfilment.

'He-He' is sarcastic laugh, usually a joke about a person.

'Hee-Hee' suggests a undisclosed giggle that comes out when a person is distrustful or nasty.

'Ho-Ho' communicates disclosure even doubt, by a person who is protesting, or is tough.

**Rules to Interpret Body Language**

- Have a holistic approach content and context
- Observe the complete person
- To be reasonably accurate at least three signals should point to the same direction

## ACCURATE PERCEPTION OF BODY'S IMAGE

This includes:

- Postures
- Gestures
- Body movement
- Facial expression
- Eye contact

## BUILD SELF-CONFIDENCE BY BEING YOURSELF

## BUILD SELF-CONFIDENCE THROUGH PREPARATION

## LET THE BODY MIRROR YOUR FEELINGS

### SMILE

The most crucial body language signal which gives the first impression is a smile. It transfers happiness.

A great smile radiates warmth that draws others instantly. A smiling person helps to empower our life, lets the sunshine in and gives others permission to smile too. A smile is an asset. The real essence of a smile makes people attractive and creates a magnetic effect of attracting people towards each other. It's always a welcome act. It makes people approachable. A smile is a stimulating and aromatic asset and comes at no extra effort and extra cost.

### Posture Development

POSTURE is the spine of an attractive figure. Develop a rhythmic walk, WHICH IS BALANCED IN MOTION, and one will develop grace in all his movements.

#### *Advantages of Body Language*

1. It helps the receiver of the message in decoding the message.
2. It adds intensity to the process of communication.

#### *Limitations of Body Language*

1. It is a non-verbal communication, relying on facial expressions, gesture, etc.
2. Facial expressions, gestures, postures, etc., become ineffective if the listener is inattentive. It is not very effective in large gatherings.

### Five Effective Ways to Make Your Body Speak

1. Obtain accurate perception of your body's image.
2. Build self-confidence by BEING YOURSELF.
3. Let your body mirror your feelings.
4. Self-confidence through preparation.
5. Read your audience.

#### *Body Gestures when Under-confident*

***Body Gestures When Overconfident***

## TYPES OF COMMUNICATION

### Formal

(a) **Oral Communication**: In this type of communication the communicator uses his verbal/talking abilities to convey his viewpoints either to an audience (public speaking) or to the other members of the participating group (group discussion).

(b) **Written Communication:** In this type of communication it is the written word which is used as the medium of communication. The success of this mode of communication depends on clarity, conciseness and correctness of the facts. A very good grasp of syntax pertaining to language used is very essential.

### Informal

(a) **Grapevine:** This is a common feature observed in organizations. The information reaches the receiver from the sender through a number of intermediaries. In the process the message gets distorted One thing which is very characteristic about this mode of communication is the speed with which the message is transmitted.

(b) **Rumour:** This form of communication occurs when people get word of an action, present of contemplated – without knowing the reason for it. In this event, false reasons are manufactured, i.e., rumours.

(c) **Body Language:** This method involves reading meaning into unconscious gestures made during oral communication, which might be significant in judging the emphasis/disinterest on the part of the communicator.

It has long been recognized that a person communicates not only with his tongue, but also with his entire body. Body language can be an important supplement to your communication skills. Each gesture is like a word in language. As the words, when structured into units or 'sentences' convey complete thoughts, the gestures, when studied in groups of related gestures, (gesture clusters) indicate with some certainty what the person is communicating.

## GUIDELINES FOR EFFECTIVE COMMUNICATION

1. Clarity of purpose
2. Shared activity
3. Common set of symbols
4. Focus on the need of receiver
5. Use feedback
6. Active listening
7. Controlling emotions
8. Politeness
9. Eliminate noise
10. Clarify assumption
11. Avoiding connotations and ambiguities
12. Socio-psychological aspect
13. Completeness
14. Conciseness
15. Proper use of body language

For oral communication, skill in interpersonal relations assumes greater importance. The assumptions, viewpoints and feelings of the speaker and the listener will vary depending on the organization relationship and the situation. These points should be given due weightage in a person-to-person communication.

### Essentials of Effective Communication

1. Understand yourself – self-analysis.
2. Understand your colleagues – seniors, peers and subordinates.
3. Understand the message – purpose and content.
4. Understand the organizational structure and policies.
5. Keep an open mind.
6. Develop the art of listening. Learn to be a good listener.
7. Overcome the sources of barriers to communication.

### Points for Discussion

1. **Communication** may be defined as "covering all methods of making known or transmitting ideas and information with the object of making oneself understood". Communication is the act of creating understanding.
2. 'Good communication' and 'effective communication' are commonly used to denote the same meaning but it is not so. 'Good' communication means that `B' has understood the concept that `A' wished to convey to 'B'. `Effective' communication means that the desired result has been obtained. Good

communication is a prerequisite but does not ensure 'effective' communication'. 'Effective communication' includes behavioural aspects like persuasion, motivation, coercion and the like.

Communication structures human relationships in such a way, that a group of people can work together to achieve a goal.

## COMMUNICATION

### Pitfalls

There are certain pitfalls in communication, such as given below:

### Cost

Reinventing the wheel: in the absence of clear communication, we normally do not get to know what is happening in other parts of the origination and with the result end up recreating things which are already existing, e.g., training modules, industry data, policies across different units, research material, etc.

### Delays in Getting Work Done

In the absence of timely communication, *n* number of delays could take place resulting not just in loss of time, money productivity but also employee satisfaction as a whole.

### Morale

In the absence of clear communication, the first thing that impacts is the employees' morale, especially in a crisis. If a company is doing well, it is imperative to share the success to boost the moral. In a situation where the performance is not good, the mantra is communication, communication and more communication. In the absence of clear direction from the top, rumour mongering starts and people start building stories around it.

### Barriers to Effective Communication

Miscommunication, noise or interference can effect the communication process. In complex and often conflicting relationships the following suggests a number of sources of noise:

#### *Sender*

(a) Sender does not know enough about the receiver.
(b) Sender picks the wrong time.
(c) Sender picks the wrong place.

(d) Sender uses the wrong method.
(e) Sender uses vocabulary that is misunderstood by the receiver.

***Receiver***

(a) Receiver is preoccupied.
(b) Receiver is not interested in the message.
(c) Receiver has emotional barriers.
(d) Receiver is distracted.
(e) Receiver pretends to understand when he doesn't.

**ARE YOUR CONVERSATIONS LIKE THIS?**

## APPENDIX

### Exercise-1 How Fast do You Speak?

Speaking too fast or too slow can cause lack of understanding. Experts agree speaking relatively slowly is better than speaking fast. A speed of about 140 words is considered ideal.

Try this little test. Time yourself reading the passage below loudly.

There is no set rule for the rate of speaking of individuals. Some people can speak at a rate of one hundred and ninety words per minute and be clearly understood, while others must speak as slowly as ninety words per minute to achieve the same understanding. Most experts feel, however, that there is more to be gained by speaking slowly. They have decided that a rate of about one hundred and forty words per minute is a safe rate. The main disadvantage of speaking too fast is lack of understanding caused by lack of clarity. However, it has other disadvantages also. The other person may get the impression that he or she is being pressurized into something. In addition, he or she may get the impression that you are very rushed and pressed for time. To be really understood – speak slowly – one hundred and forty!!

Indicate the time you took to read:

Less than a minute: ________

More than a minute: ________

### Exercise–2 Developing a Basic Communication Plan

While developing a communication plan, it would help to keep the following things in mind:

- ❒ What message do we want to convey?
- ❒ What is the target segment to whom we want to convey the message? Is it for some people or is it for the entire organization?
- ❒ What is the best approach to reach the target segment including who should convey the message and how should it be conveyed?

### Exercise–3 My Application Experience

| Date | My Application | Result | Learnings |
|---|---|---|---|
| | | | |

## Exercise–4 My Learning Today

| Date | What Was Covered? | Key Learning Points | How can I apply this back at work? |
|---|---|---|---|
| | | | |

## Exercise–5 Departmental/Divisional Action Plan

| Objective/Goals/Projects | How to achieve it? Who? | By when |
|---|---|---|
| 1. | 1.<br>2.<br>3.<br>4.<br>5. | |
| 2. | 1.<br>2.<br>3.<br>4.<br>5. | |

| 3. | 1.<br>2.<br>3.<br>4.<br>5. | |
|---|---|---|
| 4. | 1.<br>2.<br>3.<br>4.<br>5. | |
| 5. | 1.<br>2.<br>3.<br>4.<br>5. | |

## CASE STUDY

Employees of Aura Communication Pvt Ltd are undergoing special training. These trainings are specially to train the employees of marketing and sales on how to make decisions on the basis of non-verbal communication. Shalini Sehgal, the VP of the company stresses on non-verbal communication as an important part of inter- personal dealings and relations. Ms Sehgal has become interested in gestures, mannerism, body movements of individuals, as they reflect their personality. According to her, the potential employees and potential customers can be identified by reading them. The positiveness and negativeness of an individual is observed by his body language and this has a competitive advantage. It can really make a difference in the sales figures. It can also make the difference when closing the sales, and hiring new employees. During recruitment, Shalini pays attention on the candidate's eye movements, gestures, and facial expressions. She believes by observing this, one can predict if the candidate will be an aggressive salesperson or a friendly one. Now how does she do this? She observes this by looking into the eyes and the way the candidates present themselves. The first person looked into the eyes of the interviewer and made a constant eye contact, and demonstrated good communication skills. The second candidate did not look into the eyes, crossed both his hands and legs. Shalini is fully convinced that non-verbal communication plays a significant role in an organization to achieve its annual sales goals. This has helped her 'quality customers'

### *Answer the Questions*

1. How does body language signify the personality of an individual?

2. Describe the communication process used by Ms Shalini Sehgal in dealing with candidates and employees.
3. Do you think non-verbal communication is the only process that should be used in the recruitment process? Explain.

## SUMMARY

- Communication is the ability to share information with people and to understand what information others are conveying. Communication can take many forms including gestures, facial expressions, signs, vocalization (including pitch and tone), in addition to speech and written communication.
- Effective and open communication promotes an awareness of others' interests and needs.
- Objectives of communication are to provide information, order, persuasion, warning, motivation, advice, suggestion, education, raising morale.
- Communication process model is the art of encoding a message to communicate the intended message of the client/customers.
- The principles of conversation skills are clarity, brevity, simplicity, courtesy, sincerity, originality, pleasantness of tone, and flexibility of tongue.
- Oral communication is the interaction in which spoken words are used which are integral parts of the modern business world. "The ability to communicate effectively through speaking as well as in writing is highly valued, and demanded, in business."
- Power speak is your way to success: Rediscover yourself with your own speech and step towards success. There should be enthusiasm and vigour in your speech. Present in style. Be positive, and promote a positive attitude. Modulate your voice. Talk intelligently. Smile while you speak. Speak your mind from the depth of your heart. Have a sound vocabulary. Be enthusiastic. Have confidence.
- Non-verbal communication is the communication without words (anything someone does to which someone else assigns meaning). It can be structured or unstructured, i.e., more or less according to the explicit norms. It includes facial expressions, tones of voice, gestures, eye contact, and spatial arrangements, patterns of touch, expressive movement, cultural differences, and other "non-verbal" acts.
- Body language plays an important role in oral communication. It helps analyse the motion of the "intelligent' body in the context in which it is represented. Body language depicts our inner self and conveys more than our tongue.
- In face-to-face interaction 93% meaning is transferred through non-verbal communication, 55% is body and face gestures, 38% is volume, pitch and inflection, and 7% is through words.

- Five effective ways to make your body speak: Obtain accurate perception of your body's image, build self-confidence by being yourself, let your body mirror your feelings, self-confidence through preparation, read your audience.
- Miscommunication, noise or interference can affect the communication process. Barriers to effective communication are language or words with different meanings, defensiveness, unclear perceptions, blame, conversion, misrepresentation from the past, misinterpretation of body language, tone and other non-verbal forms of communication.

## QUESTIONS

### I. Explain in Brief

1. What do you mean by communication? What is the objective of communication?
2. Mention five communication elements in speaking.
3. What are the five effective ways to make your body speak?
4. Mention the non-verbal communication into four broad categories divided by G. W. Porter.
5. What does these indicate?
   - Sitting with legs crossed, foot kicking
   - Open palm
   - Gripping arms and wrist
   - Raising eyebrows
   - Dilated pupils
6. What do you mean by proxemics? What are the three basic principles of Goldhaber that summarize the use of personal space in an organization.?
7. Why is perceptual favouritism a barrier to effective communication?

### II. Answer the following questions

1. Describe five non-verbal means of communication in detail.
2. Explain briefly the principles for better conversational skills.
3. How can you describe body language as an effective means of communication? What is its limitation?
4. What are the ten commandments of effective communication?
5. Voice is called a powerful tool for transmitting the words and language. What are the different types of voice modulation used in different situations?

## PROJECTS

- Visit your library and identify books containing classic speeches. Read two of them and list down the success factors that have contributed to the greatness of such speeches. Communicate in your own style and try to evaluate yourself.
- The class is divided into 4-5 members each, read the autobiographies of successful people, who have grown from the grassroots. List down the steps involved in the success of each.
- Advertisements are generally considered the ultimate message style and act as a direct communication between the product and customer. Identify two advertisements and study the different communication strategies provided by the company to lure the customers for buying a particular product.

# 4

UNIT

# Presentation

*In sports, you don't play a game with just one part of you, for example, your arm in tennis or hands in basketball. You play the game with your whole physical being. The same is true in presenting yourself.*

**— Anne Miller**

## Learning Objectives

- Presentation Skills. "Speak for Yourself"
- Effects of Visual Aid in Presentation
- Format or Structure of a Presentation
- Communication for Employment: Resume
- The Perfect Interview
- Corporate Etiquettes

### Power Your Presentations to Create the Right Impact

In a busy street an old blind man was sitting begging for money. There was a cardboard sign, written: 'Blind - Please help' next to the begging bowl with no money.

A young advertising girl passed by the blind man. She observed that the people did not give any notice to the man and the board.

She took a thick marker-pen from her pocket and rewrote at the back of the signboard, then went on her way.

Immediately, the blind man could notice money being dropped into the cup and it started overflowing. The young writer, out of curiosity came to see the change of activity near the blind man. The blind man could hear the steps and he knew that this was the person who wrote something and hence the change.

"It says," said the stranger, "It's a beautiful day. You can see it. I cannot."

When you truly want to connect with people – your presentation is more important than your message. It's not what you want to say, but how you say it, makes the impact. This is true in any communication, and becomes still more important if you are in the field of influencing people.

**Answer the following**

1. Why did the blind man receive lot of money after the sign was changed?
2. Do you think powerful presentation creates an impact? Describe.

## 4.1 PRESENTATION SKILLS "SPEAK FOR YOURSELF"

### Presentation Skills for Emerging Managers

**Presentations are one of the first managerial skills, which a management person must acquire.** Management is the art of getting things done. A presentation is potentially a effective method.

One of the fundamental skills that every manager requires is that of the power of persuasion.

In order to achieve objectives of an organization, to motivate one's manager to greater commitment, to overcome the obstacles that the manager may face in living up to the expectations and finally, to project oneself in the corporate consciousness as LEADERS, one needs the skills of effective presentation.

Persuasive communication, in all aspects, finds fulfilment in the presentation skills. Mastery of these skills will make the managers LEADERS both within the organization and in the corporate world.

### Power Speak Your Way to Success

- Language is a success, and gives a big change to succeed.
- Increase your vocabulary
- Relive yourself with your own communication. All words do not sound same when spoken but look great when written.
- Try to read aloud, and hear your own voice while reading.
- Discover your voice by giving better modulations with speech, style and pronunciation.
- Sound is produced by your own vocal chords. Sound with enthusiasm while speaking gives confidence and energy to convince.
- Be positive and soft spoken. Speak from your mind and depth of your heart.
- Be lively, energize the listener with your presentation.
- Language should be clear and easily understandable. Don't mingle words and accent.
- Talk intelligently. Be clear, brief without any confusion. Convince the listener with your tactful speech, honesty. Be convinced with what you are speaking.

- Create an atmosphere of leadership. Create confidence with your motivational speech. Speak with knowledgeable words – it involves better understanding, curiosity, excitement, etc.
- Give presentation with style. Nurture a positive attitude by being, prepared and aware of the subject. Practise before the mirror and check your expressions.
- Pitch, tone and volume should be well adjusted. Good beginning has an happy ending. Feel happy, calm and composed and smile while speaking.
- Express your thoughts. Your inner feelings are reflection of your thoughts. Dress comfortably and according to the occasion. Have a good decent dress code.

## The Panchshila of a Good Talk

It may be about a new process, a product, a project or an idea that we want to explain effectively within a short period of time.

1. **The Purpose**
   We should be able to state in one sentence what we wish to accomplish.
2. **Preparation**
   - ❖ Analyze your audience
   - ❖ Plan your time
   - ❖ Anticipate questions
   - ❖ Take a look at the room/place
   - ❖ See if the facts/material are ready
3. **Problems**
   Answer the question "Why should someone listen?"
4. **Possibilities**
   Try to think of all choices
5. **Proposal**
   What you say should satisfy the other person(s)

### *How to Begin a Talk*

- ❒ A relationship has to be created with the audience.
- ❒ Be friendly, look friendly, sound friendly.
- ❒ Attention seeking, arouse curiosity.
- ❒ Use catchy statements.

### *How to End Your Talk*

- ➢ Say what you wanted to say, then stop
- ➢ A summary and a strong finish
- ➢ Don't let the speakers stand while the last few words are said.

### *How to Structure Your Talk*

Read a lot, fill your mind with the latest and the best.
Picture your audience. Get your thoughts together.
Make yourself interesting

- ♦ Use examples, jokes, quotes
- ♦ Go from things to ideas

A good talk should have four parts:

(i) Introduction
(ii) An indication of the structure
(iii) The body of your talk
(iv) Conclusion

Analyze the reaction of your audience.
Ponder on where you could improve.

Public speaking is enlarged conversation. There is little difference between talking to one person and to ten persons, or to a hundred. You must talk louder; but the talking that goes on around your dinner table does not differ in essence from the talking that goes on at a meeting. The only difference is that at a meeting the speaker is allowed to talk for a longer time without interruption.

Therefore, think of your speech as a conversation with the audience.

It is helpful, too, in preparing and practising your speech, to think of it as a discussion with people you know. Imagine that they have asked you an important question and you are doing your best to answer. As you do so, they put other questions to you, try to answer these. You explain, tell stories to illustrate what you mean, and cite statistics. Or someone objects, and you offer counter-arguments, and produce facts to support them. Finally, you sum up everything you've said with a "There, that's it. That's what I've been saying."

If you think of and prepare your address in these ways, it will be a good talking.

Public speaking is a purposeful communication. You talk to an audience for a purpose. You want them to feel, to think, to do something.

Therefore, during your speech, concentrate on this objective. Keep your eyes on the ball.

Don't let yourself be distracted by latecomers or noise. Don't let your talking become mechanical. If you let your attention wander, your manner will become absent-minded and you will not be able to communicate.

Think that you are saying while you are saying it. Think it hard.

Then the audience will know that you mean what you say and will listen to you.

*Beat Stage Fright*

State fright affects just about everyone who's called on to speak in public, and there is comfort in that thought alone.

Self-confidence is that wonderful, assured feeling you have just before you fall flat on your face—that was how one speech student felt about public speaking. Oddly enough, he was confident in other speaking situations.

There is a truth about speaking tensions: it only happens to the best people. Only the individual who is concerned about doing the perfect job suffers in anticipation of possible failure.

The circumstances and pressures that surround the speaking situation become a challenge to the ego. We are anxious about possible failure; we are nervous even about being nervous. Our normal reaction to all fear is either flight and fight. We must find a way to release this nervous energy in constructive expression. If we do not, it tends to perpetuate the symptoms and sensations that bring distress and discomfort to the speaker.

The speaking pressures and tensions are released because our nervous system believes we need them. It is as if we set off a false fire alarm, and now we are stuck with the apparatus – energy that is seeking an outlet. Once it is given an outlet, we can return to a relatively normal level.

First, remember that every experience is different. The dissimilarities are greater than the similarities. What reminds us of the past is entirely different from the present. Rarely, if ever, do situations in life repeat themselves. There is always a difference: time, age, mood, audience, speaker, topic, and results.

Next, we must remove the mystery labels from our feelings. Our feelings have no judgment. They respond when we need them or think we need them. Poise and control come with knowledge. The strange is fearful; the unknown brings apprehension. Conversely, with understanding comes control; with familiarity, comfort.

### *Let Your Tensions Work for You*

A teacher of public speaking was called in to observe a speaker who was unusually lazy in his speech and movements. He began with a slow paced, interminable walk to the speaker's stand. When he spoke, his pauses were wide.

When the man was interviewed, he admitted that he behaved as he did because he was very nervous about his speaking ability and wanted to hide it from the audience. He said, "I figured that if I could just slow myself down, I could hold those shook-up feelings." He had another talk to give in two months, so he went to work. His teacher demonstrated how unreleased tensions can create the impression of rigidity. The speaker learnt to put his nervous steam to work. He learned the techniques of alert gestures, accelerated speech rhythms, energetic movements, and lively expressions.

During his next talk, he amazed everyone, including himself. From the moment he stood up and walked to the platform, he was like a man electrified. He packed so much power into his enthusiastic movements and energetic speech delivery that everyone in the auditorium sat up and took notice of it. Since he used visual kids in his talk, the microphone bothered him because he had to return to it every time. Like an old pro, he confidently pushed it aside. He noticed that the room was hot, took his coat off and invited everyone else to do the same. He swept through his presentation with an astounding aliveness.

If fear and tension do nothing else but stimulate the speaker to do his homework, they have performed their natural purpose.

Fear and tension should be considered a positive influence which sharpens our strategy so that we may do our best. We are always facing difficulties. We make progress by meeting the challenge and conquering our fears. In that way out emotions motivate greater effort, which invites growth and development.

Delivering a talk or a presentation does take time to prepare. Even the more experienced speaker, whether he admits it in public or not, profits from the perspiration of preparation.

Obviously, we cannot keep a secret from our nervous system. If our nerves are stirred up in anticipation of the event, they are more tranquillized by the very fact that we have done our best to make ready.

*Ways to Reduce Physical Tensions*

- Breathe in rhythm—slowly, deeply
- Gesture and move whenever possible
- Relax your throat, jaw, shoulders.
- Loosen your arms
- Don't be perfect, just be good

The human brain is a wonderful organ, it starts to work as soon as you are born and doesn't stop until you get up to deliver a public speech.

— George Jessel

To gain confidence, take up the challenge to speak at every opportunity. In that way you can develop a new tolerance for the stresses and toughen your reactions as muscles are toughened by activity. We all have a marvellous capacity to adapt to the external environment. Use it, speak often.

Throw away all your fine excuses.

When it comes to public speaking and presentations, remember, the only way around is through.

## The Art of Presentation

### *Uses of Presentation*

- Presentation is used while an organization is launching a new product, a marketing proposal is being presented, in a seminar, workshop, diversity in business, new business plan

### *How to Make Presentation*

- Clarity of the content and occasion

- Study the audience
- Be proactive to plan the type and method of presentation
- Rehearse and rehearse
- Use proper visual aids
- Overcome nervousness

### *How Presentation Skills Add to Effectiveness*

- Teaching
- Leading
- Demonstrating
- Explaining
- Discussing/brainstorming
- Coordinating
- Consensus building

### *Types of Presentation Media*

- Overhead transparencies
- Video and film (for any size of audience)
- Slides (when designing slides choose your colours carefully as they convey different feelings and ideas).
- Computer aided presentation
- Flip charts
- Handouts

### *Essential Characteristics of a Good Presentation*

- Be clear about the introduction, body and the end of the presentation.
- Facts and figures can be represented in the form of tables, graphs and charts.
- Colours can be used to make the presentation of content attractive.
- The presenter should be properly and neatly dressed and should understand the audience and their need.
- Set up a good relationship with the audience.
- Use simple and clear language.

**How PowerPoint can add impact to your presentations**

- Structuring your topic
- Bullet notes for a talk
- Reinforce learning with visuals
- Clarify/demonstrate processes

- Build interest – entertain
- Ease of adapting message

### *Elements of a Presentation*

- Presenter
- Audience

Specific content with a definite objective to be achieved.
Think and plan the following before delivering the presentation:

- **Identify your purpose**
  This will help you organize ideas in logical order to convince the audience.
- **Analyze your audience**
  Get an idea of the number, nature, needs, level of knowledge and the attitude of the people who are going to receive the message.
- **Identify the need**
- **Collate your information**
  Structure and design your delivery, so that the audience accept your ideas.
- **Design your communication**
  Introduction
  Main body
  Conclusion
  Questioning and answering
- **Time your presentation**
- **Decide on the visual aids to be used**
- **Study the location**

### Presentation Components

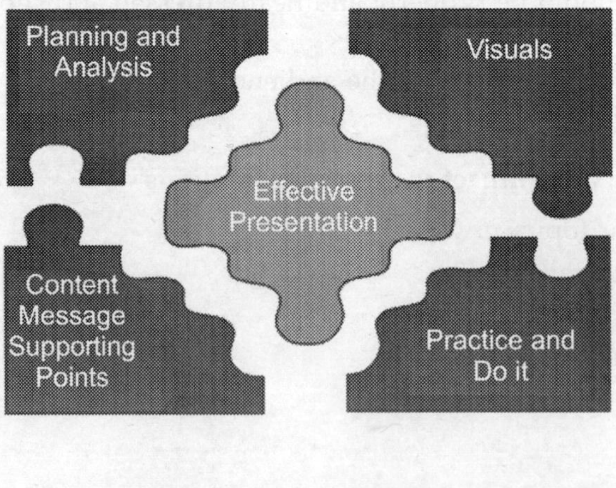

**The four components of presentation are:**

1. Planning and analysis
2. Content, message and supporting points
3. Visuals
4. Practise and do it

## *Planning and Analysis*

*Planning Your Presentation*

**Brain it!**

**Group it!**

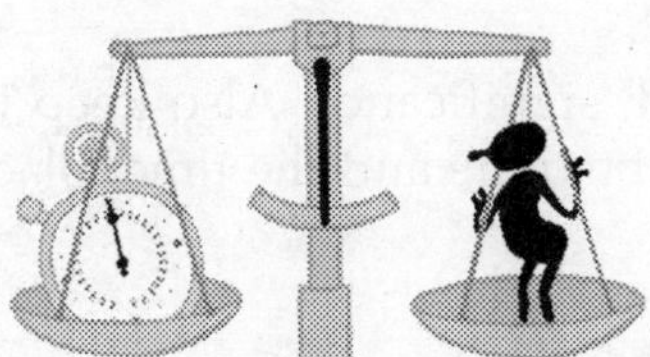

**Trim it!**

**Spice it up!**

**Do it!**

### *Use SPAM Model for Presentation*

- Situation
- Purpose
- Audience
- Method

## SITUATION

Status assessment is to be done seeing the situation, need, significance. Also keep in mind the knowledge required for delivery, the research to be done and the time, place and logistics for the presentation.

### Content

Determine and clarify: Roadblocks/hostility to your message, the best approach to make most persuasive content with facts and credible message.

To identify the content with core message to be conveyed and handouts and supporting visuals to be shown.

### *Take Control of Your Material*

1. What is the difference between 'a mission' and an 'objective'?
2. How would you define the key components of an objective?
3. What advantages can be seen from having a clear objective for your presentation?
4. The video recommends that you brainstorm your ideas when you begin to prepare you material. What other methods are open to you? Which is the best method for your organization?
5. Is it the best to memorise your presentation, or should you try to remember 'the thought behind the words'? Why?
6. Why is the opening of the presentation so important?
7. Why give the audience 'the bottom line first'? Which other professional communicators adopt the same approach?

### Logistics

Logistics will determine the overall agenda and purpose, the time needed to achieve content goals, the location of presentation.

One also has to anticipate the challenges presented by room, equipment required and who provides it, the contingencies one needs to prepare, the items required for presentation and who can provide it.

## PURPOSE

The message will clarify the core message, outcome objectives, and the key facts, ideas, benefits support this vision.

One also has to determine the examples and visuals which will best illustrate the message, the actions to be taken, the follow-up required by the participants and by you.

## AUDIENCE

**To communicate purposefully and effectively one needs to understand and analyse the audience.** Their demographics, common interests and outlook.

- What they know, don't know about topic?
- What do they need to know?
- What are their expectations, needs?
- What are influencing expectations?

Determine and clarify the information needed to provide them and at what level. What are the goals of the group you will be addressing, their attitudes, expectations related to the topic or situation.

One should also determine certain aspects of the audience, i.e, the age, sex, the occupation, intelligence and educational level and the influence of geographical experiences.

### METHOD

### Design

Use analysis to design a presentation that responds to participants' interests and focuses on a core message, flows logically, offers visuals that clarify content, promote retention, attend to non-verbal elements and provides time for discussion, and questions.

### Evaluation and Feedback

To design your evaluation one should review past evaluations, identify evaluation tools to support content, checks and corrections to support audience goals.

## CONTENT MESSAGE SUPPORTING POINTS

### Impact

**Impact is achieved by proper planning and delivery with enthusiasm,**

Impact = enthusiasm + preparation

Being natural, lively, appropriate, with supporting facts, statistics, illustrations, logic is important. This should be supported with appropriate body language and effective visuals.

**Building audience interest should be achieved by interaction with them.** The audience need to link content to personal experience, circumstances. Information applied to practise will be retained by hearing, seeing, doing.

## Audience – What They Really Want!

### Building Audience Interest

Be yourself, know and maximize your strengths, attend to nervous habits, learn from every experience and also seek feedback from people you trust.

Rehearse, rehearse, rehearse. This makes a person perfect and confident.

- Establish rapport with the audience
- Organize presentation material logically
- Offer information they can apply
- Focus on principles with illustrations
- Recognize their experience as valuable
- Adapt concepts to audience's experience
- Engage the audience – discussion, role playing, simulations, small group processes.

### *Supporting Actions*

- Posture and body awareness
- Eye contact

- Hands and gestures – animation
- Movement
- Voice and clarity – pausing/breathing
- Change of pace
- No reading, no apologies

Audience interest is influenced by

- Speaker's
  - Dress
  - Attitude
  - Mannerisms and nervous habits
  - Tone
  - Confidence

### *Content and Delivery*

- Value of information justifies time investment
  Audience interest is supported by:
- Providing benefits
- Keeping audience's needs as primary
- Covering the material promised
- Staying within the schedule
- Offering time for discussion, questions
- Visualize a standing ovation
- Stand at 45 degrees to screen
- Stand with screen to your left
- Limit pointer to critical uses only
- Break pattern with asking audience questions
- Remember – audience **wants** you to succeed!

## TAKE CONTROL OF YOURSELF

1. Why is it that people feel nervous before making a presentation?
2. What things, specifically, worry you?
3. How likely is it that any of those things will happen during a presentation?
4. Nerves affect our body language. Why is it important that the presenter be aware of this?
5. What image should you try to project when you are giving a presentation?

6. What elements in an image do we project?
7. Why is eye contact so important, both to the presenter and to the audience?
8. How much of the presentation should you rehearse?
9. Why is a rehearsal useful?
10. What things do you need to check before a presentation?
11. Why are the safety and comfort of the audience during presentations is important and who is responsible for them?

## Presentation Delivery

Albert Mehrabian, a well-known communication theorist, specifies that impact of a message can be divided into three factors:

- Body language
  - Contributes 55% towards message impact
- Tone of voice
  - Contributes 38% towards message impact
- Actual words
  - Contributes 7% towards message impact

**There are five key aspects of the human body, which deserve attention in presentation skills: the eyes, the voice, the expression, the appearance, and how you stand.**

## Body Language

- Eye Contact
  - Eye contact should be maintained with the audience and is a necessary part of interpersonal communication.
  - Gaze directly into another's eyes to establish the link.
- Facial Expression
  - The facial expression of the speaker should have a link with the communication done.
- Gestures
  - These are very expressive parts of the body. Arms, hands, body parts can be used to illustrate the words.
- Dress of the person plays a major role in acceptability by the audience.

## Tone of Voice

Two most important aspects of the voice for the public speaker are projection and variation.

- Volume in speech
- Consistent loudness—loudly or softly
- Convey life, colour and melody

Most effective speaking rate falls within the range of 120-160 words per minute. How you present the information is more important than the actual content! Organize your speech by capturing audience attention and interest;

- Use everyday language, avoid jargon.
- If you use jargon, make sure to introduce/define it.
- Use short crisp sentences with active verbs.
- Make heavy use of examples, analogies, metaphors, and comparisons to clarify and support your main points.
- Gain audience attention, win their interest and finally build understanding.

### Team Presentation

For team presentation there has to be proper coordination with the members of the team. The team leader should introduce the team.

## 4.2 VISUAL AIDS

### Effect of Visual Aids in Presentation

Effectively designed visuals should have graphics to support text, not overwhelm it, able to clarify and support content and offer a single message in a orderly and in logical manner. It should be viewed easily and provide consistently formatted slides.

#### *Impact of Visuals*

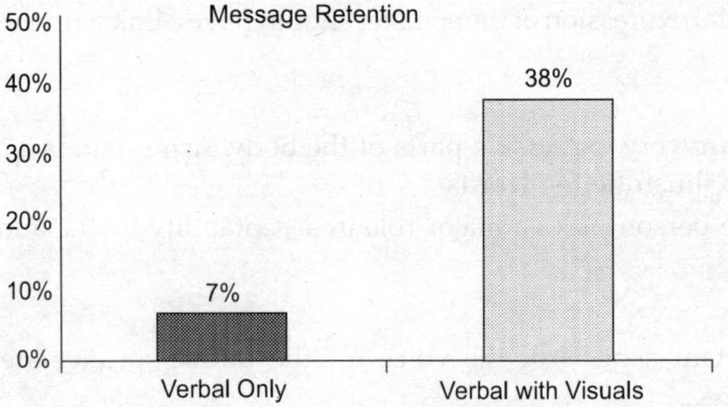

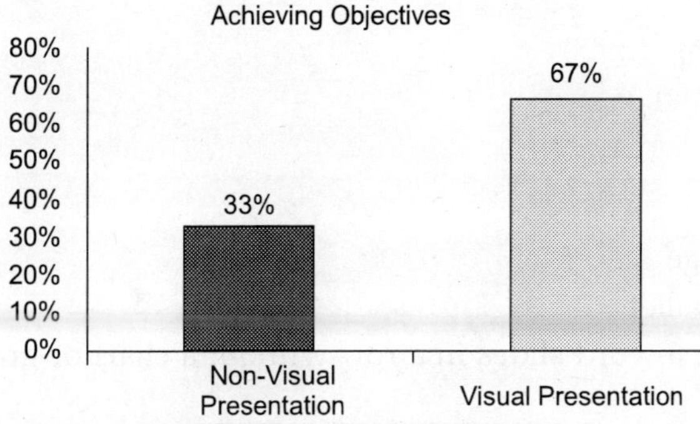


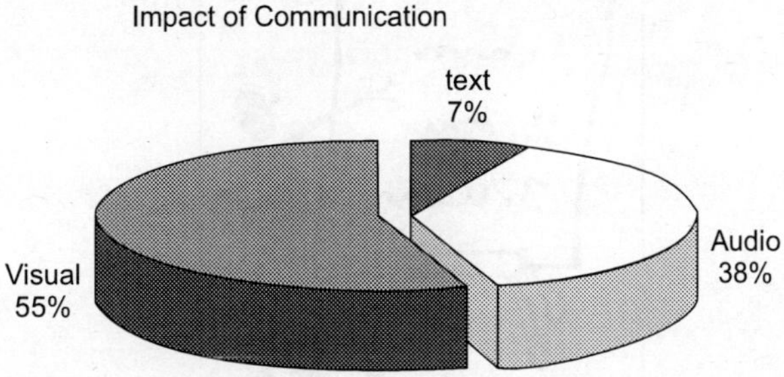


## Use of Visual Aids in Presentation

Visual reinforce delivery of any verbal message. Visual aids can be given in the form of a slide show, or even a video presentation.

The presentation should be made such as it can be read from the back of the room. Talk to the audience, not the visual aid.

For impact with PowerPoint:

- Keep content simple – headlines
- Work off the slides
- Use a non-distracting template and appealing colours
- Use "View-Master-Master Slide
  - Set title and bullet font and font sizes
  - Set default slide transitions and bullet animation
  - Place header and footer information

For audience visibility:

- Two plain fonts
  - Times New Roman for titles
  - Arial/Helvetica for bullets
- Font sizes:

– Focus on readability (20 – 44 points)

- Titles (36-44 points)
- Bullets (20-32 points)

For word slides:

- 6 – 6 – 6 Rule
  - 6 lines per page
  - 6 words per bullet
  - No more than 6-word slides in a row without a chart or graphic

***Slide Appearance***

- Assume three minutes per slide
- Avoid use of ALL CAPS
- Use landscape orientation, ample margins
- Graphics should clarify, not confuse
- Contrasting colours work best
- Test colours and graphics with projector

***What Colours Convey***

**Colour Term**

| | |
|---|---|
| Black | Authority, death, strength, loyalty, mystery |
| Brown | Action, earthiness, autumn, fellowship |
| Green | Envy, health, friendship, leisure, youthfulness |
| Red | Passion, heat, excitement, love, fulfilment |
| Orange | Warmth, action, power, aggression, fury |
| Purple | Dignity, royalty, stinginess, miserable |
| White | Holiness, cleanliness, purity, professionalism |
| Yellow | Confidence, knowledge, esteem, playfulness |

## PRACTISE AND DO IT!

### Managing Your Time

There is no alternative to rehearsal. Rehearsal in front of a mirror is important to know your style as it is the reflection of oneself. Put emphasis on your gestures and voice modulation to get used to the sound and sight of yourself.

Practice is only productive when you make a positive effort to improve, try it.

- Slide to time ratio = 3 minutes each
- Check points (agenda and clock)
- Coordinate with other presenters
- Rehearse for "time sense"
- Determine timing of questions
- Leave time for questions/discussion

**Approach: Practice, Practice, Practice**

**Handouts should be prepared and given to the participants. These are short notes of the slide handouts. It can be on paper or in the C.D.**

### Options for Handouts in PowerPoint

- 9 slides per page only for speaker
- 6 slides same as 3 with notes
- Complex content = 2 per page
- For dark graphics print "pure black and white" rather than "greyscale"
- Consider bright white paper

Common Mistakes
?
?
ΘπΣΦΩ
SRA Western - Effective Presentations
66

Common Mistakes
ΘπΣΦΩ
• Lack of planning
– Rushed job, last minute
– Wrong message for this audience
– Unresponsive to audience
– Lack of logic to points
– Poor or missing handouts
– Audience reading handouts, not watching
SRA Western - Effective Presentations
67

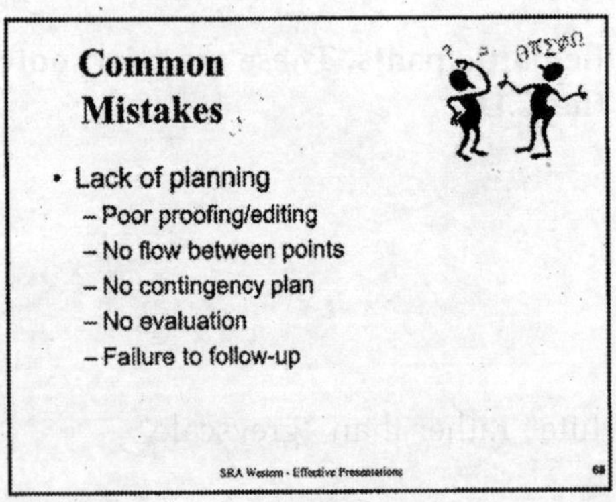
Common Mistakes
ΘπΣΦΩ
• Lack of planning
– Poor proofing/editing
– No flow between points
– No contingency plan
– No evaluation
– Failure to follow-up
SRA Western - Effective Presentations
68

## Speaker Notes

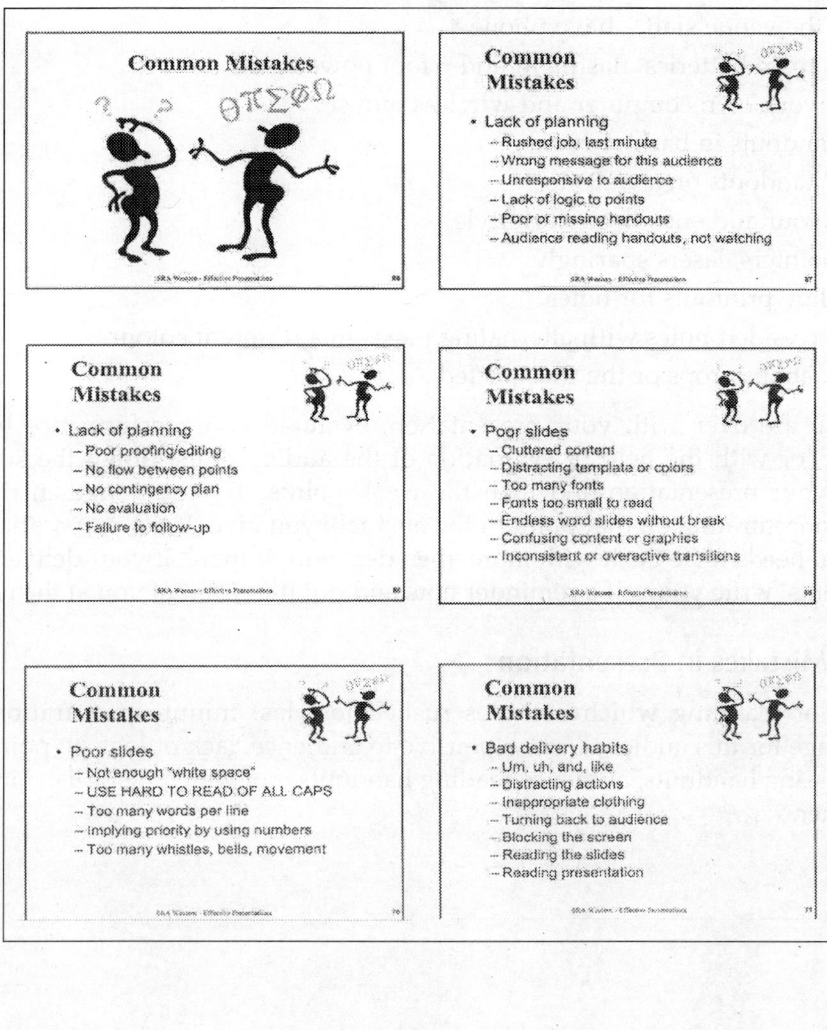

**Speaker should be introduced professionally to the participants. Purpose of speaker's introduction is to:**

- Establish rapport and speaker's credibility with the audience.
- Good introduction warms up and readies the audience for the speaker.
- Weak introductions are a disservice to the audience and the speaker.

## Presentation Tips and Tricks

- Rehearse with someone unfamiliar with the topic
- Develop a checklist
- Arrive 30 minutes early to
  - Check room
  - Layout
  - Equipment
- Meet the venue staff – have phone #
- Have spare batteries, flashlight and 6 foot power cord
- Bring your own computer and wireless mouse
- Put handouts in back of room
- Place handouts on a website
- Walk your audience (Donohue style)
- Use pointers, lasers sparingly
- Use slide printouts for notes
- Use two-sided notes with alternating pages in a different colour
- Think about props or the unexpected

Once you are over with your presentation, evaluate your performance honestly. Do it alone, or with the help of evaluation of the audience, list down the successful aspects of your presentation and then the weak points. Try to strengthen the weak points by concentrating on that point in the next talk you give. If the preparation of the presentation needs to be dealt with more, then deal with it there. If your delivery needs improvements, write yourself a reminder note and put it in front of you at the next talk.

## Common Mistakes in Presentation

➢ Lack of planning which includes rushed job, last minute preparation,wrong message for this audience, unresponsive to audience, lack of logic to points, poor or missing handouts, audience reading handouts, not watching or listening to the speaker.

- ➢ Lack of planning with poor proofing/editing, too many slides/content for allotted time, no flow between points, no contingency plan, no evaluation, failure to follow-up.
- ➢ Poor slides with cluttered content, distracting template or colours and too many fonts or too small to read, endless word slides without break create confusing content or graphics. Use of HARD TO READ OF ALL CAPS, too many words per line can create visual disinterest.
- ➢ Bad delivery habits include distracting actions,turning back to audience, blocking the screen, reading the slides, reading presentation without pausing running over schedule, no time for questions and not answering questions asked.

## 4.3 RESUME WRITING PRESENTATION FOR EMPLOYMENT

### Learning Objectives

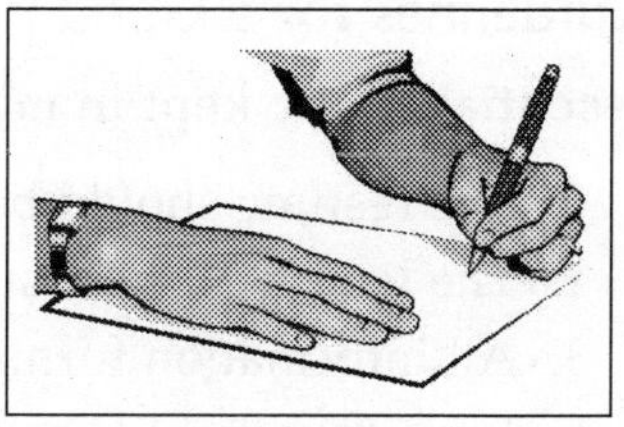

- ➢ Importance of a resume
- ➢ How to prepare a good resume
- ➢ Contents required for a resume
- ➢ Writing a resume
- ➢ Outlook of a resume
- ➢ Sending an application/cover letter
- ➢ A sample resume
- ➢ Checklist for a resume

### Writing an Effective Bio-Data

An interview situation is very similar to selling situation. For effective sale, one should have knowledge about the product and market.. Similarly, for successful interview, adequate knowledge of the employer and company is must. The interviewee must be well versed with his product (i.e., he must have good subject knowledge) in order to effectively sell himself.

**An organized and well-designed bio-data is the most important before an interview. The resume should be systematic, well organized, clear, brief and informative.**

- A resume is what a candidate sends along with the job application letter.
- A resume usually accompanies the covering letter and presents all relevant details about the candidate.
- A resume is also referred to as bio-data or curriculum vitae (CV)
- A resume or a CV is short account of one's career and qualification typically prepared by an applicant for a position.
- A resume is also understood as a personal datasheet that presents the academic qualifications, job related experience, skills and strong points of a person seeking a job.

### *Importance of a Good Resume*

- A good resume helps project the individual in proper light.
- A good resume helps bring out the basic strengths of the individual in terms of academic achievements, job related skills, attitude and aptitude and other relevant details.
- A good resume competes for attention and gets noticed.
- A good resume makes an impression even at a casual glance.
- A good resume helps you get an interview call, and move closer to getting the job you are seeking.

## Guidelines for a Good Resume

**Essentials to be kept in mind while preparing a good resume**

1. The resume should be neat and legible
2. The length of the resume should be optimum, neither too long nor too short.
3. All information furnished in the resume must be accurate and up-to-date.
4. For a favourable impression always be honest and sincere.
5. A resume should be built with the focus on employer needs.
6. The secret of an eye-catching resume is to make it appealing and distinctive.
7. Take time over your resume and choose the right format.

**Suggested list of captions or headings appropriate for resumes in general is given below:**

- Personal detail
- Academic qualification
- Academic distinction
- Work experience

- ♦ Area of specialization
- ♦ Career related achievement
- ♦ Seminars and workshops.
- ♦ Papers and publication
- ♦ Membership of boards and committees
- ♦ Guest faculty
- ♦ Consultancy
- ♦ Other relevant information
- ♦ Languages known
- ♦ Marital status
- ♦ Hobbies and interests
- ♦ References

Success in an interview depends to a large extent on the impression created by the bio-data.

## Contents of the Bio-Data

The bio-data should include the following:

- Personal data: Name, marital status, address, telephone number, etc.
- Career goals and job objectives.
- Professional experience
- Professional qualification
- Additional qualifications (if any)
- Academic honours/achievements.
- Membership of professional organizations.
- Extra-curricular activities: This includes personal achievements
- Hobbies – The person's interest in free time
- Career goals – articles/papers published, summer assignments handled, etc.
- Willingness to travel or relocate.
- Details of passport
- Languages known
- Personal abilities
- Names and address of referees.

## Resume Preparation for Interview

The bio-data should be clear, concise and reflect the career goals. Also it is a prerequisite for the interview.

The questions that may arise out of the bio-data are as follows:

1. Does the bio-data give a honest and clear description of the candidate?
2. Does the candidate have clear thoughts and beliefs and clarity of himself and the profession ?
3. Are the career objectives/goals align with the all-round preparation?
4. Is the candidate clear with the timeline for visualization to attain his career goals, realistic?

### *General Résumé Guidelines*

**Ensure that your résumé is**

- Clear and concise.
- Consistent and honest.
- Positive and aggressive.
- Careful and neat.

**Your resume should not include**

- Salary requirements.
- Reasons for leaving previous employers.
- Geographic limitations (unless necessary).
- Personal philosophies (e.g., religion).
- Any negative information

### *Resume Evaluation Checklist*

**Does the resume sell your**

- abilities and skills?
- professional experience?
- education?
- accomplishments?
- potential?

### *Does the Resume Look*

- professional?
- easy to read?
- balanced on the page?
- as polished as you look in person?

### *Will the Resume*

- catch the employer's attention?

- represent you at your best?
- leave the reader with a series of "themes" that best describe your skills sets and personal qualities?

## Writing Your Resume

### *Format and Style*

- Must look good–decision made in 45 seconds
- White or light bond paper–letter and resume on matching paper
- Laser printer only
- Everything correct
- One full page of info
- One page with references

### *Contents*

- Your strengths–your assets
- Bare essentials–name, address, education, work experience
- Don't exaggerate, but don't dwell on negatives

### *Career Objective*

- Solicited application–specific objective
- Unsolicited application–general objective
- "To obtain a job that will allow me to use my training and education" not a good objective

### *Education*

- School, major, minor, degrees and/or certificates, date of graduation
- Scholarships
- Grade point average?

### *Work Experience*

*Professional/Related Experience*

- Not simply a list of job responsibilities.
- Experience must be communicated in the context of outstanding performance and demonstrated accomplishments.
- Most recent first
- Name and location of employer
- What organization does
- Your title

- Time employed there
- Duties and responsibilities
- Significant achievements

*What is Experience?*

- Paid and non-paid positions
- Part-time and full-time
- Internships and externships
- Volunteer/community service

*Military Service*

- Relevant skills
  - Language
  - Computer expertise
  - Date available for work
- Activities and achievements
  - Speaking, writing, athletics, tutoring
  - Fund raising
  - Leadership roles in student organizations
- Personal data
  - Hobbies
  - Travel experience
- Avoid
  - Gender, sex, religion, marital status, race, colour, age
- List military service
- References
  - Name, title, company, address
  - Give title

## RESUME FORMATS

- Chronological
  - Most recent experience first
  - Most common type of resume
- Functional
  - Stress areas of accomplishments
- Targeted resume
  - Focus on particular skills

## Examples of Effective Statements

- Assisted in the implementation of a software programme which resulted in a 20% decrease in annual downtime and retooling costs.
- Worked on a marketing team that developed and implemented a plan which resulted in a three-month market share increase of 10%.
- Assisted in the development of a summer sales campaign which resulted in a territory sales ranking increase from fifth to first.

## Words of Advice

We've entered an era where talented and competent people are not getting jobs. The only remedy is to stand out and self-promote. If you do, you'll always get the nod over those who do not."

## Outlook of a Resume

**Neatness:** Never ever send a hand written resume. The resume should be neatly typed and evenly formatted.

**Formatting:** Leave space between events and details. The font size for the resume should not exceed 12 and should be preferred in Times Roman and Arial.

**Length:** The resume should not be less than 2 sheets of A4 size paper and not more than 4.

**Content:** Details on work experience, education, achievements within each and also mention the criteria of work done and also mention the depth of your work in that area. Do not mention anything superficial, as content is the basis at the interview state.

## Pre-Interview

**Your Appearance:** Dress professionally and also in the clothes that you have tried out before and are comfortable in. Stick to neutral colours. For girls, be well groomed, away from flashy jewellery; pay attention to your feet/footwear.

**Timeliness**: Reach the venue at least 10 minutes before the slotted time. Be comfortable with the venue, refreshen yourself.

Maintain your grace and cool.

## The Interview

**Listen carefully:** Respond appropriately after listening to the questions correctly.

**Measure your words:** Do not be nervous. This will allow the interviewer gain insight into the depth of your experience. Give examples wherever relevant.

## Post-Interview

**Follow-up:** If you have gone through your placement agency then do follow-up from the agency. Otherwise, follow-up over the email.

**How to Deal with a "No":** Remember, an interview is an assessment of your skills for a particular job and it is not judging you as a person. Do not interpret a "no" as a rejection of yourself.

## COVER LETTER

"A cover or covering letter is an introduction letter which is attached to a résumé or curriculum vitae"

It is a statement that tells what all you can give if hired and also shows one's interest in the job.

Cover letters are generally one page at most in length, divided into:

- Title
- Introduction
- Body
- Closing

### Dos and Don'ts

- While writing use only meaningful information highlighting the important points.
- The cover letter should not be more than one page in length and contain 2 to 3 short paragraphs.
- Use language that shows interest and motivation for the job.

There are mainly three types of cover letters:

- The application for job opening.
- The exploring letter to enquire about the possible openings and positions
- The networking letter for job search

## SENDING AN APPLICATION

Dated

**(Name of Hiring Manager, Title)**
**(Name of Company)**
**(Address)**
**(City, State Zip)**

**Dear (Mr. or Ms.) (Last Name):**

Sub: Application for the post of ______________________

Sir,

With respect to your advertisement, which appeared in ____________ dated ____________ for the post of ____________ I hereby submit my application for the post of ____________ with my resume along with relevant particulars.

I bring to the position is a combination of team leadership, strategic planning, and business development skills that I have leveraged to meet and exceed expectations. My résumé contains my accomplishments. It would be pleasure if I get an opportunity for a personal interview.

Looking forward for your perusal

Thanking You,
Yours Truly,
**XYZ**
Qualification
Address
Tel.

Enclosures:

## RESUME

**<Name>**

<Add1 with phone no>

Scanned photo

**Objective**

To be a part of working force of an institution or organization to achieve its goals and maximize one's own career potential.

**Work Experience**

Company
Designation
Duration/year
Areas of responsibility

## Professional Qualification

**I. Engineering/MBA or any Professional Degree or Diploma**

**College : <Name of College>**
**Course : <Name of Course>**
**Branch : <Branch Name>**
**Batch : <Year of passing out>**

**II. Semester-Wise Marks in Engineering College**

| Year | Marks Scored | Maximum Marks | Marks (%) | B.Tech. |
|---|---|---|---|---|
| First semester | | | | |
| Second semester | | | | |
| Third semester | | | | |
| Fourth semester | | | | |
| Fifth semester | | | | |
| Sixth semester | | | | |
| Seventh semester | | | | |
| Eighth semester | | | | |

## I. Project Undertaken in Final Year

< Details in brief>

## Academic Qualification

**II. Secondary and Senior Secondary Education**

| SI. No. | Class | School | Board | Percentage Marks |
|---|---|---|---|---|
| 1 | 10th | <school> | CBSE | <> |
| 2 | 12th | <school> | CBSE | <> |

## Skill Set/Additional Skills

Operating System : WINDOWS 98/XP.
Languages : C
Other Software : MS Project, MS Office

| Professional Memberships |
|---|
| 1. Student membership of IEEE/AIMA, etc. |

| Other Achievements and Hobbies |
|---|
| Conferences, seminars attended<br>Books or articles published<br>Sports, academic activity |

| Personal Profile | |
|---|---|
| Date of Birth<br>Gender<br>Father's Name<br>Father's Profession<br>Marital Status<br>Languages Known<br>Personality Traits | |

**Declaration**

I hereby declare that the above-furnished details are true and correct to the best of my knowledge.

**<Name and Signature>**

## Checklist for Resume

A. Contacts and Style

1. Prepare the resume before the application letter to summarize the facts the letter will be based on.
2. Present the recent qualification first.
3. Show facts and figures
4. Do not use excessive personal pronouns.
5. Do not write the desired salary, work schedule, or vacation schedule.

B. Contact Information

1. Write your name, address area code and telephone number for both school or work and home if appropriate.

C. Career Objective and Skills Summary (Optional)

1. Be as specific as possible about what you want to do.
   - State a broad and flexible goal to increase the scope of your job prospects.
   - Prepare two different resumes if you can do two unrelated types of work.

2. Summarize your key qualifications.
3. State the month and, if you know it, the day on which you will be available to start work.

D. Education

1. List all relevant schooling and training since high school, with the most recent first.
   - List the name and location of every institution you have attended, with the dates you entered and left and the degrees or certificates you obtained.
   - Indicate your major (and minor) fields in college work.
   - State your marks/grades average, if your average is impressive enough.
2. List relevant required or elective courses in descending order of importance.
3. List any other related educational or training experience, such as job-related seminars or workshops attended and certificates obtained.

E. Work Experience

1. List all relevant work experience, including paid employment and volunteer work.
2. List full-time and part-time jobs, with the most recent one first.
   - State the month/year when you started and left each job.
   - Provide the name and location of the firm that employed you.
   - List your job title and describe your functions briefly.
   - Not on-the-job accomplishments, such as an award or a suggestion that saved the organization time or money.

F. Activities, Honours and Achievements

1. List all relevant unpaid activities, including offices and leadership positions; significant awards or scholarships not listed elsewhere; projects you have undertaken that show an ability to work with others; and writing or speaking activities, publications and roles in academic or professional organizations.
2. In most circumstances, exclude religious or political affiliations.

G. Other Relevant Facts

1. List other information, such as your typing speed or your proficiency in any language.
2. Mention your ability to operate any machines, equipment or computer software used in the job.

H. Personal Data

1. Omit personal details that could be regarded as negatively or be used to discriminate against you.
2. Omit or downplay references to age if it could suggest inexperience or approaching retirement.

*Source*: C. L. Bovee and J. V. Thill, *Business Communication Today* (New York: McGraw Hill, 1995)

## CURRICULUM VITAE

NAME OF THE APPLICANT
Address
Email
Phone No

### Objective

To strive to achieve a sense of satisfaction and enjoyment from my work that is beneficial to both me and my organization.

### Professional Qualifications

Masters in Computer Application University (College)

| | | |
|---|---|---|
| | $1^{st}$ Semester | 70% |
| | $2^{nd}$ Semester | 74% |
| | $3^{rd}$ Semester | 74% |
| | $4^{th}$ Semester | 73% |
| BCA | 2001-2004 | (University, College) |

### Academic Qualifications

| | | | |
|---|---|---|---|
| $12^{th}$ | 2000-2001 | C.B.S.E | 80% |
| $10^{th}$ | 1998-1999 | C.B.S.E. | 75% |

### Software Proficiency

| | |
|---|---|
| Operating Systems | : Windows 9x, Unix |
| Web Application Tools | : HTML |
| Languages | : C, C++, Java (core), VB (6.0) |
| Packages | : Oracle 9i, MS-Office |
| DTP Application | : CorelDraw, Photoshop, PageMaker |

## Projects Undertaken

***Hotel Management System***

| | | |
|---|---|---|
| Duration | : | 4 Weeks |
| Environment | : | VB |
| Status | : | Programmer |
| Description | : | A project to have a database record for all employees, food and beverage, banquets, etc. |

***WebSite of Jammu and Kashmir***

| | | |
|---|---|---|
| Duration | : | 4 weeks |
| Environment | : | HTML |
| Status | : | Programmer |
| Description | : | A project manages all the places of Jammu and Kashmir including all temples, food and restaurants and visitors place |

***Hotel Management System***

| | | |
|---|---|---|
| Duration | : | 1 Week |
| Environment | : | OOAD (Object Oriented Analysis and Design) |
| Description | : | A project manages all the records of the employees in an hotel including all operations like deleting the information, updating the information, etc. |

## Achievements

*Won many prizes in different technical presentations.*

- Organized 'ZEPHYR' *Technical Fest (at college, year)*
- *Won prizes for scoring distinction in MCA*
- *Won 1st prizes participating in fashion show*

## Area of Interest

- Programming and database

## Hobbies

- Computer games
- Playing chess

| Personal Details | | |
|---|---|---|
| Father's Name | : | |
| Date of Birth | : | |
| Marital Status | : | |
| Languages | : | |

| Reference | | |
|---|---|---|
| Date | : | (Name of the Applicant) |

## Writing an Effective Resume

**A. PLAN YOUR RESUME**

- The purpose of employment should be clear as to meet the employers' needs.
- The strengths should be highlighted and organized.

**B. WRITE YOUR RESUME**

- Be clear and honest
- Highlight the qualification and experience which the employers are looking for.
- Career objectives, skills, achievements should be summarized.

**C. COMPLETE YOUR RESUME**

- Revise for no grammatical and spelling mistakes
- The language of the resume should be clear, concise and persuasive.
- Proof read for letter perfect
- Circulate as per employer's preference.

## Web Pages Can Work for You

Posting a web page is also a way to show yourself and your communication skills. Put details of the resume: the photos, videos and sounds. Show examples of real projects, documents, and presentations that you have done to demonstrate your skills and creativity.

You can use paid or free web pages for expressions, e.g., www.drshikhakapoor.com is expression of website to show the training and consultancy projects done by the author of this book.

You can also have YouTube channels to show your skills and achievements.

## 4.4 THE PERFECT INTERVIEW

**"Are You Good at Selling Yourself"**

We all endeavour for our growth through various means. Accepting ourselves as we are, with all the positive traits as well as imperfections, is important a goal as growth. Self-acceptance and personal growth are two sides of the same coin. One has to ascertain key strengths and focus areas for growth, both in personal and professional fields. Self-acceptance leads to acceptance of one's strength and weaknesses. One should make small measurable goals and keep evaluating the resources available at hand, skills and experience required and make personal growth plans.

### Learning Objectives

- Interview a selection procedure for recruitment
- Decisive factors of an interview
- Parameters for selection
- Preparation/checklist for the interviewee
- Essentials for an interview
- Some likely questions asked during an interview
- Formulate career plans

### The Art of Giving Effective Interviews

Interview is a face-to-face interaction of an interviewee by an interviewer for the purpose to evaluate the intelligence, aptitude of a potential employee. The purpose of the interview should be clear to the interviewee before appearing for an interview. The aim of the employment interview or selection interview is to assess the suitability of the candidate for the job/admission. Educational institution interviews are done for assessing the mental and physical abilities of the candidate for the specific course applied for.

The resume is a medium through which an interviewer assesses the interviewee on the basis of information provided by him. The bio-data provides the summary of the candidate's qualifications, experience, extracurricular activities, career objectives, family background and other personal details. The interview board uses the information provided through bio-data, tries to probe the personality to align with the profile required for the job. The interviewer assesses the intellectual qualities, the mental alertness, clear and logical description, judgment and clarity of the candidate's goal and interest, leadership ability and moral integrity.

## Decisive Factors of an Interview

The factors which play a major role in an interview are the knowledge and the power of expression of the candidate. In an interview, the candidate should be expressive, communicative, have presentation skills and content knowledge to impress upon the interviewer.

The preliminary selection is that of the academic background. The past experience and expectation from the assignment are the frequently asked questions. The questions in the opening or closing an interview asked are about describing self, achievements and personal details. The candidate should know the following:

(a) His professional and academic qualifications.
(b) The details of his past experience with its relevance to the present and future assignments.
(c) His career objectives/goals in life.
(d) Knowledge about his strengths in his personality and self-development.
(e) General awareness.

## Exercise of Profile Matching

The following are assessed and are the essential requirements for any job.

1. **Intellectual attainments**
   (a) The depth of knowledge of the subject for which the candidate is being interviewed.
   (b) Application of theoretical knowledge into practical situations.
   (c) General knowledge, social issues, newspaper headlines, etc.
   (d) The latest development in the area of job.
2. **Personal traits**
   (a) Personality: Pleasant, and cheerful.
   (b) Eagerness, alertness of the candidate.
   (c) Enthusiasm: Keenness and interest and approach.
   (d) Dress and smartness: Clean, neat dress, haircut, clean nails and polished shoes.
   (e) Confident poise: Gracefully and confidently handling self, gait, eye contact.
   (f) Punctuality.

3. **Career objectives**
   (a) Clear aim and ambition in life.
   (b) Career planning and his approach
   (c) Knowing his strengths and weaknesses.
4. **Character**
   (a) Self-discipline and moral values.
   (b) Honesty and faithfulness.
5. **Health and physical stamina**
   (a) No diseases and active life.
6. **Hobbies and interests**
7. **Developing self-interest in leisure activities**
8. **Dynamic qualities**
   (a) Self-confidence.
   (b) Leadership and initiativeness.
   (c) Hard working temperament.
   (d) Decision making abilities.
   (e) Originality.
   (f) Inspiration.
9. **Psychological factors**
   (a) Positive thinking and optimistic approach.
   (b) Absence of anti-social qualities.
10. **Social qualities**
   (a) Sense of accountability
   (b) Adaptability
   (c) Professional membership and activity.
   (d) Persuasive ability

**Expression of thought, feelings**

Our thought processes, emotions are guided by our body movements, postures, gestures, etc. These send signals and messages that often speak louder than words. These symbols convey meaning, positive/negative feelings.

## Homework to be Done before the Interview

Following steps have to be taken by the interviewee to excel in the interview.

**Visit Employers' Websites to know the statistics of the company and its prospects research in the trade journals and other publications.**

**Search the industry directories and networking about the potential organization.**

### *Market Your Skills*

After you have analyzed and researched the organization, review your qualifications for the position. Express yourself. This is the key element of effective interviewing. Your skills, interests, and work values should be assessed carefully so that you can organize your thoughts in a positive impression. A thorough self-assessment should enable you to:

- relate your personal strengths and weaknesses;
- relate your educational experience with the position you have applied for;
- express your skills and abilities;
- discuss your work and cocurricular experience;
- discuss career goals and objectives; and
- discuss variables, e.g., salary or geographical preference.

## Essentials for an Interview

### *Know Yourself*

- Be able to articulate YOUR
  - ➢ Skills
  - ➢ Values
  - ➢ Interests
  - ➢ Abilities
  - ➢ Long-term plans
- Be able to give examples of them
- Think on your feet
  - ➢ outside the box
- Use common sense
- Know your strengths and weaknesses
- Have an understanding of the company's background
- Prepare a list of "possible questions"
- Be honest
- What are my skills?
- What are my strengths?
- What are my weaknesses?

### *Review Yourself*

- Be prepared with the questions from resume.
- Be acquainted with the contents of the resume.
- Answer questions with respect to the details written in the resume.
- Questions which are asked during the interview.

- "Why should we hire you?"
- "Describe yourself."
- "How can you be beneficial to the company"
- "Tell me about one of your career goals."
- "Where do you find yourself 5 years from now"?

- Questions for organization
  - "How soon can you join our company if selected."
  - "What do you think about the future prospects of our organization."
- Interview starter questions
  - "Tell me about the company you are being interviewed /tell me about us."
  - "Tell me about your strengths."

### *Preparing for the Interview*

- Familiarity with business location is necessary before you go for the interview.
- Keep a copy of the resume updated and in folder with references included.
- Keep a few questions prepared for the interviewer if you want to know something about the company at the end of the interview.
- Visualize setting, be positive during the interview.
- Anticipate stressors.
- Decide what to wear.

### Types of Interviews

- Screening interview
- One-on-one interview
- Panel interview
- Luncheon interview
- Second interview: Second interview questions are usually deep, probing about candidate's approach to work.
- Group selection is a process where candidates are given some activity/task by the selector and they are observed by a panel of interviewers. This can be in the form of group presentations, and various other exercises to see the leadership qualities and other relevant behaviours relevant to the job.

### Day of the Interview

- Be well groomed on the day of the interview and dress professionally.
- Keep time management and reach the venue 15 minutes early.
- Eat prior to the interview, avoid too much caffeine and sugar.
- When arriving a business, be courteous to all employees.

When coming into the interview…

- Smile
- Look into the interviewer's eyes
- Sit straight
- Do not fidget

### *Approach to Answering Questions*

Be prepared

- Answer behavioural/situational questions using the STAR method
  - S – Describe the situation.
  - T – What task(s) did you identify that had to be completed?
  - A – What action did you take?
  - R – What was the result of your actions?

### *Approach to Answering Questions*

- Be honest
- Be specific
- Stay focused
- Keep position in mind
- Don't look for hidden messages
- Take your time, 2 minutes/question

### The Interview Process

- Casual conversation
  - "How was your day today?"
- Business questions
  - Employer can discuss the position applied for.
  - Continue to ask questions about skills, etc.
  - Situational behavioural questions
  - End by asking if you have questions
- Closing the interview
  - Employer initiates standing up, shaking hands
    - *"Thank-you"*

– Let employer know you are interested

- Prepare closing statement
  - *"Thank you for taking the time to interview me, I'm very interested in this position."*

### *When Leaving...*

- Thank the interviewer
- Hope to hear from you…
  - Delicately ask what's next.

### Behavioural Interview Questions

- Ask for contact information.
- Give me an example of a leadership position undertaken or conflict situation you handled ?
- Give me an example obstacle undertaken to achieve the target in your previous organization.
- Talk about a stressful situation you've experienced and handled maturely and objectively.
- Are you a team player?
- Tell me about a project or role that you've taken which is outside your job description….
- Tell me about a time when you've had to challenge authority...

### *Follow-up*

- Send a thank-you note within 24 hours
- Expect to hear within a week

### *The Verdict*

- Job is offered to you
  *"Thank you for calling, I'll get back to you with my decision by the end of the day."*
- Job is not offered
  *"Thank you for taking the time to interview me."*
- Professional/polite

### Some Likely Questions asked in the Interviews

Review these typical interview questions and think about how you would answer them.

1. **Define yourself /tell me about yourself:**
   This is the most likely question asked during an interview. Prepare a few sentences about yourself and rehearse it. Talk about your strengths, work-related items.
2. **Reasons for leaving your last job?**
   Stay positive about your previous job regardless of the circumstances. Do not speak about the management, co-workers or the organization.

3. **What experience do you have in this field?**

   Relate yourself to the position you have applied. Speak about your experience, if you have in the specific field.

4. **How far you have been successful in your career?**

   Give a good explanation of your priorities and goals, speak how you have achieved some and plan to succeed in others.

5. **What do you know about this organization?**

   Do some research on the organization before the interview? Find out the mission, vision, goals and objectives, current issues of the company and the major players.

6. **Why do you want to work for this organization?**

   Talk about the growth, learning related to the organization. Be sincere and relate it to your long-term career goals.

7. **Do you know any employee who works for us?**

   Be aware if there is a policy on relatives working for the organization. Be careful to mention a friend only if they are well thought of.

8. **What knowledge have you gained in the last year?**

   Try to include training programmes, workshops attended or conducted, or job improvements. Positive self-improvement should be discussed. You can also mention any book read and its impact on your knowledge technically or behaviourally.

9. **What kind of salary is expected by you?**

   Have some knowledge about the market trends for a particular job. Give a wide range.

10. **What are your long term plans?**

    Tell your vision/aim. Specifics can be good. This will show your planning for future, and also strategy.

11. **What is your philosophy towards work?**

    Be short and positive, showing a benefit to the organization.

12. **How can you be an asset to this organization, if hired?**

    You have now got a chance to highlight your positives, strengths and relate it to the position.

13. **Why should we hire you?**

    List your assets and how these can help to meet the organization's needs. Do not compare with any other.

14. **What is your greatest strength?**

    Stay positive. Good examples can be: Ability to prioritize your goals, use time management, your professional approach, creative problem-solving skills, your focus on task completion, your leadership skills and positive attitude.

15. **Why do you think you would do well at this job?**

    Justify talking about your skills, experience and interest.

**16. What are your strongest points?**

Talk about your positive attitude, leadership traits, work as a team player, hard work, creativity, problem solver.

**17. What has disappointed you in a job?**

Play safe which may include:

Work not challenging. Job not so responsible. My potentialities are not fully utilized in the job.

**18. Explain your ability to work under pressure.**

Give an example for yourself in tough situations and your ability to cope which helped you to come out of pressure. Also relate to the type of position applied for.

**19. What motivates you the most in a job?**

Your personal trait can be highlighted here: challenge, achievement, recognition.

**20. What do you mean by success and how far you have been successful in life?**

Give the meaning of success according to you. Standards set by you and how you have met them. Their outcomes are a success.

**21. Describe your management style.**

Some can be like progressive, consensus, or situational (manage according to the situation).

**22. What have you learnt from mistakes on the job?**

Here intention a mistake with a positive lesson learnt.

**23. Do you have any blind spots/negatives?**

This can be quite tricky. Try to speak your negatives in a positive way, e.g., if my work is not finished on time, I become quite fidgety. You can also speak about your negatives but also explain how you are working hard on it.

**24. If you were hiring a person for your company, what traits will you look for?**

Mention traits you have and then justify it with the company.

**25. Do you think you are qualified for this position?**

Describe your experience and qualification as your strengths for the position.

**26. What qualities do you look for in a boss?**

Be positive and generic. Knowledgeable, loyal, mentor and a coach

**27. Describe your work ethics.**

Emphasize determination for the completion of the job and enjoy your work, be creative and effective for the organization.

**28. What has been your biggest professional disappointment?**

Give positives from your negative feelings.

**29. Tell me about the most fun you have had on the job.**

Talk about your accomplishments in the organization.

**30. Do you have any questions to ask about the organization or the position in the organization?**

You can ask about your role profile or type of projects you will be involved in.

### *Formulating Career Plans*

An effective job search begins with careful career planning, a process that includes self-analysis, career analysis and job analysis.

*Self-Anaysis*

Remember, the resume is primarily a sales letter, selling a particular commodity, i.e., you. In order to sell yourself effectively, you need above all to identify your strengths, your interests and your achievements. Answering the questions listed below is a good way to begin your self-analysis. This will help you to get a fairly good idea of where you stand at the moment and where you want to go from there. It will also help you to provide ready answers to questions asked during an interview.

#### Self-Analysis Questions

A. The kind of person I am

1. Do I have a high level of aspiration?
2. Do I communicate well?
3. Am I dependable?
4. Am I energetic?
5. Am I free of personal habits that would interfere with my work?
6. Am I financially independent?
7. Am I a leader?
8. Am I people oriented (or would I like to work alone)?
9. Am I self-confident (without being egotistical)?
10. Do I spend time wisely?

B. My aptitudes

1. Do I have a high verbal aptitude (written and oral)?
2. Do I have a high aptitude for learning foreign languages?
3. Do I have a high mechanical aptitude?
4. Do I have a high aptitude for problem solving?

C. My achievements

1. What is my overall grade-point average?
2. What is the grade-point average in my subject?
3. In which courses have I excelled?
4. Which courses have been most difficult?
5. Have I done well in problem-solving courses?
6. What have been my achievements in extracurricular activities, in jobs I have held, or in volunteer work?

D. My interests

1. What are my favourite academic interests (the courses I liked most, not necessarily the ones in which I made the best grade)?
2. Which professional magazines or journals are most appealing?
3. What type of books or magazines do I read for pleasure?
4. To which campus and off-campus organizations do I belong?
5. How do I prefer to spend leisure time?
6. Do I like to travel?

E. My education

1. What is my area of specialization in college and when do I expect to graduate?
2. What special training have I received—internships, workshops and seminars?
3. What special skills do I possess—foreign languages, computer competency?

F. My experience

1. What part-time jobs have I held?
2. What full-time jobs have I held?

*Source:* William. C. Himstreet, Wayne Murlin, Baty and Carol M. Lehman, *Business Communication,* 10th edition (California: Wadsworth Publishing Company, 1993).

## Career-Analysis Questions

A. Type of career (such as accounting, finance sales, etc.)

1. Which aptitudes (quantitative, verbal, mechanical) would be most beneficial?
2. Is the occupation considered a "pressure" occupation?
3. Are there significant health hazards?
4. Is relocation or frequent travel expected?
5. Is the field crowded, or is it short of workers?

B. Preparation

1. What are the academic requirements (degree, major)?
2. What are the professional requirements (certificates)?
3. Are continuing education or training programmes expected and available?
4. What experience is considered a prerequisite?

C. Rewards

1. What is the standard salary of entry-level workers?
2. Are there significant opportunities for advancement in salary and responsibility?
3. What are fringe benefits?
4. What are intangible rewards?

D. Future of the field

1. Is the field expected to expand or contract?

2. Will the field be strongly influenced by changes in technology?
3. Is competition in the field increasing?
4. Will changes in political administration or governmental regulations have a significant impact on the field?

### Job-Analysis Questions

1. What are the specific duties and responsibilities?
2. Do the specified duties and responsibilities seem compatible with my personal characteristics, aptitudes, interests? Others—dependability, leadership, aspirations, desire to work alone or with others, willingness to relocate or travels?
3. Does my education satisfy requirements for the position (degrees earned or in progress, cooperative education, internships, special training programmes, directly related courses)? Would I be willing to continue my education?
4. Is my experience directly related to the job's specified duties and responsibilities? (List related part-time jobs or full-time jobs. If experience is scant, what aspects of the academic programme, school-related activities, volumeer work, or other jobs are related to the job in which you are interested?

*Source:* William. C. Himstreet, Wayne Murlin, Baty and Carol M. Lehman, *Business Communication*, 10th edition (California: Wadsworth Publishing Company, 1993).

### Tips for Building "Personal Brand"

- **Know yourself:** Know your strengths, weaknesses and differentiators.
- **Maximize your strengths**: Be master of one and jack of all trades. There is a need of multitasking today.
- **"Google" yourself**: Manage your online recognition.
- **Solicit for feedback:** Ask for feedback from your peer, family members, friends, superiors on your achievements and respect their criticism.
- **Be a good networker:** Networking helps you to be a nucleus among friends or in organization.
- **Think large:** Think big, act fast and be smart. Be passionate with your dreams and be a life-long learner.
- **Define your own crowd:** Know your competitors as it will thrive you to excel and shine.

## CASE STUDY

### Perfect Interview

A couple lived in a small cottage near the seaside. One day the woman saw a young man from her window carrying a spade, a small case, dressed in working clothes walking on a shrubby uncultivated land and he then disappeared behind the trees.

The woman again saw him the next day almost same time carrying his spade and a small case, and again he disappeared behind the trees.

The woman explained the whole story to her husband, finding this a fishy affair. The husband said that the young man probably was a farmer or may be setting traps, so it is no use to worry. This went on for several more sightings of the young man for next two weeks. The woman then convinced her husband to take a stroll to watch the hidden activity of the young man. So she left early from her house, to investigate what he was doing. To her surprise she found a long and deep trench, rough and uneven at one end, becoming much neater and tidier towards the other end. The young man arrived to see the couple near the trench. The woman could not resist her enquiry and asked him."Why are you digging a trench here – and in such difficult rocky ground?"

"I'm digging a trench," said the man, "I'm actually learning how to dig a good trench, because the job I'm being interviewed for later today says that experience is essential - so I'm getting the experience. And the case – it's got my lunch in it."

He got the job.

### *Answer the Questions*

1. Why was the woman curious about the activity of the young man? What was her apprehensions?
2. Why was the man digging a trench?
3. What are your leanings from the story?

## PRESS NOTE

Sand City Corporation is seeking an HR Manager to coordinate and conduct training programmes for the employees in the organization. The candidate should possess good communication and presentation skills, possess soft skills to demonstrate. Previous training experience with a company is desired. A degree in MBA with Diploma in Training and Development will be preferred. Please mail your resume to scshr@yahoo.com within 10 days.

## SUMMARY

- Presentations are one of the first managerial skills, which a management person must acquire. Management is the art of getting things done. A presentation is a fast and potentially effective method of getting things done through other people. In managing any project, presentations are used as a formal method for bringing people together to plan, monitor and review its progress.
- Public speaking is enlarged conversation. There is little difference between talking to one person and to ten persons, or to a hundred. You must talk louder; but the talking that goes on around your dinner table does not differ in essence from the talking that goes on at a meeting. The only difference is that at a meeting the speaker is allowed to talk for a longer time without interruption.

- A good speaker has a sense of responsibility to his listeners, to his subject, sense of leadership. He doesn't let his confidence become overconfidence. A good speaker is balanced, and keeps his sense of humour.
- Elements of a presentation are presenter and audience. The presenter should think and plan the following before delivering the presentation. Identify your purpose, analyze your audience, identify the need, collate your information, design your communication, time your presentation, decide on the visual aids to be used, study the location.
- The four components of presentation are planning and analysis, content, message and supporting points, visuals, practice and do it.
- Use SPAM Model for Presentation SPAM is SITUATION, PURPOSE, AUDIENCE And METHOD.
- There are five key aspects of the human body, which deserve attention in presentation skills: the eyes, the voice, the expression, the appearance, and how you stand.
- Useful tips and tools to overcome speech anxiety are to practise skills training, practise your speech at home (practice, practice, practice). Cognitive modification, set yourself a goal, mentally practise your speech, visualize the speech, the pace, your gestures, breathing, where you will be standing. Think about how the audience will be reacting to you, Think about how you will feel after you sit down and final image should be of you successfully completing the goal you set for yourself.
- Each presentation should have an introduction (tell them what you are going to tell them), body (tell them) and conclusion (tell them what you just told them).
- Formulas for speech/presentation organization is OIBCC, i.e, Opening – grab attention, introduction, body – bulk of the presentation, conclusion – summarize briefly points and close – last strong sentences that leave the audience with something to remember.
- A presentation consists of three most basic elements: you, your audience and your tools. Key steps for effective presentation are: know your subject matter, know your audience, develop a theme, prepare your script, the opening, the body, select the proper visual aids, prepare, a story board, produce the visuals, the summary, the closing. Rehearse—rehearse—rehearse.
- Common mistakes in a presentation are lack of planning which includes rushed job, last minute preparation,wrong message for this audience, lack of planning with poor proofing/editing, poor slides with cluttered content, bad delivery habits.

## QUESTIONS

### I. Explain in Brief

1. What do you understand by Panchshila of good talk?

2. What should be the profile of a good speaker?.
3. Suggest ways to reduce physical tension before a presentation.
4. What are the essential characteristics of a good presentation?
5. What does the basic formula OIBCC mean in presentation?
6. List down the general guidelines for writing a resume.
7. What is the importance of a good resume?
8. What are the points to be kept in mind while writing your work experience?
9. Write the checklist of content and style of a good resume.
10. What are the points to remember for the outlook of a resume?
11. What are the two important factors which play a decisive role in an interview?
12. Write down your personal and professional traits.
13. What are the parameters for selection in an interview?
14. What preparation should be done before an interview?
15. Mention five dynamic impressive qualities of an individual.

**II. Answer the following questions.**

1. What are the four components of presentation? Explain one in detail.
2. "Body language and tone of voice gives an impact to your presentation." Explain.
3. Explain the effect of colour in visual presentation.
4. Give some useful tips to overcome speech anxiety.
5. Write in details the key steps needed for an effective presentation.
6. Imagine yourself as an MBA with 2 years experience in a bank. Write a covering letter for a job in a multinational.
7. Write your own resume.
8. A resume is the reflection about the person. Comment
9. A good conversation is necessary during an interview. Comment
10. How should a candidate handle the behavioural questions?
11. Explain why is self-analysis/introspection necessary before one's interview.
12. Body language is a depiction of one's thoughts and emotions during an interview. Discuss
13. Have you ever given an interview, if yes what were the questions asked and how did you respond. Discuss

## EXPAND YOUR KNOWLEDGE

- Visit websites
- www.careerbuilder.com
- www.buscommresources.com
- Make your own blog and post your resume in it

## ASSIGNMENT

1. Prepare on 5 sentences that describe yourself.
2. Write down 10 possible questions that are asked during an interview and your answer for it.

## ACTIVITY

✓ Look into the mirror and practise the presentation assigned to you. Also record yourself and highlight the drawbacks in your presentation.

✓ Rehearse by looking at the mirror.
- Conduct a mock interview with friends
- Tell your friends to do video recording of your presentation in the class and assess your strengths and weaknesses. Make an action plan for self-improvement.
- Use networking sites to post your resume.
- Identify 5 different formats to produce your resume.
- List down the action verbs that describe your skills and experience.

✓ Choose a topic from the list below and create a powerful presentation. Your presentation should not be more than 15 slides.

➢ Cross communication

➢ Honesty is the best policy

➢ Disaster management

➢ Buying and selling online

➢ Creating a job portfolio

## PRACTICAL EXERCISE OF 3 P'S ( PROBLEM, PROCESS AND PRODUCT)

You are Prashant Suri, a Public Relations Officer in a multinational company. Your company has three communication documents – a quarterly newsletter, annual report and a semi-annual report. All of these are prepared outside by a printing company. Recently, the decision was made to switch the task of publishing to in-house.

Your superiors asked you to research the feasibility and make a presentation on your findings and recommendations to the firm's executive committee.

## PROJECT

1. Visit fresherworld.com and find out the latest interview tips.
2. Make a video presentation of the dirt and filth in the neighbourhood to awaken the MCF of the unhygienic conditions and make them aware for necessary action.
3. Make a documentary for awareness about pollution and health hazards.
4. The Japanese delegates are visiting the campus for a joint project. Make a video presentation of the institute highlighting the activities and ethics and culture of India.

# MODULE 2
# GROUP

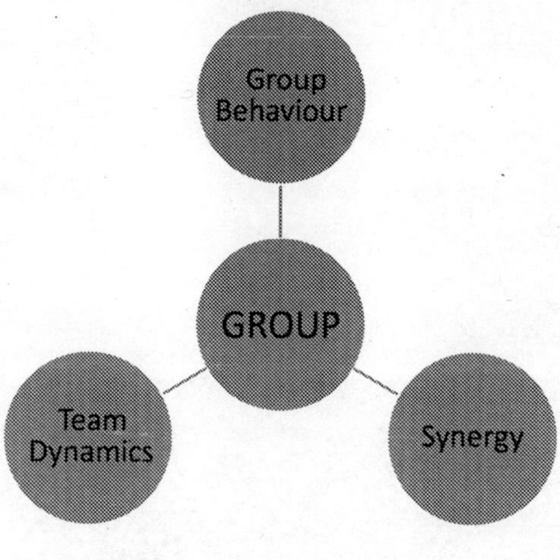

# 5 UNIT Group Behaviour

**Learning Objectives**

- Building Interpersonal Relationships
- Behavioural Patterns and Understanding Assertiveness
- Resolving Conflict

WHERE the mind is without fear and the head is held high
WHERE knowledge is free
WHERE the world has not been broken up into fragments by narrow domestic walls
WHERE the words come out from the depth of truth
WHERE tireless striving stretches its arms towards perfection
WHERE the clear stream of reason has not lost its way into the dreary desert sand of dead habit.
WHERE the mind is led forward, thee into ever widening though and action: into that freedom my father let my country AWAKE.

**Gurudev Rabindranath Tagore**

### Behaviour Speaks

Subhodh is a salesman with RO Purifies. He is an aggressive marketing person and strong target oriented. He recently became the star salesperson of the year for highest turnover record. His superior Arvind is proud of his accomplishments. Subhodh was promoted to Deputy Manager and now supervises 5 sales representatives to manage the sales target of the area.

After assuming the charge as a Deputy Manager, he called for a meeting to set the targets of each representative. The targets were communicated in a direct and detailed manner. Three of the salespersons found the target very ambitious but did not comment. After a week the targets were reviewed. Subhodh was highly dissatisfied to know that all of them were trailing behind their targets. He was very blunt in showing his disappointment with all the representatives. After the meeting the five representatives showed their displeasure in the unreasonable targets set and perceived him as a difficult person to communicate with.

The representatives went to speak to the manager about Subhodh and his unreasonable demand. The manager knew Subhodh as an efficient person, but he was lacking in people management so he called Subhodh for an informal talk and advised him to be calm with his team. Subhodh took this as a personal disrespect and turned more bitter in his approach. He directly called all the representatives and showed displeasure about the incident, and communicated about sense of commitment for the target. At the month end the brief showed that the result and the team had underachieved its targets.

**Answer the Questions**

1. 'Targets should be accomplished'. Comment.
2. If you are given the responsibility of the deputy manager, what will be your team approach?
3. Explain the behaviour of Subhodh as a leader. What should be the characteristics of a leader.

## 5.1 BUILDING INTERPERSONAL RELATIONSHIP

It is well said, "treat others the way you would like them to treat you. Respect others as you want to be respected."

The key of foundation of any relationship, personal or professional situation is interpersonal relationship. This relationship gives the basic foundation of a stronger bondage for any family, any company or any country.

To build up a relationship, flexible and adaptable approach is required for an acceptable graph to benefit the individual, the employees, and the employers. Good feelings, good results can achieve the success of the company as well as individuals can grow faster.

Healthy, open, fulfilled and mutually rewarding relationships, enhance future growth and development by becoming treasure of our life. It is, therefore, necessary to master the art of establishing healthy interpersonal relations with people we come across.

The key to healthy interpersonal relations lies in openness. The self-centred person would hardly be able to master excellence in human relations.

The seven techniques for improving relations are:

- The six most important words – "I admit I made a mistake."
- The five most important words – "You did a good job."
- The four most important words – "What is your opinion."
- The three most important words – "If you please."
- The two most important words – "Thank you."
- The one most important word – "We."
- The least important word – "I."

If a person is approached with a healthy and positive outlook, the outlook will be always positive.

## Components of Interpersonal Relations

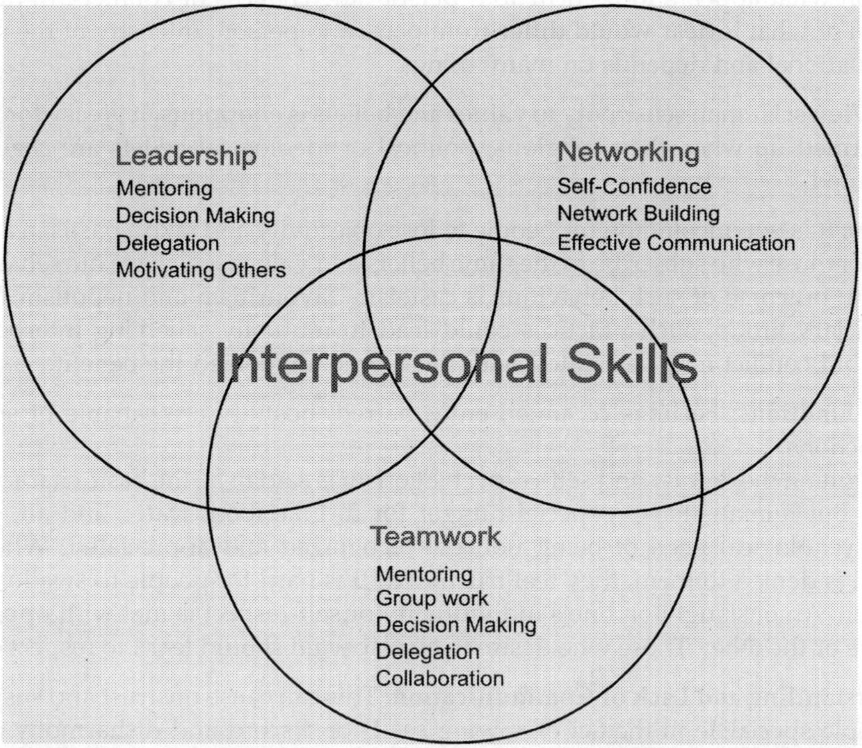


### *Leadership*

A leader influences others through his personal charisma, language, command personal and strong communication skills He successfully influences a group towards the achievement of a common goal. Leadership uses the background skills of mentoring, decision making, delegation and motivating others.

### *Networking*

It is ability to recognize and create effective contacts with others and maintain them for mutual benefit. Strong communication skills and persuasive skills are required to build networks and motivate others.

### *Teamwork*

Team work involves working together in a group towards a common goal. The prerequisite is collaborative approach, cooperation, responsive to others' ideas, and taking responsibility for developing and achieving group goals. Teamwork requires, mentoring, decision making and delegation.

## Anatomy of Unsuccessful Interaction

**Clash of Interest:** Everyone tries to protect one's own interest and whenever an onslaught is made on what appears to be dear to a person, the chances of conflict brighten up. Perception of what is dear would differ from person to person. Intensity of the conflict is also situational and depends on many things.

**Clash of Views:** Human sensitivity to values and beliefs is enormous. It is easy for people to get warmed up when their religious, political or ideological beliefs are challenged or discounted.

**Prejudices:** It is not uncommon for people to lose objectivity and take a partisan attitude in favour of those who subscribe to the same beliefs and values which we ourselves hold. The natural outcome of such behaviour is casteism, favouritism and nepotism. Within the beneficiary group, such practices could lead to mutually satisfying interpersonal relations, but conflict may be created with those who are denied the benefit.

**Negative Emotions:** Feelings of anger, envy, hatred, hostility are capable of spoiling our interactions.

Onslaught on the dignity and self-respect: Egotism is said to be the basic characteristic of all life. But humans have a special hunger for it. Like food, water, and air, people have a psychological need of being noticed, recognized and appreciated. When this basic need is denied to them, they feel frustrated. It is hard for people to swallow their humiliation. An onslaught on one's individuality or self-respect is met with opposition at one time or the other. Those who desire to be respected should learn to respect others.

**Misunderstanding and Lack of Communication:** This can cause mistrust and suspicion. Some people specialize in the act of sowing seeds of discord and disharmony among others. They create conditions for two people to fight among themselves. Conflict is a source of enjoyment for them.

**Lack of Mannerism:** Manners are picked up mainly during one's childhood and adolescence. In case these are not in congruence with the norms acceptable within the social environment one is dealing with, they can cause embarrassment and could lead to negativity.

## Building Effective Interpersonal Relations

**Build Self-Esteem**. To be effective in dealing with others, accept that you are the most important person in the world. You can reduce the sense of inadequacy and emotional turmoil that keeps you from managing effectively by developing self-esteem. You can genuinely have a high regard for others when you have a high regard for yourself.

In other words, the first order of business is to love yourself. It's pretty hard to love or care about others if you hate yourself. That self-hate tends to be projected onto others.

One way to nourish self is to allow yourself to feel satisfied when you function at your best and to acknowledge your strengths and abilities. It is harder to see the best in others when you don't see the best in yourself. Promotion and recognition often go to the people who are self-confident. Modesty can work against you when you are selling yourself to others.

### *Know How to Listen*

When your employees share a problem with you, for example, do you get the sinking feeling that it is your responsibility to solve it? If so, you are probably wasting your energy. A request for listening is usually not a request for help. Therefore, your main task is to listen non-judgmentally and with understanding.

Generally, maintaining an open, available stance while seeking information and showing concern is an effective, assertive style of communicating. Your listening may be the only help required.

Active listening alleviates the problem by giving the employees a chance to talk it through while experiencing emotional release. Given the opportunity to solve their own problems, employees tend to feel more confident in their abilities.

Employees who are listened to will not bottle up their feelings. Listening tells the employee, "Your feelings are legitimate."

**Take Risks**. Risk-taking is tied to self-esteem. If you feel good about yourself, you'll be able to take risks because you will be optimistic about their consequences.

The risks you take fall into these categories: speaking up for what you believe, asking for what you want, and expressing your expectations of others. These actions involve risk because people have the mistaken belief that others will respond to them negatively and that they will be judged adversely.

Part of risk-taking is setting limits. When you set limits, others know who you are and how you want to be treated. It is a way of gaining respect. When you don't set limits, you allow others to pick on you.

**How to Say No**. The ability to say no is crucial in two areas. The first is saying no to unwanted tasks imposed by peers and superiors. The second area in which the ability to say no is crucial for imposition of unrealistic deadlines. An impossible deadline can be negotiated for a more realistic one.

There are times when you need to say yes to encourage and develop your employees, even when you might want to say no. Constant, hostile, or aggressive refusals can intimidate creative employees, causing them to leave or to do only the minimum on the job.

**How to Give Constructive Feedback**. Providing realistic performance standards is one approach that will assist in giving constructive feedback. The standard is based on the job requirements, not on the performance of the employees. It is best what could be expected of any qualified person assigned to the job.

Another approach that will aid you in applying constructive feedback is the levelling method, or treating the employee as an equal. The intention is to create a cooperative environment that will enhance agreement and problem solving.

**Handle Criticism.** Criticisms strike at your ego and self-esteem. One of the best ways to handle criticisms is to be fully aware of your components that result in self-defeating behaviour. Awareness will diminish the possibility of shock, hurt, or defensiveness.

Separate yourself from the criticism. You are not your mistakes. It's okay to dislike your behaviour and still like yourself. Think about modifying and improving your behaviour, not labelling or judging yourself.

Another approach in handling criticism is to request negative feedback. Solicit criticism to improve and perfect your performance. When you do, listen to the criticism from the other person's point of view. Ask qualifying questions related to the data on which the criticism is based, such as, "What is it about...that could be improved?"

**How to Give and Receive Positive Feedback**. How you "stroke"—provide attention and recognition—those you manage will strongly influence and your people will work together.

**What You Want**. Often it is tempting to sit back and wish that things were different. But people who waste their energies on "if only..." Aren't doing what they need to do to be successful.

Using the assertive style assists you in making your interpersonal relationships more clear, forceful and honest. Applying an assertive approach can reduce stress and anxiety, and can help you to be less preoccupied with self-consciousness and less driven by the need to control.

## 5.2 BEHAVIOURAL PATTERNS AND UNDERSTANDING ASSERTIVENESS

Healthy pattern of thoughts, feelings and actions should be in the behaviour of an individual. Healthy thoughts are those thoughts that challenge. For example, when one friend hits another you would teach him how to resolve problems by teaching him by getting angry: walk away, etc. In order to change our pattern of behaviour we need to learn to manage our FAT (feelings, actions and thoughts).

## Behavioural Patterns of Individuals

**Reaction-Response-Fight or Face**

| Submissiveness | Aggressiveness | Assertiveness |
|---|---|---|
| Passive powerless (giving away the power) to others | Position – I am ok You are not ok | Empowering – self, others |
| Position- I am not ok | I win you lose | Position – I am ok |
| You are ok | Defense – offensive | You are ok |
| I lose you win | Disrespect for other-I lack of freedom and space create conflict | I win you win |
| | | Communication: intimacy |
| Lack of self-respect | | Respect – valuing self others |
| Suppression-repression (feeling-thoughts-needs-depression-self hurting) | Guilt-anger | |
| | Frustration | Self-discipline |
| Helplessness-hopelessness | Hurt others – sadist | Confronting |
| | Poor self-image-grandiosity | |
| Poor self image-self pity | loneliness | Resolves inter-personal conflict |
| Hyper stress-distress | Insecurity-feels out of control | |
| Feels out of control | | Positive self-image |
| Loneliness | Hyper stress | |
| | Lack of delegation | Relaxed |
| Resentment-suppressed-anger | Over-sensitive | In-charge of self |
| | Over-protection | |
| Laziness-postponing | Denial-marking | Feels in control |
| Victim position | Workaholics | Peace |
| Lack of responsibility | Insensitive to feelings and needs | Transparent – open |
| Irrational belief | | Being objective |
| Self-defeating attitudes | Expects others to change | Avails opportunities |
| Others hurt me | Hostile | |
| | | Give space to others |
| Maladjustive behaviour | Maladjustive | Examining irrational – Beliefs |
| Socially inhibited | Socially | – Myths |
| Masochist | Destructive | – Attitudes |
| | | Incorporating new options |
| | | Feels responsible – commitment |
| | | Delegating – coaching – training |
| | | Others |
| | | Adjustable |

## Behavioural Pattern (Personality Development)

### *Submissiveness*

It is "I can't change". They avoid conflict.

They are socially maladjective and inhibited. Then theme in life is:-

I am not O.K. You are O.K.

I lose – You win

They carry the board "USE ME"

### *Aggressiveness*

These people are overpowering and control others. They are human `road rollers'. They attack people. They don't take chances. They control people, are over-sensitive and over-productive. They seldom give people space to function by themselves.

They create conflict, divide and rule is their policy. They are angry people and their expression of anger is overt. They get frustrated easily. They hurt others; their poor self-image leads to grandiosity. Since they get frustrated easily. They lose opportunities. They are insecure therefore they don't delegate.

They often are cardiac-prone people being task oriented and workaholics. Their irrational belief is "others have to adjust with me".

He/she is a vehement defender of one's own rights yet violates or uses the rights or privileges' of others.

They are socially destructive – their theme in life is

I am O.K. – You are not O.K.

I win – You lose.

### *Assertiveness*

It empowers others to help oneself and others. Assertive persons are communicative and listen to self and others. They have respect for themselves and for others. They are risk takers and take life as a challenge and solve problems effectively. They are self-disciplined and discipline others. Having a good self-image, being self-charged, they are transparent at peace with themselves. They are committed and take responsibilities by availing all opportunities for success. They take decisions for self and give space and freedom and space to others to function. They are usually more extrovert and use their rights and privileges in a socially constructive and productive way.

The theme of this person's life is: I am O.K. – You are O.K.

I Win – You win

### *Tips for Better Interpersonal Relationship*

- ❖ To get respect, learn to respect others. Okness would most probably provoke Okness in the other person.
- ❖ Do not criticize — this would simply harden the attitude.
- ❖ Never argue when the other person is in a state of anger. Listen to him and let him cool down then talk.

- ❖ Appreciate others with good character.
- ❖ Try to understand the perspective of the other side. Each person behaves according to his values, attitudes, needs and expectations. In the face of similar circumstances, you too would have behaved likewise.
- ❖ When you talk to someone, say something, which would be of interest to that other person. The magic effect of this would be that the other person would start listening to you. Remember that everybody is basically concerned about his own problems and prospects.
- ❖ Search for the areas of mutual interest even if there is clash of interest and express them.
- ❖ Appeal to the sense of humanity and pride in the other person.
- ❖ Generate trust and serviceability.

### *Progress of the Conflict*

During a product strategy meeting, a marketing vice-president carelessly implied that the R&D group tended to overdesign products. The remark was intended to be a humorous stereotyping of the R&D function, but it was interpreted by the R&D vice-president as an attempt to pass on to his group the blame for an uncompetitive product. Later in the meeting, the R&D vice-president took advantage of an opportunity to point out that the marketing vice-president lacked the technical expertise to understand design limitations. The marketing vice-president perceived this rejoinder as ridicule and therefore, an act of hostility. The R&D vice-president, who believed he had evened the marketing vice-president, who, in turn, thought he was evening the score for the uncalled-for barb. These events soon led to a memo war, backbiting, and then to pressure on various employees to take sides.

The important point here is that from the first rejoinder neither party wished to escalate the conflict each wished merely to score. Nonetheless, conflict resolution would have been difficult to accomplish during this escalation phase because people do not like to disengage when they think they all owe one" to the other party. Since an even score is subjectively defined, however, the parties need to be convinced that the overall score is approximately equal and that everyone has already suffered enough.

### *Developing Conflict Management Skills*

In the presence of conflict at the decision-making or decision-implementing stage, managers must focus on generating an agreement rather than a discussion. A discussion without agreement makes the strategic direction difficult to implement. In contrast, an agreement on strategic direction doesn't require an explicit decision. In this context, conflicts have "gone away". The people involved still have interests that are somewhat incompatible. Agreement implies that these people have become committed to a course of action that serves some of their interests.

## Elaborated Interpersonal Styles

| Ego Stages | Basic Needs | I'm Not OK, You're not OK | I'm OK, You're Not OK | I'm OK, You're OK | I'm not OK, You're OK |
|---|---|---|---|---|---|
| Regulating Parent<br>Nurturing | Love Care<br>Power | Traditional<br>Over-Indulgent | Prescriptive<br>Rescuing | Normative<br>Supportive | Indifferent<br>Ingratiating |
| Adult | Rationality | Cynical | Task Obsessive | Problem Solving | Overwhelming |
| Adaptive<br>Child Reactive<br>Creative | Approval Safety<br>Aggression<br>Creativity | Sulking<br>Withdrawn<br>Humorous | Complaining<br>Aggressive<br>Bohemian | Resilient<br>Confronting<br>Innovative | Dependent<br>Intropunitive<br>Satirical |

## Non-Facilitative Behaviour

- ♦ Exploiting the needs of the participants.
- ♦ Pushing, manipulating and making rules.
- ♦ Judging and evaluating
- ♦ Believing in a single approach – being rigid.
- ♦ Centring the discussion around self.
- ♦ Giving interpretations.
- ♦ Being emotionally aloof.

## Effective Listening Behaviour

- ♦ Attention to what is being said.
- ♦ Suspending judgment until you have heard the whole story.
- ♦ Looking at the person who is talking.
- ♦ Checking for understanding.
- ♦ Retaining things in mind and dealing with them later.
- ♦ Conveying interest through facial expression.
- ♦ Maintaining proximity.

## Giving Feedback

- The goal of feedback is to describe what you have seen in the trainee and now evaluate.
- Feedback is a statement of what is, not a statement of what ought to be.

- Use tentative language.
- Make it specific.
- Clearly express views.
- Time it to be near the issue being discussed.
- Take into account the needs of the receiver.
- Check to ensure clear understanding.
- Concentrate on the things the receiver can do something about.
- Initiate by giving positive feedback first.
- Check your facial expressions and tone.

## Communication Profile and Styles

Effective communication requires self-awareness, disclosure, confidence and receptivity to feedback.

**Communication Profile:** Since communication is an exchange process, communication profile examines self-awareness, disclosure and receptivity feedback through the Johari window development by Left and Ingham (1973).

| | Known to Self | Unknown to Self |
|---|---|---|
| Known to Others | Arena | Blind |
| Unknown to others | Closed | Dark |

**Arena** – is the public self.

**Blind** – not known to self but perceived by others.

**Closed** – characteristics of self not revealed to others.

**Dark** – not known to self and others, the unconscious self.

### *Self-Disclosure*

1. Helps increase the arena.
2. Sharing information, which is appropriate and relevant to situation.
3. Is characterized by constructive openness.
4. Self-disclosure is facilitated by interpersonal trust.

### *Interpersonal Trust Cycle*

| | Constructive | Destructive |
|---|---|---|
| Person A | High Trust | Low Trust |
| Person B | Effective Communication | Ineffective Communication |

### *Receptive to Feedback*

Feedback is any information, which allows an individual to evaluate effective communication.

*Receptivity to Feedback*

1. Increase self-feedback awareness.
2. Trust the mutuality.
3. A person understands strengths and weaknesses.
4. Communication openness.
5. Receptivity to feedback depends whether it is dissonant or congruent.
6. Receiving feedback positively means:
   - Owing data
   - Self-analysis
   - Empathy
   - Exploration
   - Data collection
   - Listening and seeking help.
   - Understanding and clearing doubts
   - Sharing concerns
   - Results in self-integration

**Communication sensitivity** means being sensitive to the various contents of communication.

1. Emotional contents.
2. Information.
3. Help/support requested.
4. Direction needed.
5. Evaluation required.

Sometimes individuals are mentally set to respond to only one or two contents of the communication.

**Communication style:** Communication sensitivity generates a specific communication style.

### *Withdrawal Style*

1. Communication process is avoided.
2. No influence is sought or desired.
3. Independent approach to decision making.

### *Effects of Development of Johari Window*

1. Withdrawal and relinquishing styles increase blind and dark areas by limiting self-disclosure and feedback.
2. Withdrawal and relinquishing style reduce arena.
3. Structure and dynamic styles increase bind area by help in organizing and directing.
4. Equalitarian style increases arena and effectiveness by facilitating feedback and self-disclosure.

### *Controlling Style*

1. Communication is one way.
2. Communicator is directive, demanding and controlling.
3. Communicator uses power and authority.
4. Communicator may be manipulator.

### *Equalitarian Style*

1. Communication is two way.
2. Communicator stimulates and draws out thoughts of others.
3. Communication is free, friendly and warm.
4. Atmosphere is mutual understanding and personal interest.

### *Structuring Style*

1. Communication oriented towards systematizing environment.
2. Communicator concerned with standards, procedures, rules, etc.
3. Communicator clarifies and establishes structure of a problem.

### *Dynamic Style*

1. Communicator is brief.
2. Communicator is direct.
3. Communicator is pragmatic and action oriented.

### *Relinquish Style*

1. Communicator submits to desires of others.
2. Communicator complies with others' views.
3. Communicator receptive to other peoples' ideas and contributions.
4. Communicator shifts responsibility to others.
5. Communicator assumes a supporting role.

## Understanding Assertiveness

Assertive behaviour enables a person to have the best chance of obtaining the desired results while retaining, self-respect and respecting others.

Assertion training was originally a technique of behaviour therapy and is still practised as such by some psychologists.

### *How to be Assertive*

Being assertive rather than submissive or aggressive means getting the balance right between your needs and those of others. They will vary in every context according to, whether you are dealing with your colleague, your boss, subordinate, customer or even with your children. Assertiveness is a life skill and everyone has the right to be assertive in a wide range of contexts.

There is never one simple, single answer on what to say to be assertive. But there are a number of general guidelines which you may find helpful.

**Be Honest**: The first and the most important component of assertiveness is emotional honesty. Without being honest with ourselves and with other people, none of us would be able to achieve balanced transactions.

What prevents us from being honest? Normally, it's fear of what might happen if we are honest. One way to overcome this fear is to ask: "If I am honest with this person, what is the worst thing that can happen?" Honesty is never as dangerous as you think its going to be but it still worries us. Honesty will lead to a rational discussion between consenting adults. You may be right, you may be wrong but at least in being assertive your are being honest and people know where you stand.

Honesty allows you to criticize people fairly. Criticism whether of a colleague, superior or subordinate, can be positive provided it is done assertively and with respect. We only need to be honest about what is relevant. Deep down we are all emotional people and we all carry around a lot of old emotional baggage – resentments, prejudices, whatever. But when we try to get something done, we have to learn to differentiate between relevant and irrelevant issues.

**Stick to Your Bottom Line**: You have to decide what in a situation is negotiable and what is not. When you have decided what is not negotiable, you must stand your ground.

How do you stand your ground without becoming aggressive? One technique which is useful is to imagine you are pressing the instant replay switch on a video. State where you stand, but say it nicely and keep on repeating where you stand.

For example, consider this exchange between Ravi and Rajeev:

Ravi : "I need the first quarter figures for a meeting this afternoon."

Rajeev : This afternoon? I am sorry, I've just promised, Vimla a complete audit, by lunch time and I just want be able to do both."

Ravi : "But this is an emergency."

Rajeev : "But I promised."

Ravi : "Vimla won't mind, call and tell her the computer is busy and you will be late, this is an emergency.

Rajeev : "I simply don't have the time. I can't give you these figures by 2:00. I would if I could, but I simply can.

Ravi : "But it is an emergency."

Rajeev : "I can't do them by 2:00, I understand your problem but I can't do them by two."

Ravi : "I've got to get them by 2:00."

Rajeev : "I simply can't do it. I could probably manage something by 4:30 but I simply can't do it by 2:00."

At first you may feel a little uncomfortable as if you are rejecting the person. But you are not, you are just refusing the request.

**Make it clear that you are negotiating as equals**: Once you know what is not negotiable, everything else is negotiable.

Having stood your ground and repeated where you stand, try to be helpful. Offer alternatives, and if you reach an impasse, ask the person to come up with a solution.

You may find this difficult if the other person continues to be aggressive. Tell yourself that something awful has just happened to him, and you are the nearest person he can find to take it out on. It may not be true but if you respond as if it is, you will keep your emotions under control.

So put yourself into the right mental state to be able to negotiate as equals. By being helpful and inviting other to help solve a problem, you make it clear that you are negotiating with them as equal partners. Therefore, you share a common interest in reaching a practical solution.

**Building blocks to managing others – and yourself – assertively.**

- Arbitrariness
- Arrogance
- Failure to show appreciation or give credit
- Failure to see the other person's point of view.
- Lack of leadership
- Lack of frankness and sincerity
- Failure to delegate responsibility
- Indecisiveness
- Bias; letting emotions rule reason

One way to avoid these behaviours, which result in ineffectiveness, is to manage others and yourself assertively.

## Assertion on the Job

Do you awake Monday mornings with the I-can't-bear-to-go-to-the-office feeling?
Do you live in the constant fear of losing your job?
Do you perform work that should be done by subordinates?

### *Do You Fear Success?*

If you answer yes to any of these questions, you are unassertive about your job. Your lack of assertiveness affects not only the pay check you bring home but the way you feel about yourself.

The more assertive you are in relation to work, the more satisfaction you gain. When the structure of the job or your own psychological blocks prevent this, dissatisfaction, resentment, and alienation occurs.

### *Assertion on the Job involves Five Basic Skills*

1. An active orientation. You must think through your work goals, the steps you must take to achieve them, and how, in doing this, you can utilize your talents to the fullest possible extent.
2. Ability to do the job. Interferences, obstacles, and blocks sometimes arise in the work situation because you have not mastered the skills you need for your particular job. In addition, you may have problems with self-control. You may possess bad work habits, lack discipline and the ability to concentrate.
3. Good interpersonal relations on the job. "Most people get fired because they can't get along with other people." You must be able to relate to pears, subordinates, and superiors; make requests and ask favours; say no when necessary; handle put-downs.
4. Control your anxieties and fears. Inappropriate emotional reactions interfere with work performance. General tensions can produce fatigue, irritability, and poor judgment. Fear of a specific work situation may lead to avoidance of the very task needed to get your job done – and may keep you from achieving your work goals.
5. The art of negotiating the system. This requires a knowledge of the job society and the specific skills that will enable you to work within, through, of against it to achieve your particular goals.

Assertiveness, like any other skill, can best be development through practising. So, to start the practice, we have chosen a number of situations that people have to handle at work. The situations are ones in which you might sometimes find yourself behaving aggressively or non-assertively. They occur fairly often, so there is usually plenty of opportunity to practise them.

### Situation I: Making Requests

Do you sometimes find it difficult to make requests to other people at work, or are you very tentative or abrupt when doing so? Often, it is easier to ask a colleague for a request. Asking a superior or a subordinate is perceived to be difficult. If you are not able to make requests assertively, you can often end up missing opportunities, not taking initiatives, and not getting the best use of available resources; alternatively, you might cause others to be resentful and uncooperative.

### *Hints for Making Requests*

The aim is to make requests in a straightforward, open way.

(a) *Don't apologise profusely.* For instance, "I'm very sorry to bother you; I hope you don't mind." Or, "I hope' you won't think I'm a nuisance, but do you think you could possibly…."

(b) *Be direct.* For example, speaking to a colleague: "Sanjay, I'd really like the report on the welfare project by the end of the next week. Can that be done"? If you make hints rather than requests, people will either become suspicious or impatient or both, and say to themselves, "Why don't you get straight to the point."

(c) *Keep it short:* Long-winded explanations get confusing and increase the chances that you will start justifying yourself.

(d) *Don't justify yourself* for making the request, for example, "I normally wouldn't ask anybody, but…."

(e) *Give a reason* for you request, if you think it will help, but be sure it is genuine and keep it brief. "Verma, I need the figures for the meeting next week. Will you let me have yours by Friday?"

(f) *Don't sell your request* with flattery or tempting benefits.

(g) *Don't ply on people's friendship or good nature.*

(h) *Don't take a refusal personally,* even when the request is more of a personal nature, or when the colleague is also a friend. *Respect the other person's right to say no'.* Don't become persistent with nonassertive pleading or aggressive bullying.

## Situation II: Refusing Requests; Saying No

People usually make requests or place demands on others. You must be able to stand up for yourself by the simple process of saying no. If you can't state this simple two-letter word when you want to say it, you begin to lose control of your life.

This does not mean saying no to everything. You say yes when you want to give an affirmative response. If doing a favour for a friend or participating in a community event may inconvenience you, there is still nothing wrong with saying yes if you feel the matter is important enough to undergo discommodity for the sake of the friend or the activity. Saying yes becomes wrong when you want to say no and it is in your best interest to say no, but instead, you end up with a feeble, "OK, I'll do it."

The inability to say no has several consequences:

- It leads you into activities you don't respect yourself for doing.
- It distracts you from what you really want to accomplish. You become so burdened doing the things you don't want to do that you have neither the time nor energy for the things that are most important.
- Because you allow other people to exploit you continually, the resentment builds up and, sometimes, after years of the yes routine, you lose your temper in an inappropriate outburst. This stems not from the most recent incident, but from hundreds of happenings. What the yes sayer doesn't realize is that this behaviour often creates lack of respect rather than liking.

– It produces a lack of communication between you and others. Unless there is honest communication, people cannot understand each other. Saying yes when you mean no is not the quality of sweetness; it is dishonour.

The key to refusing requests assertively is to believe that other people have the right to ask; you have the right to refuse.

(a) *Keep the reply short.* Avoid rambling justifications, i.e., normally wouldn't say no, only........you know how it is. I hope don't mind."

(b) *Simply say:* "No, I don't want to." Or "I prefer not to."

(c) *Give a reason for refusing* if you want to, but don't invent an excuse.

(d) *Avoid "I can't" phrase.* It sound like an excuse.

(e) *Don't apologise profusely:* "I'm terribly sorry......... Do you mind very much if........"

(f) *Acknowledge the requester.* "Thank you, Anu, but I'm not ready to take a coffe break yet."

(g) *State limitations or possibilities honestly.*

(h) *Non-verbal behaviour.* Especially with short replies, you need to slow down, speak steadily and with warmth. Otherwise replies like, "No, I don't want to," can sound abrupt.

If the requester is persistent, use the instant replay technique discussed in the last session. Don't search for better reasons.

## Situation III: Disagreeing and Stating Your Views

At work and in your social life your experience different events from other people, Even with the same event, you might, experience it in different ways. All this leads you to see things from your own point of view. Assertive behaviour involves disagreeing and agreeing openly and stating your viewpoints clearly and firmly.

### *Hints for Disagreeing and Stating Your Views Assertively*

(a) *State disagreement clearly.*

(b) *Express doubts in a constructive way.*

(c) *Use `I' statements* to distinguish your opinion from fact, and to distinguish your experience from that of other people.

(d) *Give reasons.*

(e) *Be flexible.* Keep your mind open to new information. Recognize other people's point of view.

Disagreeing and stating your views assertively increases the chances that further the road, people will be able to come up with mutually acceptable situations.

## Situation IV: Giving Praise

It is quite common from people to be working in an environment where praise is non-existent. If you are unable to praise assertively, you leave people trying to guess whether the work they do meet your expectations.

In the workplace, it is inevitable that there will be times when you want to acknowledge someone for what she has done or said. In addition to showing acknowledgement, praise also has a learning function. People learn not only from mistakes but also from successes.

### *Hints for Giving Praise*

(a) *Maintain eye contact* in a relaxed way.
(b) *Keep the praise brief and clear.*
(c) *Use `I' statements.*
(d) *Make it specific* to detailed aspects of the work, wherever possible. This would give the person information about what would be useful to repeat in future and why.

## Situation V: Receiving Praise

All too often, you might feel uncomfortable or foolish when you are on the receiving end of the praise.

### *Hints for Receiving Praise*

(a) *Keep the response short.* "Thanks, Nikhil, I'm glad you liked it."
(b) *Simply thank the giver.* "Thanks, Kavita."
(c) *Agree with or accept the praise.* "Thanks, Veena, I thought the presentation went well."

If you disagree with the praise, certainly qualify your reply, but, still thank the giver: "Thank you, Deepa, .........although didn't feel too pleased with it myself."

## Listen with Empathy

Empathy means putting yourself in another person's frame of reference. You fully understand a person emotionally and intellectually.

This does not mean you agree to whatever he says.

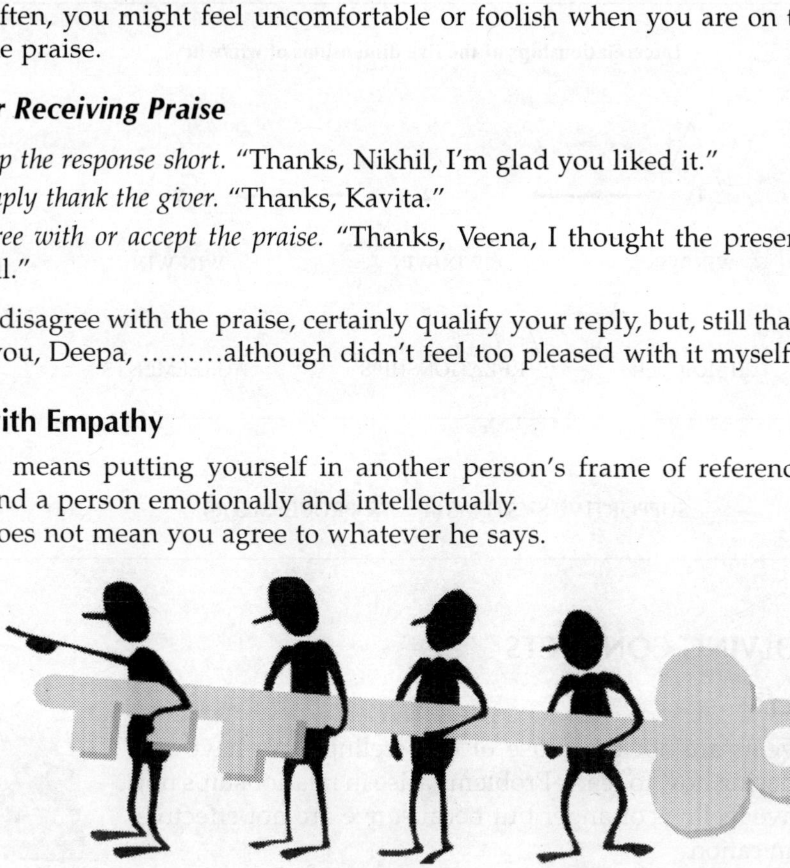

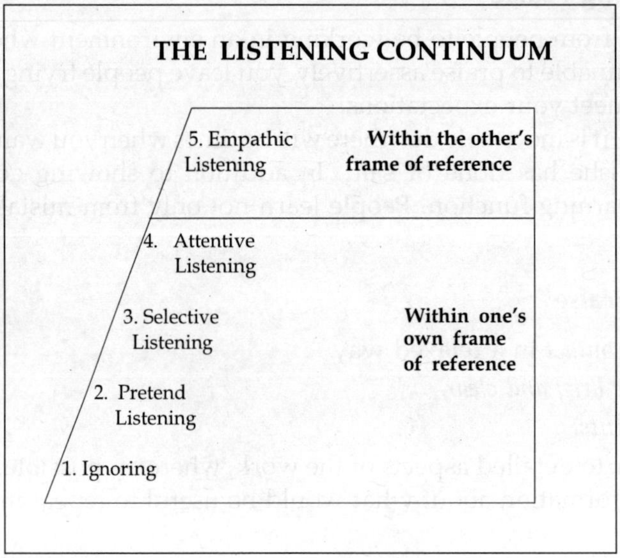


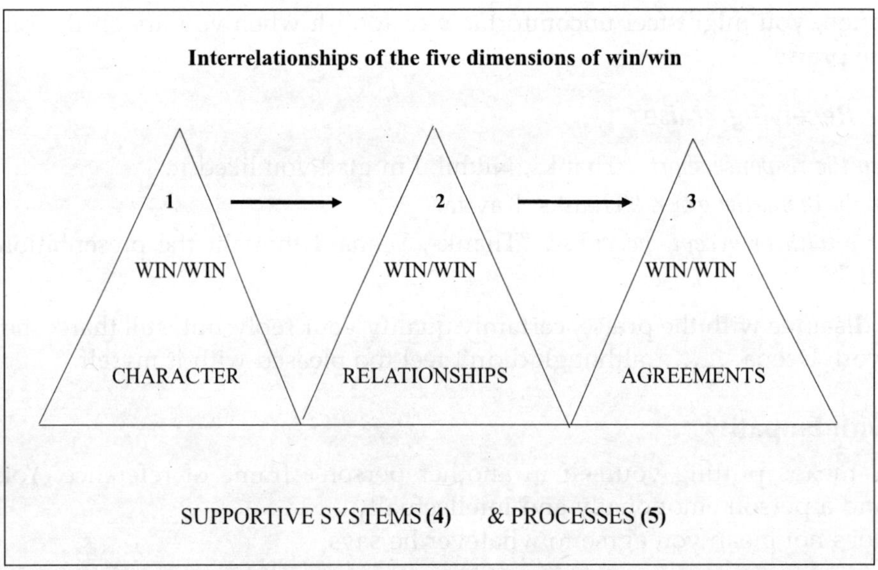


## 5.3 RESOLVING CONFLICTS

### What is Anger?

People and events are not the cause of our feelings. We have the freedom of choosing how to react. Problems arise in relationships not because we have feelings of anger but because we are not effective in our communication.

## Objectives of Expressing Anger

1. Realisation of one's own weaknesses and strengths
2. Behavioural modification of self and others.
3. Confronting rational/irrational beliefs/myths.
4. Clarification of distorted perceptions or illusion.
5. To build up a mutually agreed frame of reference for future functioning.

## Use Situational Analysis as Anger is a Positive Force

| | |
|---|---|
| Anxiety, guilt | Defensiveness |
| Defensive shame | Self-motivation for change |
| Self-motivation | Self-realisation |

1. **Own the feeling:** It is natural, healthy and not evil to express your anger.
2. **Be aware of your feelings:** Express your anger objectively whether it is justified or not. The process could be:
   (a) Displaced anger
   (b) To hurt others
   (c) To build others.
3. **Ask for clarification before expression:** Clarify your assumptions and gather facts. Let the other person explain from his frame of reference and listen and let there be congruency.
4. **Avoid Argument:** It is better not to get involved in the game of "who will win" and "who will lose" as this does not achieve anything and it is better to stop such a game for progressing.
5. **Descriptive Approach (Behaviour)**
   (a) Avoid the diagnostic approach. Labelling others makes them defensive and is disabling. Avoid 'You' response. Be aware of verbals and non-verbals.
   (b) Use the I-responses through self-disclosure of your feelings, i.e. (i) the way you are affected and (ii) the way you are perceiving the other person.

   My reaction Other person's action

   (c) Be rational in your expression. Use the adult, not the child.
   (d) Be specific with your words, i.e. (a) how you would like to be treated and what are your expectations; (b) avoid generalizations and be specific and concrete.
   (e) Be consistent and firm in your expression, without feeling guilt and shame. Express yourself.
6. **Authority Approach**

   CARE + CONFRONT + PAIN = CHANGE

   (a) 'Given authority' indicates roles assigned to us as parents, managers, authority figures with a lack of attention and care.

(b) The 'earned authority' approach expresses caring, investment of time and energy, coaching, teaching, discipleship and disciplining.

Therefore:

1. Anger is an opportunity to understand others and ourselves.
2. Anger provides energy (strength) and increases the vigour with which we act. Anger helps us to move towards action and productivity.

Anger overcomes anxiety and fear and encourages us to take action necessary for change/growth of self and others.

## Conflict Management

*An organization is more stable if members have the right to express their differences and solve their conflicts within it.*

— **Machiavelli**

- It is a natural disagreement arising between two or more people.
- It exists when they have incompatible goals and one or more believes that the behaviour of the other prevents them from their own goal achievement.
- Conflict may be:
  - (a) Intrapersonal
  - (b) Interpersonal
  - (c) Intergroup

When you become engaged in a conflict there are two major concerns you have to take into account:

- Achieving your personal goals
- Keeping a good relationship with the other person
- Given these two concerns it is possible to identify five styles of managing conflicts.

## Types of Conflict

There are different types of conflicts they can be between two individuals, within an individual, within a team of individuals, between two or more teams within an organization.

### *Causes of Conflict*

There can be conflict of aims—different goals; conflict of ideas—different interpretations; conflict of attitudes–different opinions; conflict of behaviour—different behaviours are unacceptable.

One can prevent conflict by assessing positive and negative personality traits of people.

There are different types of personalities and they determine the behaviour of a person, i.e., aggressive, submissive, assertive.

People are introvert or extroverts. Judge the behaviour and the past record of a person before the argument. Manage the language used.

Aggressive and people with negative attitude personalities can cause conflict.

**Use WAC'em Method to Prevent Conflict**

What's bothering you?

What do you want to ask the person to do?

See if what you've asked for can happen

## Styles of Managing Conflict

### *What are You Like?*

- Turtle
- Shark
- Teddy bear
- Fox
- Owl

All individuals have different styles to handle conflicts. In different situations a person handles conflict differently. A person can be like a turtle, who withdraws himself from the conflict or a shark, who is aggressive and fights back.

### *The Turtle (Withdrawing)*

- Turtles withdraw into their shells to avoid conflicts.
- They give up their personal goals.
- They stay away from the issues over which conflict takes place.
- They feel it is hopeless to try to resolve conflicts.

### *The Shark (Forcing)*

- Sharks try to overpower opponents.
- They force opponents to accept their solution to the conflict.
- Their goals are highly important to them.
- They give less importance to their relationships.
- They want to be the winner.

### *The Teddy Bear (Smoothing)*

- To teddy bears relationship is of great importance.
- Their own goals are of little importance.
- They want to be accepted and liked by others.
- They think that conflicts should be avoided in favour of harmony.
- They do not want to hurt anyone.

### *The Fox (Compromising)*

- Foxes are moderately concerned with their own goals and relationships with others.
- They seek to compromise.
- They give up part of their goals and also persuade others in conflict to give up part of their goals.
- They seek solutions in which both sides gain something.

### *The Owl (Confronting)*

- Owls highly value their goals and relationships.
- They view conflicts as problems to be solved.
- They seek a solution that achieves both their goals and the goals of the other person, thus satisfying both the parties.
- They are not satisfied until tensions have been fully resolved.

WHAT ARE YOU LIKE?

## Reactions to Intense Conflict Situations

### *Psychological Responses*

— Inattentiveness to other things
— Lack of interest in work
— Job dissatisfaction
— Work anxiety
— Estrangement or alienation from others
— Frustration

### *Behavioural Responses*

— Excessive smoking
— Alcoholism
— Undereating or overeating
— Aggression towards others or work sabotage
— Decreased communication
— Resisting influencing attempts

### *Physiological Responses*

Psychosomatic disorders such as:

— Peptic ulcers
— Respiratory problems like asthma
— Hypertension
— Headaches
— Coronary problems

## Five Modes of Resolving Conflicts

1. **COMPETING: Appropriate situations:**
   - When quick decisive action is vital—emergencies
   - On important issues where unpopular actions need implementation, e.g., cost cutting, enforcing unpopular rules, discipline, etc.
   - On issues vital to company's welfare when you know you're right.
   - Against people who take advantage of non-competitive behaviour.
2. **COLLABORATING: Appropriate situations:**
   - To find an integrative solution when both sets of concern are too important to be compromised.
   - When objective is to learn.
   - To merge insights from people of different perspectives.
   - To gain commitments by incorporating concerns into a consensus.
   - To work through feelings which have interfered with a relationship.
3. **COMPROMISING: Appropriate situations:**
   - When goals are important, but not worth the effort or potential description of more assertive modes.
   - When opponents with equal power are committed to mutually exclusive goals.
   - To achieve expedient solutions under time pressure.
   - As a backup when collaboration or competition is successful.
4. **AVOIDING: Appropriate situations:**
   - When the issue is not important or more important issues are pressing.
   - When you perceive no chance of satisfying your concerns.
   - When potential disruption outweighs the benefits of resolution.
   - To let people cool down and regain perspective.
   - When gathering information supersedes immediate decision.
   - When others can resolve the conflict more effectively.
   - When issues seem to be tangential/symptomatic of other issues.
5. **ACCOMODATING: Appropriate situations:**
   - When you find that you are wrong to allow a better position to be heard, to learn and show your reasonableness.
   - When issues are more important to others than yourself, to satisfy others and maintain cooperation.
   - To build social credits for later issues.
   - To minimize loss when you are outmatched and losing.
   - When harmony and stability are especially important.

## SUMMARY

- The key of foundation of any relationship whether it is personal or professional is interpersonal relationship. This relationship gives the basic foundation of a stronger bondage for any family, any company or any country.
- The ability to get along with others is immensely helpful for getting success in almost all walks of life, the manner in which we interact with people determines the life is buoyant or miserable.
- For effective interpersonal relations following things are important: build self-esteem, know how to listen, take risks, know how to say no, know how to give constructive feedback.
- Assertive behaviour enables a person to have the best chance of obtaining the desired results while retaining, self-respect and respect for others.
- Assertion training was originally a technique of behaviour therapy and is still practised as such by some psychologists.
- Being assertive rather than submissive or aggressive means getting the balance right between your needs and those of others.
- Handle criticism, know how to give and receive positive feedback, know what you want.
- Assertion on the job involves five basic skills: 1) an active orientation; 2) ability to do the job (interferences, obstacles, and blocks sometimes arise in the work situation because you have not mastered the skills you need for your particular job); 3) good interpersonal relations on the job; 4) control of your anxieties and fears; and 5) the art of negotiating with the system.

- Use WAC'em method to prevent conflict what's bothering you? What do you want to ask the person to do? See if what you've asked for can happen or not.
- Styles of managing conflict: The turtle (withdrawing), the shark (forcing), the teddy bear (smoothing), the fox (compromising), and the owl (confronting).

## QUESTIONS

**I. Explain in Brief**

1. What is interpersonal relation? What are the seven techniques of improving relations?
2. Mention three negative behaviours.
3. What do you mean by constructive feedback?
4. I am not OK, you are OK. Write down the behaviour pattern.
5. Write down five building blocks for managing others – and yourself – assertively.
6. Mention five factors that stop us from achieving our goals.
7. Use WAC'em method to prevent conflict. Expand WAC.

**II. Answer the following questions**

1. What are different types of behaviour? What is the difference between aggressive and assertive individuals? Explain giving example of situation.
2. Explain the different styles of managing conflict. Write the difference between the turtle (*withdrawing*) and the fox (*compromising*)?

# 6
UNIT
# Team Dynamics

**Learning Objectives**

- Team Building
- Effective Leadership
- Group Discussion

## 6.1 TEAM BUILDING

Team building is a dynamic way by which a group of individuals with a mutual drive is engrossed and affiliated to accomplish a definite assignment or consistent outcomes.

**Team Work**

Two men working as a team will do more than three men working as individuals!

Team work makes the Impossible possible!

## Why Teams are Essential?

- For disruption of individuality.
- To inculcate the "we feeling".
- Perform task collectively.
- To adapt synergy for success and proficiency.
- To satisfy the organizational and invidiviual needs of its members.

## Achieving More – Through Creative Cooperation

- ACCEPTING Each Others' DIFFERENCES
- RESPECTING Those DIFFERENCES
- GAINING from each others' STRENGTHS
- COMPENSATING for each others' WEAKNESSES
- Making IMPOSSIBLE POSSIBLE
- Together everyone achieves more

## Strengths of a Team

- Capability to transform
- Achievement of task/tasks
- React to the rapidly changing surroundings
- Judge and analyze the perspectives to the problem or opportunity
- Evaluate and analyze the situation
- Nurture cooperation
- Build long-lasting linkages
- Concepts and principles flow more swiftly
- Actions implementation in task
- Holding together the team with high standards due to peer pressure

## Tips for Working Successfully in a Team

- **Meet people appropriately.** Starts with the introducing self, exchange contact and phone numbers
- **Find things you have in common.** Find something in common with another person, and start from that baseline
- **Make meeting conditions good.** Select a room which has a large surface to write on, is quiet and warm enough, and that there aren't lots of distractions. **Let everyone talk.** Let the talking come from each person of the team to know each other's viewpoint. **Do not interrupt while in discussion.**

- **Check your egos at the door.** Write down the ideas coming out of discussions in a descriptive way.
- **Praise each other.** Focus on the goodness of discussion, praise it whenever required. If any objection, clarify it.
- **Put it in writing.** Always write down the responsibilities of each member. Be specific. Arrange meetings by email, and establish accountability. Always intimate the group members in the form of cc in emails.
- **Be open and honest.** Talk about a problem if any. Forgiving people for their mistakes, but raise the issues when they come up.
- **Avoid conflict at all costs.** Avoid conflicts and misunderstandings. Clarify and apologize, if required. The goof the team is to work together. Be the peacemaker.
- **Create clear goals**: The goals should be shared and their importance should be believed by all members of the team. The accomplishment of task should be a joint effort.
- **Encourage Teams to Go for Small Wins**: Set attainable goals by building effective cohesiveness and confidence in teammates. Aim at small victories first then the big ones.
- **Build Mutual Trust:** The team should be well informed about the development of the task. A climate of openness should be maintained so that members feel free to discuss problems without fear of retaliation. Be truthful towards one's own problems and limitations.

  Be open minded and humble to attend to team members' ideas. Be reasonable, unbiased, reliable, and trustworthy.
- **Ensure mutual responsibility and a sense of collective purpose:** All members must feel responsibility—for both achievements and disappointments. They must share responsibility.
- **Training:** Train to build skills if teammates require it. Training may be in problem solving, communication, negotiation skills, conflict-resolution skills, and group processing skills.

### *Cultivate Harmony in the Team*

- Motivate individuals
- Define roles and responsibilities
- Encourage creative, constructive and innovative environment
- Listen and acknowledge others' points of view
- Add variety to one's organizational life
- Provide diagnostic information to prevent occurrence of similar problems
- Facilitate understanding and win-win situation

## 6.2 EFFECTIVE LEADERSHIP

### Leadership is Influencing – Nothing More, Nothing Less

Leadership denotes unleashing energy, building, freeing and growing.

— *Tom Peters*

Leadership is an art of getting from people more than they are capable of giving.

— *Sir Raymond Lygo*

Management is about doing things right, leadership is about doing the right things.

— *Warren Bennis*

The leader's unending responsibility must be to remove every detour, every barrier to ensure that vision is first clear, and then real.

— *Jack Welch*

Leadership is a universal human activity in which leader influences followers to act in order to attain goals that represent the motives, needs, wants, hopes and expectations of both—leader and followers.

### *Leadership is Leading and Developing Others*

- **Showing Sincere Concern** – Open importance in individuals, principles and their contribution, advances their strength, has affirmative opportunities of what his teammates can accomplish.
- **Enabling** – To trust others to take decisions on important matters, delegates effectively an develops the potential of the team members.
- **Being Accessible** – Desires in personal communication, approachable and not status conscious.
- **Inspiring Change** – Boosts creative thinking, inquiring and also new approaches to solutions to problems with strategic planning and thinking.

## LEADERSHIP IS A UNIVERSAL HUMAN

### Basic Qualifications of a Leader

1. A complete mastery over the five basic fears, like:
   (a) Fear of disapproval
   (b) Fear of ill health
   (c) Fear of loss of life
   (d) Fear of old age
   (e) Fear of death
2. The leadership must be willing to subordinate personal interest for the good of their followers. Complete mastery over flattery and greed.

3. The singleness of purpose denoted by a convinced programme of leadership which harmonizes with the needs of the time.
4. The considerate and the submission of the mastermind principles through which authority may be attained through coordination of efforts in a spirit of agreement.
5. A self-confident leadership in its highest form.
6. Capacity to reach conclusions rapidly and to stand by them firmly.
7. Lssseadership must imagine sufficiently in advance to enable them to expect the needs of the time and to produce plans for providing these needs.
8. Creativity is the essence and it should be in the strongest form.
9. Passion and the capacity to convey it to their followers.
10. Self-discipline in its highest form is most important.
11. Always willing to render more service than that for which direct compensation is received.
12. A attractive and compelling personality.
13. The ability to think precisely and to be a good speaker.
14. The ability to cooperate with others in essence of coordination.
15. The determination to ponder opinions and determination on a given task until it has been completed.
16. The aptitude and "for sight" to profit by faults and disappointments.
17. Patience in its highest forms.
18. Self-restraint in all of its form.
19. International trustworthiness of both purpose and deed.
20. Last but by no means, least, firm loyalty to the true principles as the basic of all relationships with others.

## Traits of a Leader

- Ambition
- Cheerfulness
- Cooperation
- Courage
- Dedication
- Dependability
- Drive
- Emotional stability
- Energy
- Faith
- Fairness
- Flexibility
- Foresight

- Humour
- Initiative
- Integrity
- Intuitive
- Justice
- Personality
- Respect
- Sensitivity
- Sympathy
- Tact
- Tenacity
- Toughness
- Will power

## Leadership is Leading the Organization

> A team with a leader exists because the task or purpose for which the team exists cannot be achieved by one person alone. Neither can it be most effectively achieved by a group of people.

- **Interacting and Attaining** – Gains assurance and support of various groups through thoughtfulness to necessities and accomplishing organizational goals. Thought-provoking communication of the image of the organization.
- **Focusing Efforts** – Explains purposes and boundaries, team orientation to problem-solving and decision making and to identify values.
- **Constructing Collective Vision** – Has a strong and strategic vision and draws others for achieving the vision.
- **Supportive Progressive Culture** – Encourages feedback and supports when mistakes occur and stimulates corrective measures.
- **Enabling Change Thoughtfulness** – Sensitivity to the impact of change on different parts of the organization, maintains a balance between change and stability.

### *The Action Centred Leadership*

A leader who consistently fails to achieve the task is unlikely to remain a leader for long!

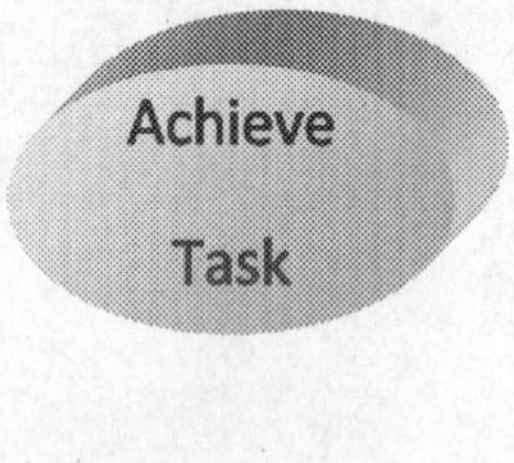

### *Task*

**Never to fail is probably never to take risk.**

| PURPOSE | Am I clear what the task is? |
|---|---|
| RESPONSIBILITY | Am I clear as to what mine tasks are? |
| OBJECTIVES | Have I agreed these with my boss? |
| PLAN | Have I worked out to reach objectives? |
| RESOURCES | Are these adequate? |
| TARGETS | Have targets been clearly defined/agreed? |
| LEADER | Do the people know who they report? |
| TRAINING | Are there any gaps in the team ability? |
| PROGRESS | Do I check this regularly and evaluate? |
| PRIORITIES | Have I planned the time? |
| AUTHORITY | Are all lines of authority clear? |

A team with a leader exists because the task or purpose for which the team exists cannot be achieved by one person alone. Neither can it be most effectively achieved by a group of people.

BUILD TEAMS

**It is a team and teamwork, which achieve task.**

### *Teams*

| OBJECTIVES | Does the team understand them? |
|---|---|
| STANDARDS | Do they know what is expected? |
| QUALITY | Have the appropriate standards agreed? |
| TEAM MEMBERS | Are the right people working together? |
| TEAM SPIRIT | Is the job structured to encourage this? |
| DISCIPLINE | Are the rules seen to be reasonable? |
| REVIEW | Is it regular? |
| TEAM MEETINGS | Are there regular team meetings? |

**Each team member is an individual**

### *Individuals*

| | |
|---|---|
| TARGETS | Have they been set and quantified? |
| INDUCTION | Do they really know the organization? |
| RESPONSIBILITY | Have they got the job description? |
| AUTHORITY | Do they have sufficient responsibilities? |
| TRAINING | Has adequate provision been made? |
| RECOGNITION | Do I emphasize people's successes? |
| GROWTH | Do they see the chance of development? |
| PERSON | Do I know the person? |

## Kinds of Leadership

**Authoritarian:** This type of leadership dominates the discussion, speaks loudly, issues orders and commands, suggests his authority to support his/her position.

**Leaderless:** Here the leader delegates all direction and decision-making steps to others. The person supports shared leadership and allows high ability people to run the meeting. Though this can be sometimes successful, but some guidance is needed and some positive feedback to the group.

### *Democratic, Participative*

We are living in democracy; the group in such an environment has the final authority to make decisions. Here the main goal is not to force decisions but to make the best decision possible and facilitate productive group discussion, invite minority opinions, evaluate unsupported generalizations, and clarify.

## The e-Leadership Challenge

| Industrial Age | Knowledge Age |
|---|---|
| An office | A workspace |
| Quiet | Noisy |
| Single task | Multitask |
| Focused | Directed |
| Lifetime employment | Lifetime learning |
| Wages | Ownership |
| Unions | Teams |
| Culture | Environment |
| Accuracy | 80% solutions |

| Play on weekends | Play at work |
|---|---|
| Seniority | Performance |
| Tangible products | Intangible products |
| 9 to 5 | 24/7 |
| Office buildings | Anywhere, anytime |
| Knowledge is power | Knowledge sharing |
| Competitors | Networked alliances |

## 6.3 GROUP DISCUSSION (GD)

### Learning Objectives

After reading the unit you would be able to:

- Why group discussions
- How to make group discussion effective.
- Importance of agenda.
- Methods of group discussions.
- Methods of decision taking after the discussions.
- Evaluation parameters of group discussion
- Types of group discussion

Group discussion is an efficient way to discuss an issue from various prospectives. When a topic is open for brainstorming in a group, they come together to give their ideas. With consensus a conclusion is made. It is also seen as a tool to measure one's behavioural, emotional and psychological attributes.

### Why Group Discussions

(a) Democratic society is run by groups. Govt industry – educational institutes.

(b) Discussions are there in one form or the other in everybody's life – even in home discussions about future of children.

(c) Group discussion are largely used in the selection process for admission into institutes – admissions to business schools and professional organizations.

(d) *Examiner wants to test how* effectively an individual can participate in a group – individual gives importance to group objective or his own – how good a listener to other point of view and how he accepts opposite views.

(e) What a group wants to accomplish and how should you talk to influence others.

(f) Only learning about groups is not enough but participation in discussion is more important. By observing others one can improve one's errors and change his behaviour.

(g) The discussion involves an exchange of thoughts and ideas among members of the group.

(h) This is to test the listening, inter-human, persuasive and presentation skills.

### *Reasons for Employing a GD*

- **Value for Time**

  GD helps in establishing an opinion about candidates within a short period of time.

- **Skills Assessment**

  GD helps in assessing definite skills that cannot be appraised even in a personal interview. These skills include team membership, leadership, interpersonal and listening skills.

## How to Make Group Discussion Effective?

In group discussion different ideas and points are discussed by a group of people to represent an idea and solve a problem. Following points are to be kept in mind to make a group discussion effective.

1. Discussion should be target oriented.

   The effectiveness of any group discussion depends on the quality of participation and on the consensus of the issue by the members of the group. It should be intended to accomplish the goal.

2. Sharing of responsibility for the group's effectiveness.

3. Cooperation for a purpose with positive attitude should be the motto rather than conflict.

   Conflicting situation should be resolved at the earliest, provided it is healthy. Every decision need not be arrived at by consensus.

4. An effective discussion requires leadership.

   In a group discussion a member has to act as a leader to keep the discussion in the right direction.

### *The value of an Agenda (applicable to discussions based on case studies)*

For any formal discussion there should be an agenda for systematic thorough investigation necessary for wise decision making. It is as follows:

1. *Understanding the subject:* Why is the group in existence? What is there for it to do? What form does its output take. Who gets it? What is to be done with it?
2. *Accepting and wording the questions:* What is the group enquiring about ? Are the methodical arguments and topics clear to the members?
3. *Information outcome:* What is the cause of the symptoms? What is the remedy and the fact finding ?
4. *Setting standards and restrictions:* What is the possible solution look like?
5. *Discovering and choosing clarifications:* What are the alternatives, that should be selected? What evaluation plan can be used to measure and effectiveness of the solution?
6. *Preparing and present the final reports:* What must be written down? What must be said? What, where and to whom? How can the final report be most persuasively presented?

### Understanding the Fundamentals in a Group Discussion

In order to be able to take part in a successful group discussion it is necessary to understand the element/s features of interaction. These are:

1. *Verbal Communication:* This is the most important influence on how a group operates and what it achieves. Talking and listening are the substance of problem solving.
2. *Non-Verbal Behaviour:* Non-verbal messages form a major part of communication. Behaviours of the face and gestures are transmitted through non-verbal messages. Facial gestures, physical position, eye contact and tone of voice indicate feelings and levels of interest form the non-verbal communication.
3. *Norms and Conformity:* Norms are standardized patterns of beliefs, attitudes, communication, and behaviour within groups.
4. *Power:* In an organizational situation, power comes from occupying a position in hierarchy. The advantage of having power in a group discussion is that powerful members are the centres of communication in a group they talk.
5. *Cohesion:* This leads to the we feeling and team orientation in the group. The opinions on achieving these 'goals' are discussed at length.

**Decision Making Styles:** There are three distinct ways by which decisions can be made.

- **Consensus:** It means an unanimous agreement by all members.
- **Negotiation:** It involves bargaining among members to build a solution that honours each person's position on particular issues.
- **Voting:** The obvious advantage of such a decision making process is its efficiency.

## Evaluation Parameters of Group Discussion

### *Quality of Content*

Comprehension of Core Ideas/Creativity/Data Generation/Analytical/Ability/Reasoning/Assimilation

- **Knowledge in Your Area of Specialization**
  This may include your academics, your job, details of the organization in which you work, your hobbies, etc. Understanding of the fundamentals of each of these areas contributes immensely to your confidence
- **Self-Awareness**
  Knowledge about self, including strengths, weakness, career goals, personal aspirations, etc.
- **Background Awareness**
  Contextual awareness refers to one's knowledge about the context to which one belongs – the school, the college, the company, the family, the country, etc.
- **General Awareness**
  This is nothing but an extension of one's immediate context. The political system, the economic situation, the human rights movement, world war II, etc.
- **Experience**
  Past experience has an impact on the level of confidence.
  Successful experience adds positively to one's level of confidence and failures lower the level of confidence.

Comprehension of core idea is essential to deliver a high quality content. This is judged from the relevance made by you, the supportive examples.

Logical reasoning which includes understanding the topic, generating quality arguments, analysis and a progressive approach to a justifiable conclusion.

### *Content vs Process*

- The content is all about 'what' or the 'matter' spoken in the GD, whereas the process refers to 'how','when' and 'why' of GD.
- Both are equally important and need adequate attention at all stages.
- High quality content contribution by one with no regard to the 'process' is as suicidal as a contribution.

**Critical Success Factors**

- Cognitive skills or knowledge:
  The most important aspect of your contribution to a GD is the quality of content (QOC)

### *Behavioural Personality*

Attitude/Aggression/Rapport Building/Participation/Team Membership/Confidence/Persuasiveness/Accommodation

### *Communication*

Articulation/Listening/Body Language/Eye Contact/ Presentation

- One of the most critical factors that contributes to the success at the personality assessment stage is the skills of communication comprising both articulation and listening skills.
- Do not equate communication with articulation.

  Good and active listeners, generally, add greater value to a group discussion.

### *Vision/Goal Orientation*

Goal Clarity, Effective Utilization of Resources, Driving towards issue Resolution

### *Confidence*

Motivation/Action Orientation, Proactiveness

Confidence, perhaps, is the single most important attitude that contributes to the 'personality' of an individual.

Confidence is the result of various factors. Let us consider a few of them in the context of personality assessment by the business schools.

## Types of GD'S

1. **Structured GD**

   A structured GD is one that is most commonly used.

   A group is given a topic for discussion with 10-20 minutes

   There is no leader appointed for the group.

2. **Unstructured GD**

   Unstructured GD can be built into a discussion by giving no clear instructions.

   The group is expected to achieve some objective(s) during the course or by the end of the GD.

   The tasks of choosing the topic for discussion, appointing a leader or a chairman, etc.

### *Case Study*

- This is a specialized technique in which a short situation is given and the participants have to discuss the situation and recommend appropriate course of action.
- Equal level of information about the situation is given to all, since the same case is given to everyone.

- Here, the evaluators test the information processing and analytical skills after processing the information, and suggest ways of tackling the problem. For this, you need to be abreast with current affairs, should regularly read newspapers and magazines.
- Your group behaviour and communication skills are on test, i.e., how you convince others and how clearly you are able to express your points of view?
- You should be articulate, generate ideas, not sound boring, should allow others to speak and, adopt a stand on a given subject.
- Additional marks may be given for starting or concluding the discussion.

*Consensus GD*

- The task given in a GD is open-ended.
- The group is not expected to arrive at a consensus unless specified by the panel, at the outset.
- GDs can be **topic based** or **case based**.

  Topic based GDs can be classified into three types:

1. Factual topics
2. Controversial topics
3. Abstract topics

### Factual Topics

**Factual topics** are about current issues and day-to-day facts. These topics test the awareness and also visualize the sensitivity of the participant with the real-life situations, such as global warming, sixth pay commission, new education policy, and so on.

### Controversial Topics

**Controversial topics** involve argument and high level discussion. The maturity of a person is judged and the logical argument is viewed without getting personal and emotional, such as women make better managers, reservation system should not be there.

### Abstract Topics

**Abstract topics** test involves out of the box thinking/lateral thinking and creativity. These are about intangible things, such as Red, Blue Whale, Number 10, Dot.

*Case-based*

In this method of discussion a case is given which tries to stimulate a real situation and the group is asked to resolve the situation. In this situation participants give their views which can be incorrect or perfect solutions. The purpose is to think of solution from all points of view and angles.

**A group discussion consists of:**

Communication skills
Knowledge and ideas regarding a given subject
Capability to coordinate and lead
Exchange of thoughts
Addressing the group as a whole
Thorough preparations
The first aspect is one's power of expression.

It is necessary that you should be precise and clear.

- About knowledge on a given subject, clarity of thought
- You should speak as much as necessary, neither more nor less.

*Group Discussions are not Debating Stages*

- Ability to listen is also judged by the evaluators.
- One should listen carefully to others and then react or proceed to add some more points.
- Behaviour in the group is also important, i.e., how you interact with fellow participants.
    - Thoughts should be conveyed in such a manner that convince other participants in the group.
- Confidence and levelheadedness in doing so is necessary. These add value to your presentation.

### *Knowledge and Ideas Regarding a Given Subject*

Knowledge of the subject under discussion and clarity of ideas are important. In-depth knowledge makes one confident and enthusiastic, it also makes one sound convincing and confident.

### *Leadership and Coordinating Capabilities*

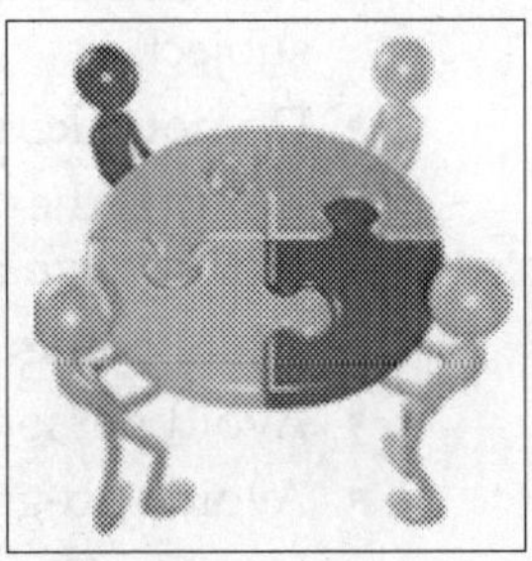

The basic aim of a group discussion is to judge a candidate's leadership qualities: tactfulness, skill, understanding and knowledge on varied topics.

*Exchange of Thoughts*

The number of participants in a group can vary between 8 and 10. Mostly a topic or a situation is given to group members who have to discuss it between 10 and 20 minutes.

- The purpose is to get an idea about candidates in a short time and make assessment about their skills.

  A note is made of your contributions to the discussion, comprehension of the main idea, the rapport you strike, patience, assertion, accommodation, amenability, etc. Body language and eye contact too are important. Addressing the group as a whole confidence and coolness while presenting your viewpoint are of help.

**Knowledge is strength**. A candidate should be aware of current affairs and sound knowledge on different topics like politics, finance, economy, science and technology is helpful. Power to convince effectively, clarity in speech and expression is yet another essential quality.

A GD is not a debating stage. Language used should be simple, direct and straight-forward. Don't interrupt a speaker or try to cut others short.

- Maintain rapport with fellow participants. Eye contact is needed as it shows confidence. Non-verbal gestures, such as listening intently or nodding while appreciating someone's viewpoint speaks of you positively.
- Communicate with each and every candidate. Do not look at one member and speak. Speak to the group.

1. **Personal Skills**

   Self-confidence, depth of knowledge, group and level of understanding of the subject, the ability and logical development of thought should be possessed by the candidate. A candidate should be pleasant, courteous and cooperative.

2. **Group Skills**

   Willingness to listen to logic and reason, besides his ability for sustained interest. Ability to contribute original points, ability to steer the group into discussing ability to make consistent efforts to relate with others in the group.

3. **Leadership Skill**

   Ability to influence and persuade others, his ability to encourage and also to compromise, ability to coordinate and summarize, ability to build up the confidence of the group and ability to encourage silent members into discussion.

4. **Guidelines for the Candidates**

   - Remember to keep the discussion on the subject, or to bring it back to the subject.
   - Do not take the discussion on a tangent by adding irrelevant points.
   - Control the overtalkative member. Do not allow one or two members to monopolize the discussion.
   - Make points that enhance the quality of the discussion.
   - Avoid personal arguments.
   - Avoid sub-grouping tendencies.
   - For effective leadership in group discussions conclude each argument at the right time and in the right manner. You should be able to review the highlights of the discussions that the group arrives at during the discussion.

- A group discussion can be a very powerful screening device to judge the candidates. The steps proposed above can go a long way in enhancing the quality and effectiveness of this technique if followed in the right spirit.

**What skills are judged in group discussion?**

- How good are you at communication with others.
- How do you behave and interact within a group.
- How open-minded are you.
- Your listening skill.
- How you put forward your views.
- Your leadership and decision making skills.
- Your analysis skill and subject knowledge.
- Problem solving and critical thinking skill.
- Your attitude and confidence.

## Dos for Group Discussion

- KISS – keep it short and simple. Always use brief statements in place of long description to retain the focus of participants
- Even contribution made by participants should be evenly spaced. Try to avoid being the first speaker when not knowing the topic.
- Don't hurry while delivering points, in case you speak fast participants would keep probing issue and may not appreciate true impact of the idea.
- Others may speak against during the course of your presentation, tackle such situation in a polite and decisive manner by using "please and "excuse me".
- Support your points with examples and incidents.
- Do not speak when someone else is speaking. Be attentive to details and sensitive to feelings and ideas of others.
- Keep eye contact while speaking.
- Initiate the GD.
- Allow others to speak.
- Speak clearly.
- Make sure to bring the discussion on track.
- Positive attitude.
- Speak sensibly.
- Listen carefully to others.
- Positive body language.

### *Don'ts*

- Don't speak loudly or scream in case others are unable to hear you above loud noise in group discussion. A pushy tone creates a negative impression on participants as well on monitors of GD.
- Avoid taking a negative stance against any participant however incompetent or ill-informed he may be.
- Avoid negative gestures during discussion.

- Examples of negative gestures
  1. Sitting one leg folded
  2. Sitting cross-legged
  3. Shaking legs
  4. Too much flaying of hands
  5. Draping the arm around head of chair

### *Sitting Posture Don'ts*

## Group Discussion Evaluation Sheet

| S. No | Name | Quality of Content | Behavioural Personality | Communication | Vision/Goal Orientation | Confidence |
|---|---|---|---|---|---|---|
| | | | | | | |
| | | | | | | |
| | | | | | | |
| | | | | | | |
| | | | | | | |
| | | | | | | |

## Some Group Discussion Topics

1. Should there be job reservations in the private sector?
2. Is America a rouge superpower?
3. Are minorities safe in India?
4. Will caste system ever die in India?
5. Is cloning ethical?
6. MBA stands for Manager by Accident
7. Women literacy in India
8. Women emancipation in India, myth or reality
9. Is India on the path of an intellectual revolution?
10. India a developing country
11. Legalization of homosexuality in India
12. Terrorists and India
13. India host to Common Wealth Games
14. Pollution in India
15. Ecology and tourism
16. Is globalization a threat to India?
17. Reservation of women in parliament
18. Efficiency and corruption lives in hand in hand
19. Growth and integrity are poles apart
20. The impact of Internet on Indian society
21. Impact of globalization in India
22. Environment – Global warming and India's role
23. Nothing Succeeds Like Success
24. Strategic thinking in turbulent times
25. Creativity and Innovation in Business Enterprises
26. Work Life Balance
27. Relevance of Gandhi's Policies in today's Management
28. New Education Policy – No Board Exams
29. Euthanasia (mercy killing) – Is it morally right for society
30. A ship docked in harbour cannot face the storms
31. Reality shows – Do they really lead to stardom
32. Metro Railways is a boon or a bane
33. Attitude not aptitude determines your altitude
34. RED
35. GREEN
36. BLUE WHALE

37. DOT (.)
38. Is China a threat to Indian industry
39. Today youth is in hurry, worry and curry
40. Mumbai terrorist attack is a lesson
41. Art of Living
42. Professional Tax to be imposed by MCD
43. Money speaks but God is silent
44. Communication – A powerful tool
45. Media – A mixed blessing
46. Is the consumer really the king in India?
47. India of my dreams
48. Is youth prepared to face the future
49. Plastic carrybags still debated issue
50. Is India the path of an industrial revolution?
51. Financial recession – Its Impact in India
52. Blue Elephant
53. Regression Therapy – A way to know past life
54. FDI and the retail sector
55. Every cloud has a silver lining
56. We need more entrepreneurs than managers
57. Good things come with good thinking
58. Lokpal bill and corruption in 2020
59. Health is wealth
60. Will India be a super power
61. Value based politics is the need of the hour
62. Foreign television is destroying our culture
63. Fill it, shut it, forget it
64. Advertising is a form of brainwashing
65. Honour killing – Khap style of management
66. Reality TV
67. Money is sweeter than honey
68. Are security cameras infringing our privacy
69. Sky is red
70. Inequality of income in India
71. Yellow metal at all time high
72. Indian economy and recession

## SUMMARY

- Tips for working sucessfully in a team: Meet people properly, find things you have in common, make meeting conditions good, let everyone talk, check your egos at the door, praise each other, put it in writing, be open and honest, avoid conflict at all costs, create clear goals, encourage teams to go for small wins, build mutual trust, ensure mutual responsibility and a sense of common purpose, training.
- A team with a leader exists because the task or purpose for which a team exists cannot be achieved by one person alone. Neither can it be most effectively achieved by a group of people.
- Leadership is a universal human activity in which the leader influences followers to act in order to attain goals that represent the motives, needs, wants, hopes and expectations of both leader and followers.
- Kinds of leadership – authoritarian, leaderless, democratic, participative
- Group discussion requires that a number of persons with different ideas and points of view come together and talk in order to solve a problem they have in common
- Types of GD's – **1. Structured GD:** A group is given a topic for discussion for 10-20 minutes. There is no leader for the group. **2. Unstructured GD:** Unstructured GD can be built into a discussion by giving no clear instructions. The group is expected to achieve some objective(s) during the course or by the end of the GD. The tasks of choosing the topic for discussion, appointing a leader or a chairman, etc.
- **Dos for group discussion** – KISS – keep it short and simple. Always use brief statements in place of long description to retain the focus of participants.

## QUESTIONS

### I. Explain in Brief

1. What is a team? Describe with examples.
2. What are traits of a good team?
3. Why is group discussion used as a selection criteria?
4. What are the essential skills required by a candidate for a good group discussion?
5. Why is non-verbal communication, one of the evaluation parameters of GD?
6. Name different types of group discussion. Which type of GD is commonly used?
7. Name two abstract topics.

### II. Answer the following questions

1. What is leadership? What are different kinds of leadership? Explain with examples.
2. Team work makes the impossible possible! Discuss.

3. What makes a group discussion effective?
4. What are the different evaluation parameters of GD?
5. A GD is not a debating stage. Comment.
6. Mention some guidelines necessary for a GD.
7. Describe quality of content as a evaluation parameter for GD.

## ASSIGNMENT

1. Make group of 6-7 students. Brainstorm about a recent problem. Practise again and again taking different topics.

# UNIT 7

# Synergy

**Learning Objectives**

- Goal Orientation
- Involving Others in Time Management
- Develop Trust and Collaborations

## Well Said Quotes

Holding your head high, And being the best you know you can be
When life seems to fall apart at your feet,
Facing each difficulty with the confidence
That time will bring you better tomorrow
And never giving up,
............... means CONFIDENCE

To the question of your life,
You are the only answer.
To the problems of your life,
You are the only solution.

When you keep saying you are busy,
Then you are never free.
When you keep saying you have no time,
Then you will never have time.
When you keep saying you will do it tomorrow,
Then your tomorrow will never come.

Time is like a river.
You cannot touch the same river twice,
The flow which has passed will never pass again.
Enjoy every moment of life...................

Treasure every moment that you have because...
"Yesterday is history.
Tomorrow is a mystery. Today is a gift.
That's why it's called the present.'

Winning doesn't always mean being first,
Winning means you're
Doing better than you have done before.....

## 7.1 GOAL ORIENTATION

"Discipline is a bridge between goals and accomplishments."

"Goals give direction, purpose, and meaning to life."
The basic rules of goal setting are:

- Know what you want?
- Find out what it takes to get it?
- Action it and preserve.

**Why are Goals Important**

Goals are the focus that lights up the determination and the power of concentration.

**Goals Must be SMART**

**S**: Specific
**M** : Measureable
**A**: Achievable
**R**: Result-oriented
**T**: Time bound

Goals can be short term up to a year, usually up to 3 years and long term up to 5 years. Goals can also be longer than 5 years. Such long-term goals are called "purpose of life".

**Goals Must be Balanced**

1. Family: Our loved ones are reason to live and make a living.
2. Financial: That includes career and things that money can buy.
3. Physical: Our health, without which nothing makes sense.
4. Mental: It represents knowledge and wisdom.

5. Social: Every individual and organization has social responsibility without which society starts dying.
6. Spiritual: Our value system represents ethics and character.

**Goals Must be Consistent to our Values**

Goals lead to purpose of life.
Goal setting is the starting point of success.
Goals must be full of quality and not quantity.
Action plan for goal setting.
Make definite goals.
"Goals and actions must meet".
"Goal 'setting' is important….. Goal 'doing' is more important".

## Ten Facts about Goals

1. A person going nowhere can be sure of reaching destination.
2. Abraham Lincoln was great because his goals got him out of it.
3. The size of accomplishment is measured by the obstacles you had to overcome to achieve the goal.
4. Visualize long-term goals, but make short-term goals also to achieve long-term goals.
5. Many people have good aim in life, but for some reasons they never pull the trigger.
6. It is not enough to make progress; we must make it in the right direction.
7. One must have the attitude to accomplish his goals.
8. To achieve happiness, we must make it certain that we have a definite goal.
9. Some people look backward than forward because it is easier to remember where you had been than to figure where you are going.
10. An achieved goal is the starting point for future progress.

### *Probability of Completing a Goal*

- 10% if you hear an idea.
- 25% if you consciously decide to adopt it.
- 40% if you decide when you will do it.
- 50% if you plan how you will do it.
- 65% if you commit to someone else you will do it.
- 95% if you have a specific accountability with the person to whom you committed.

## Common Causes of Failure and Mental Blocks

The factors that stop us from achieving success are:

1. Lack of specific goal or choosing wrong goals.
2. Carry the past as burden.

3. Fear of failure (not trying the unknown).
4. Blaming others or justifying already made opinion.
5. Living in one's own reality/limiting visions and beliefs.
6. Using short-cut approach to long-term goals.
7. Allowing energy sucking emotions to drain out energy (not forgiving attitude).
8. Not learning from mistakes.
9. Pleasing others to look good in other's eyes than listening to self.
10. Reaching the comfort zone. Illusion of success.

## 7.2 INVOLVING OTHERS IN TIME MANAGEMENT

1. **Your Boss:** If your boss is one who calls you for every trivial thing, has unnecessarily long meetings, you might feel frustrated and wonder how your "time management" can solve this 'live' problem.

   You could cultivate and practise the art of cutting short long discussions. "I know, you would want to be left alone now", "I don't want to waste your time", "I" ll get started on completing the project, so I can give it to you on time". May be, giving him a few notes on time management may be a subtle hint. Otherwise you can sit with him and genuinely try to find out his concern. It is possible he is not sure of you and whether you are able to give him the results. You could also discuss with him your priorities and how you are spending your time.
2. **Your Subordinates:** Avoid being like your 'boss'. Have a clear job output description for your subordinates. Explain to them clearly what you expect of them. Delegate authority and define their job responsibility in terms of results.

   Encourage them to work on their own without running to you for every trivial matter. It is important, however, to monitor progress and spend time with them so that they know you are concerned about them and willing to help out.
3. **Your Secretary:** Train him/her to handle a lot of your C-category activities. Routine handling, sorting of mail, answering standard letters, filing, organising good paper storage and retrieval system, handling and screening phone calls, can be some of the things you can delegate. Behind ever efficient "boss" there is an efficient secretary.
4. **Your Colleagues:** Try to avoid unnecessary interruptions and advice seeking sessions. Agree to meet them at a certain fixed time. Avoid too much pleasantness. Be pleasant yet stick to the point.
5. **Visitors/Clients/Contacts:** It may not always be good to have an open-door policy. As a rule, see people only after prior appointment but be flexible about it, otherwise you might miss important opportunities. Ask your secretary to screen calls/visitors or ask your subordinates to handle routine visitors.

The important rule to remember is that while protecting your time is important to maintain good interpersonal relations with others in the office. ***Your skill as an assertive manager who can balance his/her priorities and yet be good with people is really going to be productive.***

## Six Thinking Hats

Edward DeBono (1985) wrote a wonderful book titled *Six Thinking Hats*. The book was written to help people in business and industry break out of their traditional thinking so that problems and innovations could be approached from a fresh perspective. The ideas work well in the classroom, where we so often get "cookie cutter" type ideas from students. Another advantage of using this technique in the classroom is that it is a non-threatening way to get usually negative-thinking students to think in another direction.

### *How to Use in the Classroom*

Assign each group in the classroom a different hat. Based on the definition of the hat, the group approaches the assignment only from the viewpoint of the hat they have been given.

For our lesson on hunger, the assignments might be thus:

**Group 1: White Hat Thinking**

This group looks only at the facts about hunger in the United States. They are not concerned with "I think" or "I feel" perspectives, only with data.

**Group 2: Red Hat Thinking**

This group is concerned with hunches and feelings about the problem of hunger in the United States. These hunches do not have to be backed by hard data. The members will report their opinions about the problem.

**Group 3: Black Hat Thinking**

This group will report all the reasons why efforts to end hunger in the United States will not work. Their answers will be based on logic from a negative viewpoint.

**Group 4: Yellow Hat Thinking**

This group will report all the reasons that efforts to feed the poor will work. They will focus on the benefits of the efforts to end hunger and the constructive thinking that can make it happen.

**Group 5: Green Hat Thinking**

This group will focus on the innovative ideas that are being considered to end hunger. Their emphasis will be creative, new, and innovative.

## Preparing for the Journey for the Transformation

How do you and your team share responsibilities for the transformation process?

### *Team Action Plan*

1. Meet once a week at a time when it is most productive to review all the projects that are in your plan.
2. Team mates are open and honest about the real progress that has been made.
3. A sensible time-frame for this session should be worked out; encourage short updates, not debate. If issues are to be discussed, arrange to identify resourcing and time-frame issues.
4. Use project planning tools with detailed project plan and an agreed timeline,which is vital for any transformation process.
5. Identify what is to be achieved, with the time schedule. Approach is to get together to see what is happening on a regular basis. Be realistic with the time-frame in the first place.
6. Mapping out a detailed action plan, effectively working through all the actions before they happen, questioning, challenging the assumptions, exploring the 'what ifs' and building a contingency plan.
7. Tasks are allocated, regularly reviewed and absolutely no assumptions are made. Communication across all parts of the project is well maintained and the best-fit people are allocated key roles.
8. If things do go wrong, ensure that the impact on the problem is minimized. Without this attention to detail, when things do go wrong the impact is much more serious.

## Checklist for Managing Time Thieves

Some of the typical time thieves and their remedies are listed below, while the time thieves may be universal, the causes and solutions may be different for each person.

| Time Thief | Possible Remedies |
|---|---|
| 1. Work not getting done in time/piling up. | • Set priorities<br>• Set deadlines<br>• Make realistic time estimates. |
| 2. Trying to handle too much at a time | • Set priorities and tackle tasks accordingly<br>• Do one thing at a time.<br>• Learn to say 'no'<br>• Delegate more. |
| 3. Getting involved in too much detail. | • Delegate more<br>• Don't be a perfectionist all the time. |
| 4. Postponing unpleasant tasks/ procrastination | • Set a time table and stick to it.<br>• Get unpleasant tasks over quickly so that you feel better. |

*Contd.*

| | |
|---|---|
| 5. Insufficient time to think | • Reserve blocks of time for thinking. Allow no interruption. |
| 6. Crisis management/overshooting deadlines. | • Plan better, allow more time. |
| 7. Doing things hastily. | • Take time to get it right the first time<br>• Distinguish between urgent and important. |
| 8. Constant visitors/interruptions. | • Make appointments and see that people stick to it<br>• Block reserve times when no one can interrupt you<br>• Use secretary to interrupt unwanted visitors or delegate them to necessary subordinates<br>• Say 'no' if modify open-door policy<br>• Keep the discussion brief and to the point<br>• Don't do other people's thinking for them. |
| 9. Telephone calls/interruptions | • Secretary to screen and divert calls if necessary<br>• State you will call back when convenient<br>• Keep time – slot for making outgoing calls.<br>• Be brief. Stay uninvolved with all but essentials. |
| 10. Time spent in conversation meetings. | • Decide in advance what you want to achieve when you meet someone. |
| 11. Paperwork/reading. | • Get secretary to sort out into: urgent/ordinary information.<br>• Only ask for written memos and reports when they are really required.<br>• Delegate routine to subordinates<br>• Ask for summaries rather than reports.<br>• Read selectively. |
| 12. Letters/memos to answer/dictate. | • Use telephone more often<br>• Keep a slot for dictating letters.<br>• Use handwritten notes/post its slips.<br>• Delegate routine letter writing.<br>• Ask secretary to answer routine mail. |
| 13. Cluttered desk. | • Set aside half an hour everyday to clear up urgent paper work.<br>• Handle each piece of paper only once.<br>• Aim to clear 90% of paper on your desk everyday. |

| | |
|---|---|
| 14. Lost papers | • Good filing and retrieval system.<br>• Have list of files/file nos typed and keep them near for ready availability. |
| 15. Meetings | • Get yourself taken off committees if your presence is not important or delegate to subordinates.<br>• Avoid calling unnecessary meetings<br>• Set time limit, no repetitions, allow discussion but stick to agenda. |
| 16. Travelling | • Use phone or mail<br>• Delegate more<br>• Ask yourself if really required?<br>• Get the other party to come to you<br>• Plan quickest way<br>• Use a good travel agent<br>• Use journey time productively to catch up on reading, writing letters or analyzing reports. |
| 17. Routine/Trivia | • Concentrate on priorities first<br>• Delegate routine to subordinates.<br>• Keep aside 1/2 hr for routine work. |
| 18. Lack of planning | • Review work every week.<br>• Focus on important results and not merely on activity. |
| 19. Not clear about goals and priorities | • Write down KRA's and priorities.<br>• Discuss priorities with subordinates. |

## Exercise-1: Planning Your Time

Managing and planning your time requires some thought everyday. It is important that you are clear about what you would like to achieve every day.

| | Yes | No |
|---|---|---|
| 1. Do you have a diary noting appointments and meetings for the days ahead? | ___ | ___ |
| 2. Do you spend time everyday thinking about what you would like to work tomorrow? | ___ | ___ |
| 3. Are you clear about your KRA's? | ___ | ___ |
| 4. Do your work-plan in a place that you can see every day? | ___ | ___ |
| 5. Is your work-plan in a place that you can see every day? | ___ | ___ |
| 6. Have you prioritized between things, that you must do and things you could do? | ___ | ___ |

## Guidelines for Scheduling Tasks

1. **Use your Energy Variations to Your Advantage:** Every person has a unique pattern of energy ups and downs. Some people are at their best in early mornings while others work best towards late evenings. It is important to identify your peak energy patterns and work on demanding jobs during those periods. Attack difficult things when you are mentally sharpest.
2. **Break big projects into small components:** When we look at the entire project, it sometimes appears formidable and impossible to achieve. However, chunking it into smaller components and handling each small component separately is easier and more productive. Keep some major projects on your schedule everyday.
3. **Look for signs and symptoms:** If you find yourself slowing down or feeling tired, take a break, very often, working on the same task, gets quite exhausting. While scheduling, see that there are different tasks to be done every day, so that different skills are used and boredom and fatigue do not set in.
4. **Build your day around high-priority activities:** Devote large chunks of peak time to activities which are high on your list of priorities. Low priority items like routine telephones, routine mail, etc., can be scheduled into the extra time.
5. **Keep time for creative work:** Apart from scheduling time for your important priorities and routine activities, see that you keep time aside every day for creative/ development work. This aspect of work/personal development very often tends to get neglected in the normal scheduling of activities.
6. **Keep Time for Emergencies:** Don't overschedule every minute of your day. Keep some time aside as a buffer for emergencies. A too-tight schedule is unproductive at times and it appears as if the schedule is our master instead the other way round.

   ***Time management is only a tool. It must not become a prison which blocks our spontaneity and openness to possibility. Many excellent things in life happen outside the schedule.***

   ***They key here is to balance ACTION with AWARENESS.***

## Exercise-2: Scheduling Time

This exercise will help you to actually plan and schedule for achieving one of your objectives.

**KRA:** ..........................................................................................................

**OBJECTIVE:** ..............................................................................................

**ACTION STEPS** **BY WHEN**

1. ..........................................................................................................
2. ..........................................................................................................

3. ..........................................................................................
4. ..........................................................................................
5. ..........................................................................................
6. ..........................................................................................
7. ..........................................................................................
8. ..........................................................................................
9. ..........................................................................................

(You can do the same for all your other objectives. The dates set for the activities should be transferred to your diary.)

## 7.3 DEVELOP TRUST AND COLLABORATIONS

We usually trust people who respect us and treat us well. In the time of need we don't have to search them they are there for us. Personal or professional relationships are importantly based on trust. Trust is vital for determining the quality and the depth of a relationship. Studies show that lack of trust have a positive correlation with employee turnover, employee performance, productivity, income and profits. It determines how we interact with others.

Many times trust is destroyed due to negative perceptions and behaviours. Trust in such situations needs to be restored by creation of a positive working environment. This may require a well thought out plan of trust building. Many companies give top priority to rebuilding trust as its low levels lead to low morale, decreased turnover, lower productivity, etc.

The role of trust in any organization is critical and crucial. It helps organizations sail through successfully the periods of uncertainty. It is crucial for building effective relationships in working environment.

There is lack of consensus on the definition of the term trust among scholars.

It is defined as a party's willingness to be vulnerable to another party based on the belief that the other party is competent, open, concerned and reliable. It involves three dimensions, i.e., keeping commitments, negotiating honestly and avoid taking excessive advantage.

TRUST plays a key role in ensuring relationships are stronger, cemented and concrete. The following factors can build trust:

**Dependability:** It is an essential factor in relationship. For maintaining trust one has to rely on others completely.

**Stability:** It is a vital factor, for maintaining relationship there should be a consistent approach to each other's needs and expectations without it the relationship dies down.

**Respect:** One must respect people, religion, caste, creed, sex for ensuring mutual trust and greater relationship between individuals. Respecting one another's viewpoint is a powerful tool to build up trust. Negative thinking and negative actions are results of disrespect.

**Equality:** Being just gives a positive impact to relationships. Fairness in relationship leads to long time gains.

**Honesty:** There should be honesty and there is a need to be open and transparent. For constant trust to be built up one must admit mistakes and can give an honourable situation.

**Competency:** Building trust needs competency of people in acknowledging the relationships, this leads to stronger relationships. Competent people can ensure safe and healthy bondage of positive reinforcement of trust.

**Integrity:**. Truthfulness and honesty are the reinforcing powerful impacts on healthy relationship.

**Recognition/Acknowledgement**: When a good job is done, acknowledgement and recognition plays an important part. It gives a feeling of trust and reinforces one to work with full force.

Collaboration is defined as:

1. to work jointly with others or together especially in an intellectual endeavour;
2. to cooperate with or willingly assist an enemy of one's country and especially an occupying force; and
3. to cooperate with an agency or instrumentality with which one is not immediately connected.

TRUST IS EARNED WHEN OTHERS
BELIEVE YOU WILL:
DO WHAT IS RIGHT
DELIVER AS PROMISED
BE CONSISTENT REGARDLESS OF
CIRCUMSTANCES

## How to Build a Collaborative Organisation

In order to succeed in collaborative business world one has to see onself as a curator. In this networked age.

1. **Have an innovation platform**

   Organizations can develop their performance by innovation. Building open and intelligent networks for innovation will enable communities to form around shared problems.

2. **Rethinking the commons**

   All organizations share some of their assets within their business networks or even beyond. Because sharing is about attaining growth, innovation and profits. It is true that companies need to protect critical intellectual property (IP), but at the same time they would not be able to collaborate effectively if their IPs are hidden.

3. **Create a culture of collaboration**

   Organizations cooperate and part information, and direct the organization toward a common goal. For a collaborative workplace relentless communication is needed to make enhanced collaboration a success, sustain the momentum, and then describe the next steps.

4. **Find and strengthen the vanguard (the leading position of a movement, field, or cultural trend, or the people who are foremost in a movement, field, or cultural trend).**

   Core group of leaders who establish the vision and community values, should be strengthened.

## SUMMARY

- **Common causes of failure and mental blocks** – The factors that stop us from achieving success are: Lack of specific goal or choosing wrong goals. Carry the past as burden. Fear of failure (not trying the unknown), blaming others or justifying already made opinion, living in one's own reality/limiting visions and beliefs. Using short-cut approach to long goals, allowing energy sucking emotions to drain out energy (not forgiving attitude), not learning from mistakes.
- Seven important things necessary to plan your time: 1: Set an aim, 2: Set your objectives, 3: Work out key result areas. (KRA), 4: Planning of time, 5: Time blocks, 6: Recording of time, 7: Take stock of time.
- **Goals must be SMART – S**: Specific, **M:** Measureable, **A:** Achievable, **R:** Result-Oriented **T:** Time bound. Goals can be short-term up to a year, mid-term up to 3 years and long term up to 5 years. Goals can also be longer than 5 years. Such long-term goals are called "purpose of life". Goals are often easily achievable, if they are broken in smaller ones.
- TRUST plays a key role in ensuring relationships are stronger, cemented and concrete. The following factors can build trust: dependability, stability, respect, equality, honesty, competency, integrity, recognition/acknowledgement.
- Trust is earned when others believe you will: Do what is right, deliver as promised, be consistent regardless of circumstances.
- The level of trust in a company is measured by the level of customer focus, 2. Level of transparency, 3. Level of collaboration.
- Developing a strategy that builds trust.
- Trust is not built overnight. It takes time but can be broken in an instant as a result of a single bad decision. The strategy needs to be focused on: 1. Build trust into your values and beliefs, 2. open and honest communication, 3. keep your word.

## QUESTIONS

### I. Explain in Brief

1. Experts agree we have entered a "collaborative economy". Explain.
2. The keyword to remember while setting objectives is SMART!
3. "Without trust, you may be able to coordinate, you may even be able to cooperate, but to truly collaborate with team members, customers, suppliers, and other stakeholders, you must have trust." Comment.
4. What do you understand by respect, as an important factor in developing trust?
5. "Trust is a key to social collaboration." Explain.
6. How do you measure the level of trust in your company?

### II. Answer the following questions

1. According to a Gallup survey, the best partnerships are almost all characterized by mutual trust, while in poor partnerships, less than 3% strongly agree that they trust each other. In most situations mutual interest is not enough to override mutual distrust. Comment.
2. List down five techniques for managing time thieves and their remedies.
3. What is time log? What are its benefits? What is IDU?
4. Prepare a time log and mention various activities conducted by you.

# MODULE 3
# ORGANISATION

# 8 UNIT

# Managing Change

*The secret to successful change lies beyond the visible and busy activities that surround change. Successful change, at its core, is rooted in something much simpler: How to facilitate change with one person.*

**— ADKAR – Jeffery M. Hiatt**

## Learning Objectives

- Recognizing Sources of Change
- Identifying the Demand for Change
- Structure, Technology, and People as Targets of Organizational Change
- Effective Change Management
- Skills for Managing Change
- Eight Steps to Transforming an Organization
- Proactive and Reactive Responses to Change
- Change Managers
- Transition Management Terms

*"If winter comes can spring be far behind"*

**— P.B. Shelley**

*"Change" is eternity.*

## STORY OF AN EAGLE AND ITS STRUGGLE FOR SURVIVAL

The eagle has the longest lifespan of its species.

It can live up to 70 years
But to reach this age, the eagle must make a hard decision
In its 40s.

Its long and flexible talons can no longer grab prey which serves as food.

Its long and sharp beak becomes bent.

Its old-aged and heavy wings, due to their thick feathers, are stuck to its chest and make it difficult to fly.

Then, the eagle is left with only two options: die or go through a painful process of change which lasts for 150 days.

The process requires that the eagle flies to a mountain top and sits on its nest.

There the eagle knocks its beak against a rock until it plucks it out.

After plucking it out, the eagle will wait for a new beak to grow and then it will pluck out its talons.

When its new talons grow, the eagle starts plucking its old-aged feathers.

And after five months, the eagle takes its famous flight of rebirth and lives for 30 more years.

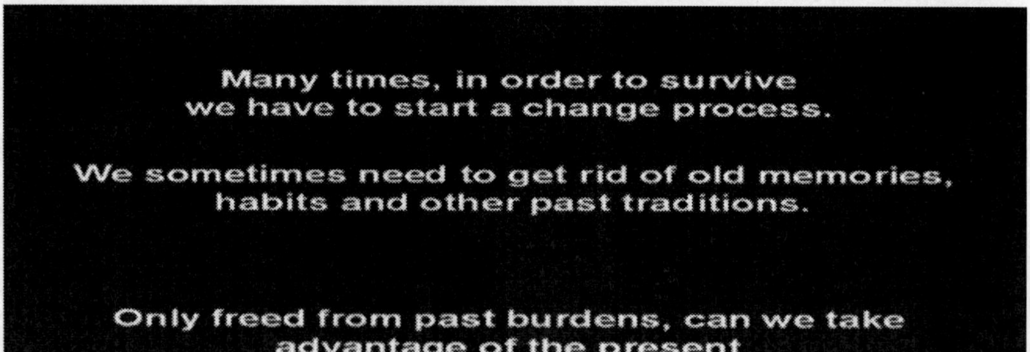


If you don't change you will become extinct.

To deal effectively with increasing rates of change, one needs to understand the underlying causes:

- If you find you are resisting change, ask yourself why…
- Write down any change you like – and plan for them.
- Seek out people who welcome change, and be their ally.
- Respond positively to uncertainty rather than avoiding change.
- Cultivate curiosity: try to become the best-informed person you know.
- Master use new information technology – do not avoid it.
- Bear in mind that technology is changing more quickly.

Successful organizations understand the predictable impact of change on the people and manage the process so that they can create the competitive advantage. Organizations can only change in a successful manner when business strategies are promoted by their employees. For this a stronger competitive team, company's sales and profitability increase, and provides better customer service and therefore repeat customers are needed.

All areas of the business world are experiencing increased need for change. They are experiencing increased complexity, globalization, demographic changes, technological and scientific improvements, new values set by employees, customers and other stakeholders.

The above factors lead to increased competition, in fact today we use the expression "hyper competition". The change process:

Is more: See, feel, change than it's: Analyze, think, change.

## 8.1 RECOGNIZE SOURCES OF CHANGE

Changes can come from many directions: from superiors or subordinates within organizations from personal initiative, and from outside.

- Always respond positively to changes outside your organization.
- Take suggestions on change projects and encourage subordinates.
- Look at both short-term and long-term contexts when analyzing.
- Be innovative and have a niche in the area of competition.

### Planning Change

If managers do not know where they are going, they cannot change to get there. If they do not know where they are they cannot start on the right road.

- Assess your organization's strengths and weaknesses realistically.
- Change corporate culture through individuals.

## 8.2 IDENTIFYING THE DEMAND FOR CHANGE

Success centres on agreeable customers: dissatisfied customers will find other suppliers.

- Attempt to satisfy the needs of both employees and customers.
- Appreciate customers who complain: their complaint should be to restructure and change.
- Remember that quality of products depends on quality of process.
- Use objective measures of customers reaction.

### Selecting Essential Change

Change programmes must be fully comprehensive if they are to last.
Prioritize change in key areas, then focus attention more widely.

- Be clear about the purpose of any change you plan to make.
- Focus on limited practices that really count.
- Plan solid and an integrated change programme.

### Evaluating Complexities

To plan and manage change effectively, one needs to make realistic estimate of its complexities and whom will it affect – directly or indirectly.

- Try proposed changes on small scale first.
- If it takes complex reasoning to justify change, abandon it.
- Use critical path analysis to help plan tasks.

Those affected by change will vary in their attitudes. It needs carefully drawn plan whom to involve in setting the change and in what ways to involve.

## 8.3 STRUCTURE, TECHNOLOGY, AND PEOPLE AS TARGETS OF ORGANIZATIONAL CHANGE

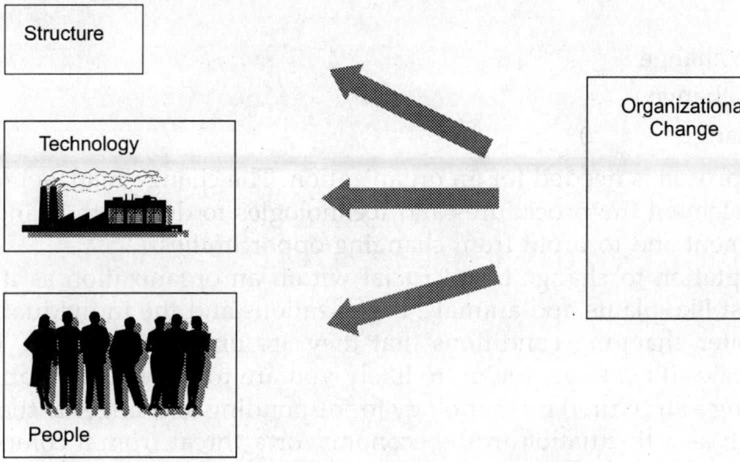


## 8.4 EFFECTIVE CHANGE MANAGEMENT REQUIRES TWO PERSPECTIVES

Individual perspective – How does one person make a change successfully?
Organizational perspective – What tools do we have to help individuals make changes successfully.

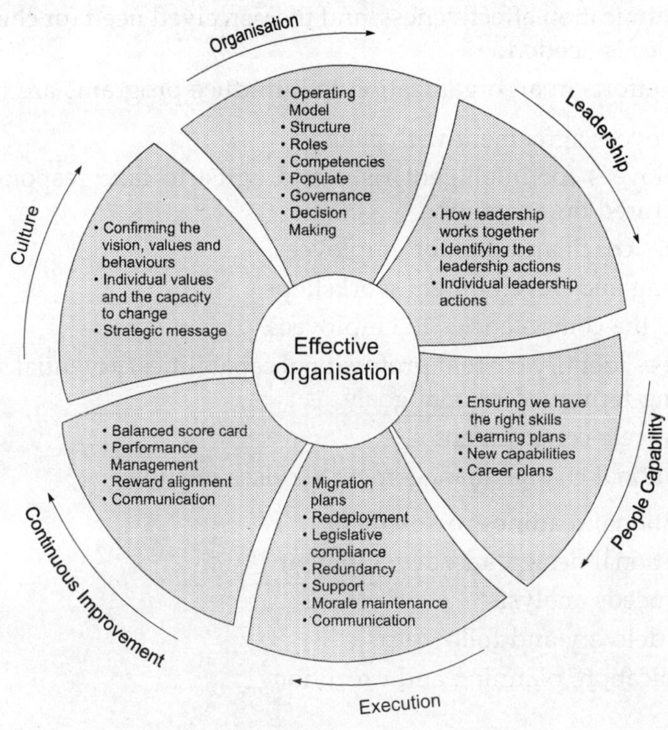

Change management is a systematic approach to deal with change, both from the perspective of an organization and on the individual level. Three different aspects include:

- Adapting to change
- Controlling change
- Effecting change

A proactive approach is needed for an organization. The change management needs to define and implement the procedures and technologies to deal with changes in the business environment and to profit from changing opportunities.

Successful adaptation to change is as crucial within an organization as it is in the natural world. Just like plants and animals, organizations and the individuals in them inevitably encounter changing conditions that they are unable to control. The more effectively you deal with change, the more likely you are to thrive. Adaptation might involve establishing a structured methodology for responding to changes in the business environment (such as a fluctuation in the economy, or a threat from a competitor) or establishing coping mechanisms for responding to changes in the workplace (such as new policies, or technologies).

Change management processes may include creative marketing to enable communication between change audiences, but also deep social understanding about leadership styles and group dynamics. Organizational change management brings into line groups' expectations, communicates, integrates teams and manages people training. For this performance metrics, such as financial results, operational efficiency, leadership commitment, communication effectiveness, and the perceived need for change to design appropriate strategies is needed.

As restructuring efforts in an organization to introduce programs are that:

1. Support employees agreement with change.
2. Counsel employees for intelligent risks and agree to take responsibility in the newly restructured organization.
3. Help managers coach and mentor employees.
4. Career planning and development workshops.
5. Communicate the competencies to employees.
6. Help employees identify current professional capabilities, potential skill gaps, and short- and long-term professional goals.
7. Validate a concrete commitment

   ERP organizational change management services include:

   - Organizational readiness assessment
   - Organizational design and development
   - Training needs analysis
   - Training delivery and follow-up
   - Communication, planning and execution

## 8.5 SKILLS FOR MANAGING CHANGE

1. Political skills
   Diplomacy, ability to engage a large group
2. Personal skills
   Communicating, listening, understanding different viewpoints
3. Analytical skills
   Workflow operations, systems analysis, financial analysis
4. Systems skills
   Technological and how people, industries and economies interact
5. Business skills
   Understanding how the business works so you can understand how it will change

## 8.6 EIGHT STEPS TO TRANSFORMING AN ORGANIZATION

1. Establishing a sense of urgency
2. Forming a powerful guiding coalition
3. Creating a vision
4. Communicating the vision
5. Empowering others to act on the vision
6. Planning for and creating short-term wins

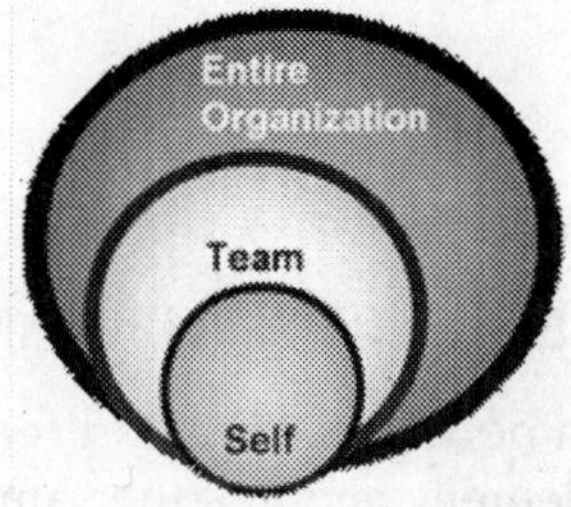

7. Consolidating improvements and producing still more change
8. Institutionalizing new approaches

## 8.7 PROACTIVE AND REACTIVE RESPONSES TO CHANGE

Proactive change involves actively attempting to make alterations to the workplace and its practices. Companies that take a proactive approach to change often try to avoid a potential future threat or to capitalize on a potential future opportunity. Reactive change occurs when an organization makes changes in its practices after some threat or opportunity has already occurred. As an example of the difference, assume that a hotel executive learns about the increase in the number of Americans who want to travel with their pets. The hotel executive creates a plan to reserve certain rooms in many hotel locations for travellers with pets and to advertise this new amenity, even before travellers begin asking about such accommodations. This would be a proactive response to change because it was made in anticipation of customer demand. However, a reactive approach to change would occur if hotel executives had waited to enact such a change until many hotel managers had received repeated requests from guests to accommodate their pets and were denied rooms.

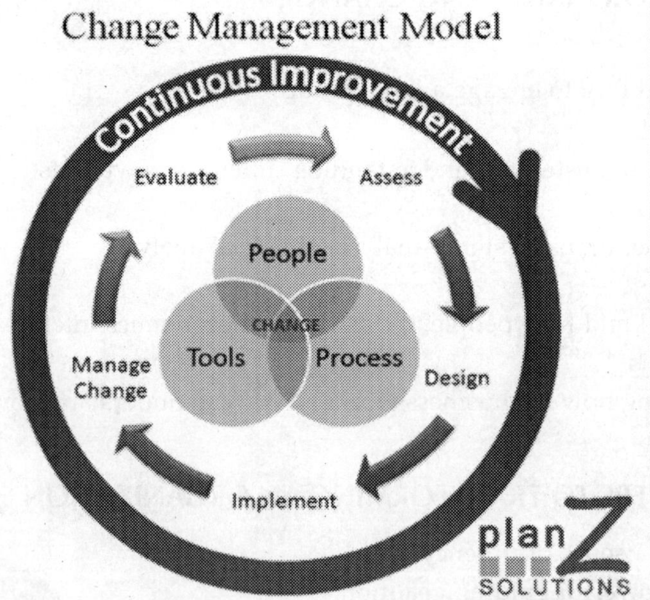


## 8.8 CHANGE MANAGERS

In both proactive and reactive responses to change and in every model of change, one element remains the same: the need for change managers. There are different types of change managers and their roles encompass a variety of duties. Managers may have the responsibility for change that is not ever formally dictated or outlined, or a person or group may be specifically chosen to enact or facilitate change. Described below are two formal ways in which change managers can be identified: transition management teams and change agents. Some responsibilities of change managers are described below.

## 8.9 TRANSITION MANAGEMENT TEAMS

In some organizations that are experiencing change, a specific group of managers is chosen to coordinate change throughout an organization. This transition management team typically consists of eight to twelve people whose full-time responsibilities are to manage and facilitate the change process in the organization. Transition management teams are responsible not only for the structural and procedural changes that occur, but also for managing emotions and resistance to change. These teams typically report to the chief executive officer of the company on a regular basis.

Transition management teams do the day-to-day work involved in change management, and they are not simply another layer of management between top management and line employees. Furthermore, they are not the planning committee; these teams do not develop the plans for the change, they only facilitate the change that is being enacted. Neither are they responsible for determining when and where change is needed, or how it will be brought about. Instead, they manage changes that have been identified and implemented by senior management. Finally, these teams are not permanent. They exist only while the organization is in flux, and they are dissolved once the company has successfully changed.

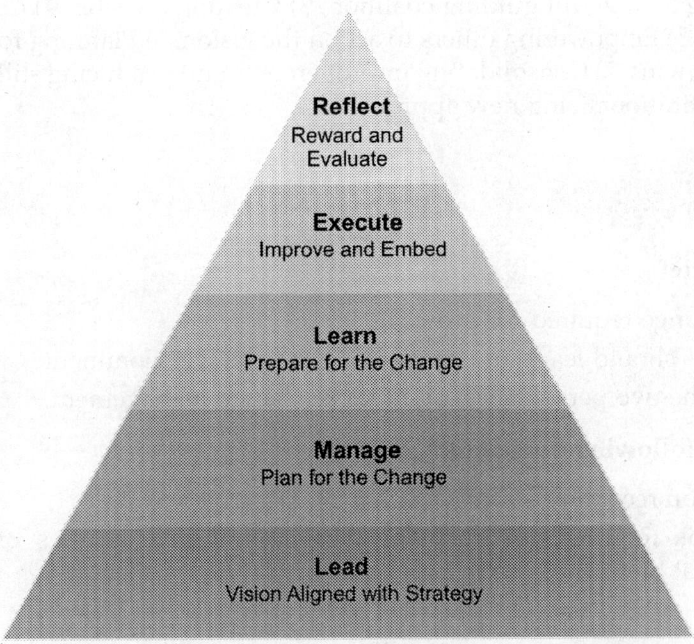

## SUMMARY


- The secret to successful change lies beyond the visible and busy activities that surround change. Successful change, at its core, is rooted in something much simpler: How to facilitate change with one person.
- Organizational change is successful only when employees 'buy into' and support new business strategies. Their backing is essential to building stronger teams, becoming more competitive, increasing the company's sales and profitability, and providing better customer service and therefore returning customers.
- Changes can come from many directions: from superiors or subordinates within organizations, from personal initiative, and from outside.
- Change management is a systematic approach to deal with change, both from the perspective of an organization and on the individual level. A somewhat ambiguous term, change management has at least three different aspects, including: adapting to change, controlling change, and effecting change.
- A proactive approach to dealing with change is at the core of all three aspects. For an organization, change management means defining and implementing procedures and/or technologies to deal with changes in the business environment and to profit from changing opportunities.
- Successful adaptation to change is as crucial within an organization as it is in the natural world. Just like plants and animals, organizations and the individuals in them inevitably encounter changing conditions that they are powerless to control.
- Eight steps to transforming an organization: 1) Establishing a sense of urgency, 2) Forming a powerful guiding coalition, 3) Creating a vision, 4) Communicating the vision, 5) Empowering others to act on the vision, 6) Planning for and creating short-term wins, 7) Consolidating improvements and producing still more change, and 8) Institutionalizing new approaches


## QUESTIONS

### I. Explain in Brief

1. Why is change required for growth?
2. Companies should learn and prepare for the change. Comment.
3. Describe the two perspectives of effective change management.

### II. Answer the following questions

1. How do you recognize sources of change. Describe.
2. "Change is required for survival. "Explain with examples of personal or professional life.

3. What do you understand by organizational change? What are the influencing factors of change? Explain with relevant examples.
4. What are the different types of changes which occur in an organisation? Why are changes essential? What are the influencing factors of change? Explain with relevant examples.

# 9

UNIT

# Creativity in Organization

*"Imagination is the beginning of creation. You (first) imagine what you desire; you (then) will what you imagine, and at last, you create what you will".*

**— George Bernard Shaw**

## Learning Objectives

- Art of Thinking and Creative Visualization
- How to Achieve Your Goals by Thinking
- What is Creativity?
- Creativity! What do I need to Have?
- Elements of the Creative Process
- Characteristics of Creative People
- Basic Steps for Effective Creative Visualization
- Aids and Blocks to Creative Thinking

## Problem Solving: The Creative Way

The Japanese have a great liking for fresh fish. But the waters close to Japan have not held many fish for decades. So, to feed the Japanese population, fishing boats got bigger and went farther than ever. The farther the fishermen went, the longer it took to bring back the fish. The longer it took them to bring back the fish, the stale they grew.

The fish were not fresh and the Japanese did not like the taste. To solve this problem, fishing companies installed freezers on their boats. They would catch the fish and freeze them at sea. Freezers allowed the boats to go farther and stay longer. However, the Japanese could taste the difference between fresh and frozen fish. And they did not like the taste of frozen fish. The frozen fish brought a lower price. So, fishing companies installed fish tanks. They would catch the fish and stuff them in the tanks, fin to fin. After a little hashing around, the fish stopped moving. They were tired and dull, but alive.

Unfortunately, the Japanese could still taste the difference. Because the fish did not move for days, they lost their fresh-fish taste. The Japanese preferred the lively taste of fresh fish, not sluggish fish. The fishing industry faced an impending crisis! But today, it has got over that crisis and has emerged as one of the most important trades in that country!

1. How did Japanese fishing companies solve this problem?
2. How do they get fresh-tasting fish to Japan?

## 9.1 THE ART OF THINKING AND CREATIVE VISUALIZATION

The art of thinking is the greatest art of all, for "as a man thinketh in his heart, so is he". The quality of thought generated within you will help you in creativity and innovation and will help in building your future.

Thinking helps a man to control his own self and be independent in his decisions. He uses his intellect to control his own mind. He verifies the truth and builds his life upon it.

The power of thoughts has no limitation He sets no limitations on the power of thoughts he recognizes that big thinking precedes big achievement.

He creates mental picture of his goals, then works to make those pictures become realities.

He knows that everything starts with an idea and that the creative power of thought is the greatest power in the universe.

He sees with the "single eye" of intense concentration, seeking facts just as a powerful searchlight penetrates the darkness.

He keeps an open mind, observing, analyzing, considering, questioning looking for the hidden key which will unlock the problem.

He thinks of his mind as a factory and gives it the raw material, the facts and data, from which ideas are fashioned.

He thinks both objectively and subjectively: he gathers mental power both from the world without and the limit mind within.

He uses the magic power of his subconscious mind, commanding it to come up with the ideas while he sleeps: he knows that thought, like a tree, grows night and day.

He studies the laws of cause and effect and strives to work in harmony with them.

## 9.2 HOW TO ACHIEVE YOUR GOALS BY THINKING

Realistic, measurable and time-bound goals, make a great start. You must not leave your goal alone up in the air, as it were, but you must surround it with a web, from getting side-tracked, but constantly reinforces your motivation. Here are some guideposts:

1. Make a list of your goals and pin it up in such a place where you can read them daily (next to your mirror, or on your wall or desk).
2. Regularly believe in your goals. How much are they important in your life? How much you have to work achieve them?
3. Exploit your thoughts. This will help and give you the power to project your vision to create a better future. Imagine your feelings and happiness on achieving your goal? Then imagine your feelings not achieving their goal. Picture your feelings of dissatisfaction.
4. Be realistic on the challenges you will have to face: Exploit your inner and external obstacles. Think how you would overcome them.
5. Pen down the steps and actions will you take. Remember that the longest journey starts with one small step.
6. What helps are at hand to aid you in achieving your goal? What people and other resources can you call upon?
7. Talk your goals with the professionals of your field to get a realistic outlook.

## 9.3 WHAT IS CREATIVITY?

Creativity is the ability to produce new and original ideas and things. Innovation makes the idea practical and usable. The innovative activity in any business enterprise depends on the creative contributions of its members. It also depends on how the organization taps the creativity of its members.

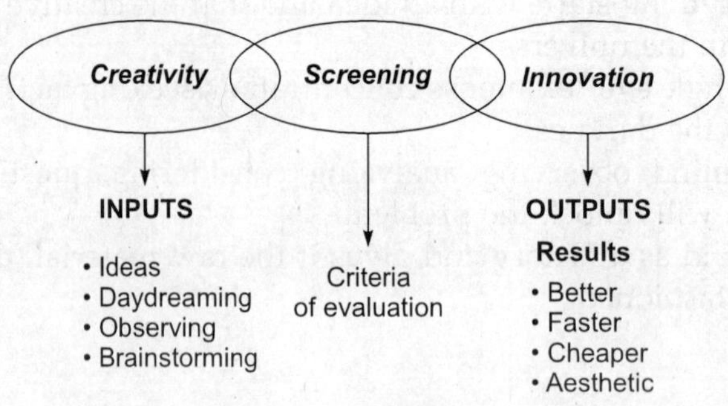

## CREATIVITY IS.........!

Creativity is the ability to formulate unique approaches to problem solving and decision-making.

— Fred Luthans

- Unexpected association of ideas
- Mental action due to insights

- Inability to create something new
- An attitude in mind

Creativity is all about generating of more and more ideas

## 9.4 CREATIVITY! WHAT DO I NEED TO HAVE?

- Sensitivity to problem

- Fluency of thinking

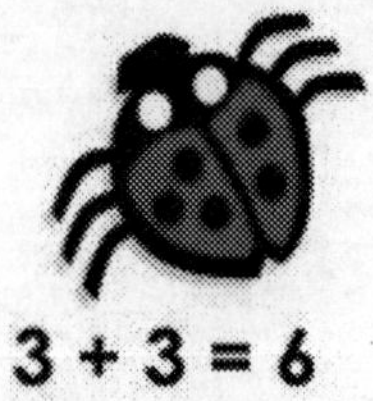


- Flexibility of thinking

- Originality

- Redefinition

- Elaboration

Creative thinking is a skill, it can be developed and improved if one practises by bits and pieces……..!

## 9.5 ELEMENTS OF THE CREATIVE PROCESS

The overall creative process has the following elements:

I. Incubation
I. Illumination
III. Verification

### *I. Incubation*

Incubation requires partially turning off the process of conservative thinking. This involves holding of or keeping in check the normal tendency to criticize and judge the value of what is taking place in the flow of thought. A lot of free thinking without any constraints should be encouraged in the stage.

### *II. Illumination*

If incubation is successful, there follows the moment of illumination, which often is like a flash of lightning. The sudden insight of people is linked to a mystical experience. People who have experienced illumination have generally expressed as "Ah-ha" effect.

### *III. Verification*

The final stage of creative process is verification. Here the mind returns to the pursuit of more conventional patterns and works out the creative solution in detail, polishes it in a more final form, and chooses some test or method of proof so that the idea becomes creditable and accepted.

### *Challenge the Impossible*

It is not unusual to find the birth of a great idea in the minds and words of someone ignorant of the specialized field. Perhaps they don't know enough to know that it can't be done.

**You don't have to be an expert.**

- The bell was invented by an astronomer – **Edmund Halley**
- The pneumatic tyre was invented by a veterinarian – **John Dunlop**
- The safety razor was invented by a salesman – **K.C. Gillette**.
- The vaccum cleaner was invented by a bridge builder – **Hubert Booth.**

## 9.6 CHARACTERISTICS OF CREATIVE PEOPLE

- Optimistic about future
- Open to alternatives
- Daydreamers
- Highly curious and observant
- Independent thinkers
- Good at turning innovative ideas into practical solutions
- Take action and make things happen
- Adventurous with multiple interest

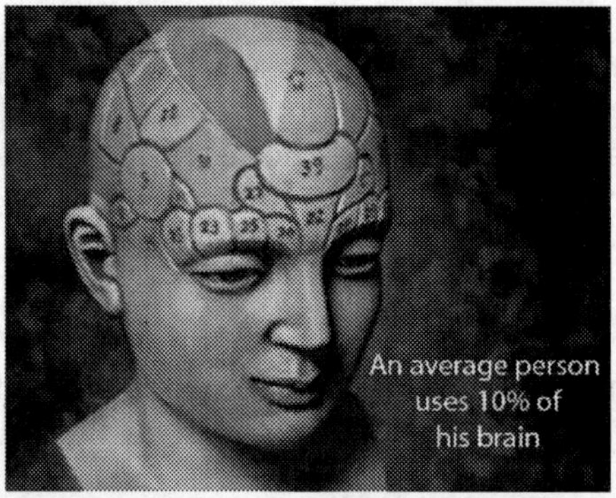


## 9.7 BASIC STEPS FOR EFFECTIVE CREATIVE VISUALIZATION

### Innovate not Emulate

#### *1. Position and Prioritize your Goal*

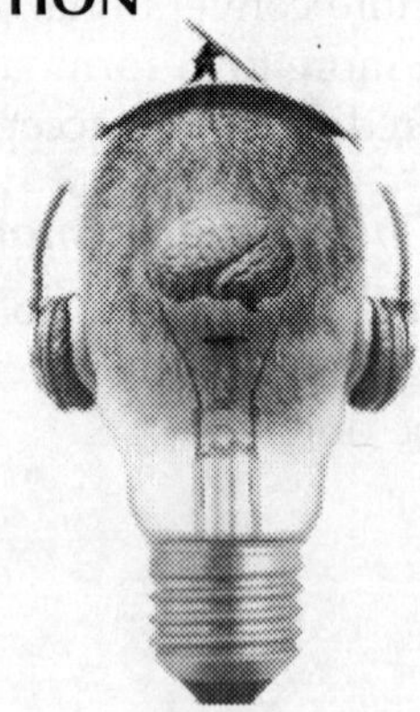

Make up your mind on something you would like to achieve, and look yourself in it. Decide on something you would like to have, work towards, realize, or create. It can be on any level. At first, choose goals which are believable and achievable. Being realistic will help you in dealing with it positively and maximize your feelings for achieving for success. This way you are learning creative visualization. Difficult or challenging problems can be achieved by practice.

### 2. Create a Clear Idea or Picture

Develop a mental picture of the idea or the object or situation as you want it to be. Visualize the idea in a pictorial way in the way it is existing presently and later the way you want it to be and keep on adding the details

Include as many details as you can. You may wish to make an actual physical picture of it as well, by making a treasure map (described later). This is an optional step, not at all necessary, but often helpful (and fun).

### 3. Keep it as a Focal Point

Visualize the idea in your mind regularly throughout the day during leisure times. This way it will become successfully integrated part of your life. Do not strive to hard and put excessive energy into it but keep a focus on it in a light, gentle away.

### 4. Impart it with Positive Energy

Think your goals in a positive encouraging way. Generate positive affirmations to yourself. See yourself receiving or achieving it. Suspend any worries or skepticism you may have, and practise you are desiring something which is real and achievable.

Continuous yearning to achieve will lead you to a process till you achieve your goal. Human has the longing for change and growth so remember not to change the goals before they are realized. Utilize your energy and keep an interest on it. Make it a zeal of your life.

If you feel that you want to relook on your goals as per the changing scenario, be sure to acknowledge that to yourself. Be clear on the new goals. Reorient the cycle on the previous to the new.

Acknowledge yourself on achieving your goals. Often after success on achieving things we desire and visualize and we forget to acknowledge it and appreciate ourselves. Thank the universe and give a pat on the back, and reward yourself for fulfilling your requests.

***A frame can limit your potential. The choice is yours....!***

## 9.8 AIDS TO CREATIVE THINKING

- Encourage creativity and put a value to it.
- Encourage a variety of experience.
- Reading and exposure on other viewpoints.

- Problem solving, quizzes, calm breathing
- Problem solving quizzes, brain teasers
- Ask searching question limits
- Use checklists like the one given blow:

  S – Substitute, subtract, streamline......

  C – Combine, combine, condense change......

  A – Add, amplify, adjust......

  M – Multiply, mix, modify......

  P – Perforate, purify, pull apart .........

  E – Elaborate, reverse, reduce ..........

  R – Rearrange, reverse, reduce ..........

- Structure the problem so that it is well understood.
- Generate as many new ideas as possible by thinking together in a group.
- During brainstorming do not criticize or evaluate ideas.
- Random assumptions of any two thoughts of ideas.
- Challenge assumptions and ask questions which test the limits.
- Fantasize impossible solution to the problem to radically alter familiar trains of thought.
- Draw analogies from nature.
- Use analogies and descriptions.
- Having generated a large number of ideas or solutions. Identify the ones with the greatest potential by some sort of an assessment and selection procedure.

## 9.9 THE BLOCKS TO CREATIVE THINKING

Barriers to creativity

- Be as practical as you can
- Follow all the rules
- That is not logical
- I am not paid to think
- Someone else may already be doing it
- To make a mistake is wrong
- If I share my ideas someone else may steal

(a) **PERCEPTUAL Blocks:** These result from our mental set or predisposition towards seeing the problem or situation in the way we want to or are used to:

(i) Difficulty in solving the problem
(ii) Imposition of self-restrictions
(iii) Inability to see the problem from varied forms of reference
(iv) Mental set
(v) Difficulty to solve the problem
(vi) Saturation of senses
(vii) Failure to utilize all sensory inputs, etc.

**(b) INTELLECTUAL Blocks:** These arise from our inability to restructure the problem and/or our existing knowledge.
(i) Preference for verbal forms
(ii) Inadequate use of problem solving strategies
(iii) Lack of correct, relevant information
(iv) Inability to identify hidden assumptions
(v) Need for closure – forcing incomplete/incorrect inferences, etc.

**(c) EMOTIONAL Blocks:** These frustrate our problem solving efforts and common source of fear. They have their origin in the childhood experience and are usually irrational.
(i) Fear of making a mistake, of taking risks of failing
(ii) Fear of criticism, of being changed of insecurity
(iii) Inability to tolerate ambiguity
(iv) Preference for judging rather than generating ideas
(v) Inability to incubate
(vi) Difficulty in visualization, etc.

**(d) CULTURAL Blocks:** These blocks derive their sustenance from over-anxiety to conform:
(i) Fantasizing is a waste of time
(ii) Work and play cannot mix.
(iii) Reason is rational. Intuition is irrational
(iv) Scientific thinking is the answer, etc.

**(e) ENVIRONMENTAL Blocks:** These blocks rise outside ourselves and are results of the environment about us:
(i) Compulsion towards conformity
(ii) Boss's idea is the best
(iii) Over-reliance on expertise
(iv) Frequent distractions, etc.

## CASE STUDY

### Eureka! Lessons from the Ranch

Creativity is a term that evolves an image of warm and fuzzy artistic expression. Many organizations are realizing that creativity, in the form of cold, hard, innovative that is related to business results, is a necessity for competing in crowded and turbulent markets. Linking creativity to business performance is a special niche of a unique place called the Eureka Ranch.

The Eureka Ranch is an operation started by Doug Hall, a former marketing executive for Procter and Gamble. What sets Eureka Ranch apart from other creativity training programmes is that it is based on careful statistical analysis of companies that generated business ideas and inventions. Through research on clients such as Pepsi, Nike, the Ranch has identified some key factors related to creativity that lead to a business payoff.

Factors that fall under the general categories of marketing and creativity are summarised.

### Marketing

***Benefit.*** The product or service has to have an obvious benefit. It has to be something that cuts through the information overload of customers.

***Credibility.*** The benefit has to be believable due to, for example, the company's reputation, guarantee, or testimonials.

***Uniqueness.*** The product or service needs to be different from what is already available.

### Creativity

***Related and Unrelated Stimuli.*** Ideas can be generated by things that are related and converge as well as by things that are unrelated and diverge.

***Diversity in Thinking.*** Mixing together people who are diverse in their ways of thinking and problem solving, not necessarily diverse in demographics, can lead to more and varied ideas.

***Fear Elimination.*** Fear can be eliminated if creativity and effective implementation of new ideas are to be successful.

### *Answer the following Questions*

1. A creativity programme at Eureka Ranch costs a lot of many for the organization. How can a creative training programme help the company to grow? Do you think the training is worth it?
2. Creativity is something that sounds like a positive and desirable characteristic. Are these situations in which you would not want employees to be creative. Describe these situations.

3. Consider each of the key factors promoted by Eureka Ranch. How could you apply them in efforts in your own organization to generate ideas for products or services that will add to the bottom line?

## SUMMARY

- Creativity is the ability to produce new and original ideas and things. Innovation makes the idea practical and usable.
- Creativity is "new" idea in combination of old elements. It is your ability to combine ideas in a unique way.
- The overall creative process has four elements: preparation, incubation, illumination, and verification.
- Creative people are optimistic, open to alternatives, daydreamers, highly curious and observant, independent thinkers, good at turning innovative ideas into practical solutions, take action and make things happen, and adventurous with multiple interests.
- Basic steps for effective creative visualization are innovating not emulating, positioning and prioritizingone's goal, creating a clear idea or picture, keeping it as a focal point,and imparting it with positive energy.
- Creative people and companies aren't always easy to deal with, but an experienced, knowledgeable manager can smoothen the process and get consistently high quality results.
- Creative people can be said to have: a particular style, originality, competence, experience, determination, flexibility and positive outlook.

## QUESTIONS

### I. Explain in Brief

1. What is creativity? Why is creativity needed?
2. Name the four elements of creative process.
3. Are you creative? What are characteristics you possess that make you creative?
4. Name four blocks to creativity.
5. Why is change needed for growth?
6. Name two sides of the brain and its functions for learning

### II. Answer the following questions

1. Explain what happens during incubation and illumination of the elements of creative process.
2. Explain the basic steps for effective creative visualization.

3. How does intellectual block create a block to creative thinking.
4. Explain "INNOVATE NOT EMULATE" with examples.
5. How do you recognize sources of change. Describe?
6. "Change is needed for survival". Explain with examples from personal or professional life.

## ASSIGNMENT

1. Make a list of activities you had undertaken which helped to take out your creative potential.

## PROJECTS

1. Make groups of 4-5 students. Make a project by doing a survey of 5 schools in your area which are using different techniques to imbibe learning through creativity.
2. Collect different articles on innovations done by people (use newspaper, magazines etc.) and make a file.
3. Inventions and innovations have made the world what it is today. Make a list of 10 scientists and their inventions in details.

# 10 UNIT Business Communication

*"It is the recipient who communicates. The so called communication, the person who emits the communication, does not communicate. He utters. Unless there is someone who hears, there is no communication. There is only noise."*

**— Peter Drunker**

## Learning Objectives

- Communication in Organizations
- Listening: A Tool of Communication
- Delivery of Speech
- Public Speaking
- Business Etiquette
- Need for Interpersonal Communication

### Motivation is the Key

A company had every thing going for it. Lot of orders, latest machinery, trained staff and good workers. Still the company could not scale heights. There seemed to be a non-vibrant feel about the company. Something was missing.

The company was manufacturing auto components, had a good R&D and developing new products. It also had a few competitors.

The manufacturers's son joined the company after completing his MBA. He observed that the company was successful, the works at various departments were running smoothly but still the employees were not happy. He found this as something strange and started talking to the employees. He found something surprising.

The factory had only a few competitors and hence the employees could not change their job even if they desired. They were dependent on the factory for their livelihood and felt helpless sometimes. This led to the downbeat mood in the factory.

The young man took the task to himself to put life into the factory. He devised training modules on time management, personality development, stress management, computer awareness. He conducted a satisfaction survey and understood most of the employees wanted to know more about computers. The employees were also sent to external training programmes. He also started inter-departmental games and activities. This helped employees to come together and form teams. This also encouraged better interpersonal relations. A plan was prepared for the future and all the employees were given a role to play.

**Answer the Questions**

1. Send a congratulation letter to the owner's young son for his achievement.
2. Write down an action plan prepared by the owner's son for putting life into the company.
3. Design a communication strategy for the employees of this company.

## BUSINESS COMMUNICATION

Have you ever thought about the most important activity at your workplace? The likelihood is that the answer will be communication. It is an activity which consumes that most of the time of an individual. It is thus important to make communication effective so that it takes less time of the receiver.

Herta A. Murphy and Herbert W. Hildebrandt wrote in their book *Effective Business Communications*. "Knowing the content of the functional areas of business is important, but to give life to those ideas—in meetings or in solo presentations—demands an effective oral presentation."

Communication is always purposeful. The purpose of oral communication is aimed to bring forth immediate and desired response. Written communication is to facilitate informed decisions and actions. Thus, while the objective of oral communication is to earn listeners, written is to earn a reader.

Communication consists of:

- Speaking skills
  - Speech/lectures
  - Conversation
  - Counselling
- Writing skills
- Presentation/briefing skills
- Actions

### Communication and the Four Management Functions

- Planning
  - Gather information
  - Write memos, letters, reports
  - Meet to formulate plans

- Organizing
  - Gather info about the state of organization
  - Communicate new structure
- Directing
  - Communicate plan and strategy *(how and why)*
  - Motivate employees
- Controlling
  - Feedback, "How are we doing?"

## 10.1 COMMUNICATION IN ORGANIZATIONS

Without proper communication nothing much would happen in an organization. Good communication oils the wheels of activity in an organization and facilitates action. The paperless office does not mean that oral communication is or will be more important than 'written'.

Even an 'e-mail' has to be written. All the 'files' attached are also written.

Good business writing does not just happen. It needs a lot of thought and effort. When a sentence does not make sense or a point fails to get across or a description confuses rather than clarifies – it is because of inadequate thought.

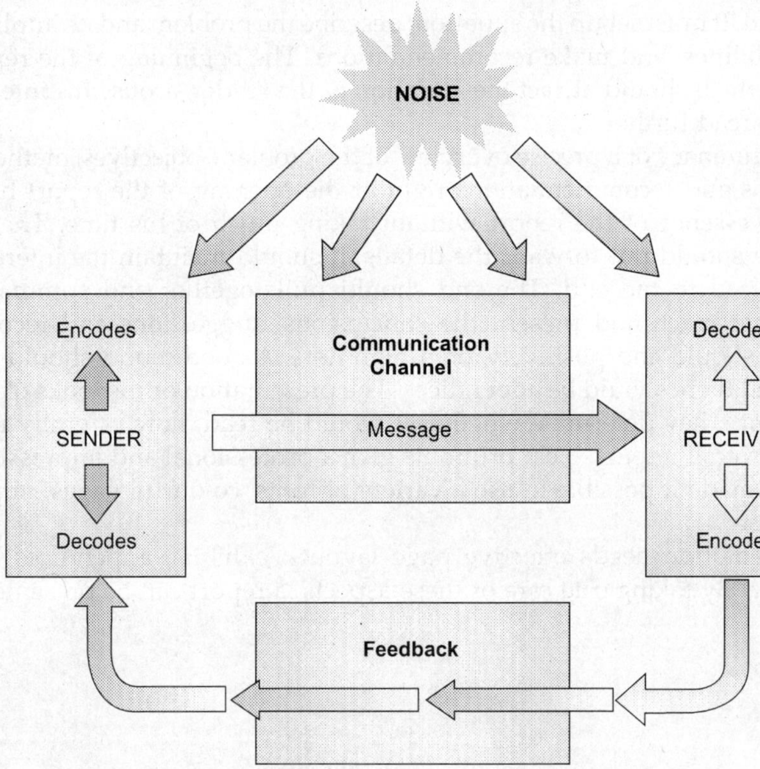

## Reader's Perspective

Understand the readers – who they are; how they think; how they view the topic; what their experiences with the issue are; what their expectations are and how they would react to your comments. The reader's perspective will help in setting clear objectives and also give the report a proper shape. The report should be early to read and to understand. For this it needs to be well structured, in language understandable by the reader, precise and clear. A good report helps contribute to the image of the writer and the organization.

**Writing good reports is important to enhance the effectiveness of office communication and create the right impression**

Business writing depends on its purpose. For example, the purpose of a memo is to set up meeting (internally). A letter is meant to respond to a query (externally), while a report is aimed to present a case, which may be a problem, an analysis or a solution.

What is important is to communicate effectively. This is difficult to achieve. An effective written communication involves better structure language, tone, style jargon and spelling. But it is also a matter of consciousness, interest and practice. Business writing is not subject to certain rules.

In case of oral communication, there is less time to think, but you can still clear the doubts.

A report is presented in a logical manner, and it usually, consists of a beginning, a middle and an end. It must set up the situation; describe the problem and its implications; review the possibilities; and make recommendations. The beginning of the report has an introduction which should attract the attention of the reader, arouse his interest and create a desire to read further.

An executive summary or a precise overview of the problem, objectives, methodology, analysis, solutions and recommendations right at the opening of the report helps the reader grasp the essence of the report without taking much of his time. The middle part of the report should put forward the details, it should maintain the interest, gain acceptance and lead to the end. The end should pull together and summarise the contents. It should reach and present the conclusions, suggestions and recommend further action. It should end positively, on a high note. A good report should not end here. After the end there should be appendices. The presentation or the looks of a report are also important. They determine whether it would be read, how carefully it would be read and the overall impact. Neat printouts give a professional and impressive look. Computers have made it possible to use a variety of fonts, colourful pages, impressive tables and graphs.

Effective presentation needs effective page layouts: exhibits, appendices and the overall packaging. By taking due care of these aspects, a report can be presented.

| Method of Communication | Factors to Consider |
|---|---|
| DETAILED REPORT<br>The whole plan, including the planning process and change in projects. | • Documentation should be clearly laid out and backed up with the analysis information.<br>• Only superiors and key team members should receive the plan in its entirety. |
| OUTLINE REPORT<br>A one-page outline of the strategy; extracts of the plan relevant to the stakeholder. | • This report should be personalized for stakeholders, stressing factors that will have direct effect on them.<br>• Any other parties who might benefit from the information can receive an outline report. |
| PRESENTATION<br>A summary of strategy and implementation plan using visual aids. | • Presentation material must look professional and convincing.<br>• Team members, internal stakeholder and manager's peer group should be invited. |
| NEWSLETTERS<br>Updates on the process of the strategy and plan. | • Reports should be brief and circulated to team members and stakeholders regularly.<br>• Preparing newsletters can be delegated to a key team member. |
| LETTERS AND E-MAILS<br>Specific extracts from the strategy and plan, or updates on change in projects. | • These are quick to produce and useful for keeping a large number of people updated.<br>• Stakeholders with a limited interest in the strategy need only minimal information. |

## The Seven C's of Communication

To make communication effective, we have to observe a few rules. In so far as written communication is concerned without elaborating on it, it may be observed that effective writing comprises the seven C's.

1. Clarity
2. Completeness
3. Concreteness
4. Conciseness
5. Consideration
6. Correctness
7. Courtesy

1. Clarity
   - It means accurately
   - Interpretation, ideas, experience are associated with words
   - Precise, concrete and familiar words should be chosen
   - Build effective sentences and paragraphs

2. Completeness
    - Complete the messages which are to be communicated
    - Help in better job of building goodwill.
    - Can help avert costly lawsuits that may result if important information is missing.
    - Communication that seems less important can be remarkably important if the information they contain is complete and effective.
3. Concreteness

    It means being specific, definite and vivid rather than vague and general.

    *Guidelines for composing concrete, convincing messages*
    - Use facts and figures
    - Position action in your verbs
    - Select intense, image-building words
4. Conciseness
    - If the messages are concise time is saved so is the expense for both sender and receiver
    - Eradicate worldly terminologies
    - Contain only appropriate material
    - Evade needless duplication
5. Consideration

    It means preparing every message with the receiver in mind, try to put yourself in their place

    *Specific ways to indicate consideration are:*
    - Focus on "you" instead of "I" and "We"
    - Show audience benefit or interest in the receiver
    - Emphasize positive, pleasant facts
6. Correctness
    - Proper grammar, punctuation, and spelling
    - Use accurate level of language
    - Check accurateness of figures, facts, and words
    - Keep suitable writing process
7. Courtesy
    - It involves perspective of others and their feelings.
    - Politeness gives respect and concern for others
    - A courteous tone
    - Be tactful, thoughtful and appreciative
    - Use expressions showing respect
    - Select non-discriminatory words

Certain rules are applicable to verbal communication only. They are:

- In verbal communication, always wait for your chance to speak, i.e., never interrupt the speaker.
- Always try to maintain eye-contact with the speaker.
- The tone and pitch should reflect respect for listener/audience.

## Four S's of Effective Communication

1. Shortness.
2. Simplicity.
3. Strength.
4. Sincerity.

### *Shortness*

- Long sentences lead to frequent wandering of attention.
- Lack of shortness makes listening an extremely painful exercise.
- Flooding messages with high sounding words does not create an impact

### *Simplicity*

- Simplicity both in the usage of words and ideas reveals a clarity in the thinking process.
- Simpler the message, easier it is to comprehend.
- Important to elicit an effective response from the audience.

### *Strength*

- The strength of a message originates from the credibility of the sender.
- If the sender himself believes in a message that he is about to transmit, there is bound to be strength and conviction in whatever he states.

***Sincerity***

- A sincere approach to an issue is evident to the receiver.
- If the sender is genuine, it will be reflected in the manner in which he communicates.
- If there is an element of deceit involved in the interaction or on the part of the sender, a keen and observant receiver will sense the make-believe situation.

## Need for Communication in Management

Every organisation, small to the multinational, needs an effective communication system to enable it to function and flourish. In an organisation, communication is a means to:

- increase employees' job performance and effectiveness by updating their knowledge;
- promote employees' sense of belonging and commitment;
- effect changes smoothly;
- motivate and create a sense of identification with the organsiation's goals;
- inform and convince employees about decisions and the reasons behind them;
- develop employees' understanding their roles and future growth opportunities in the organisation; and
- empower employees with information on development and activities.

Therefore, a dynamic communication system is vital for the health of an organisation. The atmosphere of understanding and good-will would prevail in the workplace. If there is a continuous sharing of ideas and interactive meetings between the management and workers. The decision-making has to be transparent for the employees to understand it and accept and implement them.

The following three advantages accentuate the need for communication in management.

**Creates a sense of belonging**. If the employees have an understanding of their roles and career paths in the organisation they will feel part of the organisation.

**Resolves disputes.** All disputes within an organization are due to miscommunication which leads to huge losses of time, money and human relations.

**Develops sense of understanding of situation.** An effective communication helps in making the people perceive the things that are happening around them. Through communication, employees not only "imagine" but also "witness" realities as part of the total business scenario.

Communication has become an important component of an organisation in the changing business environment of multinational competition and globalization. Like the functional areas of organization such as production, marketing and finance, communication too is shaping into a distinct area, i.e., corporate communication.

A integrated form for all communication activities is done by different areas such a marketing, public relations, good image building and developing human capital. Communication speaks about the organisation outside and within it in a single voice.

Attention should be paid to communication as an important tool of successful management.

The modern age is also known as the age of information– telephone, radio, television, communication satellite, computers and so on. It is an era of knowledge management and values, sharing of information with others helps in empowering self and others.

All employees and workers are considered to be the human component of business. Their attitudes, interest and welfare constitute a major part of management to achieve targeted goals and objectives. Hence, there has to be a live channel of communication between the employees and the management.

**Corporate etiquette.** Top corporate executives are increasingly sensitized about the importance of knowing etiquettes. They realize that management executives should learn the rules of etiquette. These include:

- How to greet
- How to shake hands
- How to dress for success
- How to present cards
- How to listen
- How to converse with seniors/ladies and clients

The training, which is a part of communication skills, develops corporate etiquette to be observed and practised for success in international/multinational/or big national ventures. Good business manners speak of the culture of the organisation.

Changing organisations need to have an effective communication system and also equip the managers with these skills.

Communication is a powerful tool in business and maximum time is spent by managers either speaking or writing to their colleagues, their seniors, their juniors, or their clients. Success of a manager depends largely on his ability to communicate to his colleagues such objectives as what has to be done, and why it is to be done.

To be able to do this, a manager has to devote his time to:

- Receive and interpret information from other managers and departments.
- Send information to other department managers.
- Pass information and suggestions on new plans/ projects upwards to senior/top management.
- Send information downloads.
- Develop a positive attitude.

To a large extent, the success of an organisation depends on the atmosphere in which there is a free flow of information – upward, downward and horizontal. A manager has to give instructions and guidelines, supervise and monitor and do periodic reporting. He has to involve with all the employees from the highest to the lowest levels by allowing every level of worker/employee to suggest/offer ideas, views and experiences. Effective information system across the organization can only be transferred by communication.

An analyzed by Henry Mintzberg, a manager needs effective communication skills to perform the following interrelated roles:

- Interpersonal
- Informational
- Decisional

**Interpersonal role**. For effective operative organization's system and to maintain proper relationships within the organization and with the outside clients, suppliers and other functionaries interpersonal skills are required and it ensures effective, internal systems run smoothly. For example, human resource functions within an organisation require a manager has to inspire confidence, win support and guide workers

**Informational role.** All the internal information systems such as stock control, personnel functions, financial systems, and quality control should be made effective by proper transfer of information. This will help in rectifying the problems and shortcomings and help in remedial actions to be taken. Timely monitoring and instructing can help in proper maintenance of product, and service standards can be ensured.

**Decisional role.** Decision-making is based on receiving and interpreting all relevant and necessary information. Decisions may turn out to be unrealistic if not provided with necessary information, relevant and latest information correctly and accurately should be given to be able to take decisions and act rationally, fairly and to the satisfaction of all concerned.

## Key Principles to Effective Internal Organizational Communication

Internal communication is essential for every organisation, and this is an essential tool for bonding the organization, improving the morale, counselling and promoting open door policy and reducing grievances. The root cause of most of the problems is due to ineffective communication within the organization. Internal communication should have good delivery mechanism to be clear and understandable and supported by action. Communication creates trust, relationship, control and delegation. It ensures knowledge sharing by supporting and driving the long-term and the short-term objectives for better productivity in the organization.

1. Communication should be proactive rather than reactive: An organisation should have high degree of communication for proper flow of information to reach to each and every employee. This helps in better grievance handling.
2. Effective internal communication starts with effective skills in communication, including basic skills in sensing, listening, speaking, questioning and sharing feedback.
3. A key ingredient to developing effective communications in any organization is each person taking responsibility to ask for information and suggestion when and how someone could communicate more effectively.

## Effective Internal Communication requires both Downward and Upward Communication Channels

Communication which flows from the top of the organizational hierarchy to the lower hierarchical level (from the superiors to subordinates) is known as downward communication.

Downward communication can be directly face to face or it may include notices, circulars, instructions, orders, letters, memos, bulletins, handbooks, annual reports, announcements and group meetings. Communication from superior to subordinate can be through written memorandums, orders, job descriptions, etc.

### *Downward Communication*

1. Ensure every employee understands the organization's mission, vision, values statements, goals and strategies.
2. Personnel policies and employee handbook to all employees.
3. Develop a basic set of procedures and standard operating manual.
4. Ensure every employee understands his role and has a copy of it.
5. Regular hold top management employee interface meetings at least once a quarter even if there's nothing pressing to share.
6. Departmental meetings to review the major accomplishments, concerns, etc.
7. Communicate and celebrate accomplishments, so that the employees perceive what's important, gives them a sense of direction and fulfilment.
8. Build informal channels of communication, understand what people are looking for.

### *Upward Communication*

1. Ensure all superiors meet face to face every month with their employees to discuss their concerns.
2. Ask for feedback. To seek information of any reported problem or suggestion, etc.
3. Act on feedback from others. Implement on the reported problem or suggestion, etc.
4. Respect the "grapevine. It's probably one of the most prevalent and reliable forms of communication."

### *Common Causes of Problems in Internal Communication*

1. If I know it, then everyone must know it. It is the most common mistake that management thinks that if they are aware of some information, then everyone else is, too. Usually, people are not aware unless management makes a deliberate attempt to carefully convey information.
2. I have passed it to some people and it will percolate down. Even when the intentions are to let everyone have the information, normally the information is passed to some people assuming that it will cascade down the line.
3. Did you hear what I meant for you to hear. Quite a few times, the information that is conveyed is conveyed with the conveyer's point of view and the background of data available to him. Quite easy for the receiver of the information to interpret it in a different manner going by his perception. Therefore, it is important to convey a vital information clearly and uniformly across the board. Moreover, it would also help to supply background to that information to avoid confusion.
4. The times are tough and we may dishearten everyone else by sharing it: this could be the most easy block to communication. But no matter what, bad news travels faster. In the absence of a clear message from the management, it could lead to rumour mongering and different assumptions. This leads to chaos, confusion and could ultimately result in low morale of employees.
5. So what is there to talk about. There could be situations when there is nothing much to share in the words, no fire and no problems. Management could feel that they do not need to communicate on anything but this is far from true. At any stage, maintaining open channel of communications pay in building relationship with all employees.

## Communication is Information

### *Other Sources of Communication*

- E-mail
  The instantaneous transmission of messages on computers that are linked together.
- Instant messaging (IM)
  Interactive, real-time communication that takes place among computer users logged on to the computer network at the same time.
- Voice mail
  The system digitizes the spoken massage, transmits it over the network, and stores it on a disk for the receiver to retrieve later.
- Fax
  Machines allow transmission of documents containing both text and graphics over ordinary telephone lines.
- Electronic data interchange (EDI)
  A way to exchange documents (invoices or purchase orders) with vendors, suppliers, and customers using direct, computer-to-computer networks.
- Teleconferencing
  Can be conferred simultaneously using telephone or e-mail group communications software.
- Videoconferencing
  A simultaneous conference during which meeting participants in different locations can see each other over video screens.
- Intranets
  An organization's communication network that uses the Internet but is accessible only to the employees.

- Extranets

  An organization's communication network that uses the Internet and allows the authorized users in the organization to communicate with certain outsiders such as customers or vendors.
- Wireless communications
  - Allow users to send and receive information from anywhere as signals sent without a direct physical connection to a hard-wired network system.
- Knowledge management
  - Cultivating a learning culture in which employees systematically gather knowledge and share it through computer-based networks and community of interest teams.

## Videoconferencing

It is a technology and a medium of communication that enables people to meet and collaborate through sight and sound medium. They can be located anywhere in the world. Videoconferencing allows two or more locations that can be used for interaction by the way of video and audio transmissions simultaneously. Videoconferencing is a need of the hour.

Video conferencing is conducted

- When live chat is needed.
- View of presentation on the other side of the conversation is crutial.
- People involved in a discussion cannot physically come to the same location.
- There is no time or budget.

Planning to ensure a great virtual meeting.

- Arrive before time to see the arrangements are in order and the equipment is working properly.
- Dress up appropriately for confidence and appropriate look.
- Understand the profile of person interacting in videoconferencing.
- Appoint an organizer. A videoconferencing can go out of control due to the Internet traffic.

- Do not move. Adjust your seating to ensure your visibility on the other side.
- Be loud and clear.
- Look straight for proper eye-to-eye contact.
- Be at ease.
- Have a clear visual medium. Make sure that the presentation materials such as agendas, charts, PowerPoint presentations, etc., are made in suitable fonts.
- Rehearse. Have a brief practice session.
- Have an emergency plan, back-up computer in case of any problem.
- Exercise patience. Wait for people on the other side to go offline and then sign out.

### Communication Skills

| Communicating | Listening |
|---|---|
| When communicating are you able to attract attention by your voice, style, body language? | When communicating are you able to attend without feeling distracted? |
| Is your communication clear precise, and easy to understand? | Are you able to follow without breaking the link of your thoughts? |
| Is your communication making an impression on listener's heart? | Are you able to reflect upon what has been communicated? |
| Can others summarize what you have said? | Are you able to summarize what has been said? |
| Is your communication unbiased towards others? | Are you able to empathise with the speaker with an open mind? |

## 10.2 LISTENING: A TOOL OF COMMUNICATION

To listen is to pay attention to what someone is saying. It is a deliberate act of attentively hearing a person speak.

Let us picture a class on Business Communications. During the course of lecture, a girl in the last row is busy writing on the notebook without even once looking at you, a student is doing silent reading from a book. In the middle row, a half-asleep boy struggles to keep his eyes half-open. In the front two rows, the students are paying attention to what you have been teaching. These students have been also taking notes from time-to-time. When asked, questions the last row girl, the silent reader and the dozing boy have no idea as to what your question is about. The front row students are ready with answers and answer you correctly.

## Why is it So?

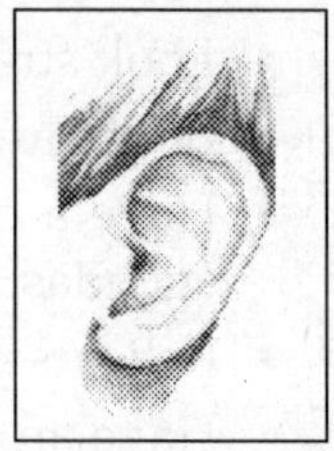

They all have been together subjected to the same lecture. Then, how some students have missed you to a large extent. It seems as if they were not present in your lecture. But how could that be?

You were loud enough to reach everyone. Clear enough to be understood. And logically ordered in your conversation.

The fact is that, those who failed to answer you, had only heard you, but did not listen to your exposition of the variables and their relationships. They heard you, for they could not fail to hear you. They were not deaf. But their minds did not absorb what you spoke. They did not listen to your lecture. They just heard it.

## Listen, Listen, Listen

Listening is important. An employee who listens properly can efficiently pass the instructions.

Good listeners are impressive for a company and make it a more effective organization. They have better rapport with others, they better understand the needs of others in meetings and conferences.

Hearing or listening has marked differences.. We hear lazily but we listen to the messages clearly. Study has revealed that 75% times people are not listening which means that people listen only 25-30% times. Also people listen if they want to listen. Hearing involves our ears, but listening involves our ears, eyes, heart and mind. It is rightly said that listening is an essential component of communication.

Some hurdles are there which we have to overcome to be a good listener. Steps should be taken to conquer these hurdles. They are:

- Accentuate the positive
- Listen to comprehend, not prove false
- Focus your thought
- Concentrate on the content and take notes
- Restrain the desire to suspend
- Review and appraise
- Good listening is demanding, requiring omission of personal bias as well as external distractions. With a positive attitude and active involvement through personal summaries and evaluation, you can have a fruitful listening experience.

## Meaning

- ➢ Listening is a vital component of communication. It is determined by the extent to which listening and comprehension take place in the course of an interaction.

- Important aid of communication
- Promotes awareness about the organization
- Helps to make better policies
- Pacifies the complaining employees
- Is important for the success of the open-door policy
- Helps to spot sensitive areas

## Advantages of Listening

- Helps to know the organization
- Helps to make better policies
- Modifies the complaining employees
- It is important for the success of the open-door policy
- Helps to spot sensitive areas before they become explosive
- It creates a positive environment and motivates the communicator.

### *Stages of Listening*

- *Hear* – listening is more than reaction to sounds
- *Focus on Message* – block out distractions
- *Comprehend/Interpret* – attach meaning
- *Analyze/Evaluate* – view nothing in isolation
- *Respond* – Feedback
- *Remember*
    - Repetition
    - Mnemonics (mind memory)
    - Take notes

## Process of Listening

Listening is an integrated process. It consists of the following phases:

- Undivided attention
- Hearing
- Understanding
- Interpreting
- Evaluating
- Empathizing
- Conceptualizing

### *Undivided Attention*

Listening requires a certain frame of mind. Attentively hearing the message is the root of listening and requires concentration without distractions, no interference of thoughts, ideas not related to the message. The listener, in this phase, enters into the focus of conscious consideration and discriminates between thoughts, ideas or images that belong to his/her focus of attention.

### *Hearing*

Attentiveness of the listener is with familiarity with the sound of words and the spoken rhythm of speech. For hearing attentively pitch, voice modulation, and quality of sound are equally important.

### *Understanding*

Understanding what is said, this requires us to hear words and understand their intended meaning. For understanding what you say, your body movements, gestures, facial expressions, eye movements and variations in tone and pitch of voice are also noticed.

### *Interpreting*

Interpreting is how you comprehend what is said by understanding it. While comprehending the message our own knowledge and experience are also taken into account.

### *Evaluating*

Communication involves our critical ability to evaluate and value of what is heard and discussed. Our feeling of interest and sense of worth closely follow the argument or theme of communication which is shared.

### *Empathizing*

While listening the message is seen as a speaker's point of view and still you let the other person speak what he wants to say.

### *Conceptualizing*

Lastly, the listener incorporates what he has heard and creates his ideas by editing with his own knowledge and experience. Therefore, listening is a requisite for perfect communication.

## Deterrents to the Listening Process

Listening can get easily affected by some internal or external factors and work as barriers to good listening.

### *Lack of Concentration*

There may be several reasons for not concentrating. This can be due to external factors such as noise coming from outside the room or music played nearby. We can shut off the external factors, but interference can be within the listener's mind. One has to overcome internal factors which can be internal or personal.

**Our brain causes interference in our concentration.** We talk 120 to 125 words per minute and our brain is capable of receiving 500 to 600 words per minute. So this causes gaps between the words and the gap tends to be filled up by other thoughts and images.

### *Attention to Speaker than the Speech*

Sometimes listening is distracted because we are more attracted to the personality of the speaker or manner of delivery than his/her message.

### *Listening Too Closely*

The purpose of listening is to grasp the meaning of what is said. So, our attention is lost in details when we try to remember whatever is said by the speaker. Each and every word cannot be retained by our memory.

### *Halo Effect*

Sometimes the impression of the listener and not the intrinsic worth of the message affects the validity of the speaker. This is because the speaker is trusted, is honest and held in high esteem. This creates a halo effect in business where the buyers go by the trusted seller than their own judgment of the product quality.

### *Complexes*

Oral interaction may be prevented by either lack of confidence or a sense of superiority between persons differently positioned. If a sense of inferiority prevails the person will fail to take initiative or involve himself/herself in conversation/dialogue or any other form of communication. Some persons may feel humiliated to listen or talk to. This may block effective listening.

### *Blocked and Overconfident Mind*

One's curiosity to know things also affects listening. Some persons think they know everything so their mind refuses to listen to other sources. Some persons feel too satisfied with their own ways and don't want to change. Eagerness/enthusiasm is needed to enter into a dialogue.

### *Deprived Retention*

During oral communication specially two-way communication, the sequence of thought and conveying it is important. One has to remember the structure of thought, sequence of ideas for comprehension. The structure of thoughts must be received and retained by the listener to understand arguments. If the listener fails to hear what was said before and cannot relate with the previous one the whole conversation is lost.

### *Premature Listening*

Sometimes, pre-judging the intention of the speaker, picking up a few shreds of information, own assumption, distorts the real intended meaning of communication. This distorted interpretation is when the listener does not listen patiently until the speaker completes his/her arguments.

### Selective Listening

This is when some part of the discussion is lost or missed and partially received. Exchange of information is partially received. In this listener listens and focuses his attention and gives his point of view on some aspects of the conversation. The rest of the communication is missed.

### Cognitive Barrier

At times, the listener does not accept or respond to statements which are communicated due to old belief and knowledge. He wants to escape from interpreting and restructuring it. This may lead to several analyses of a new message. Due to cognitive conflict, the listener does not use the skill, ability and flexibility of rational thinking to promote in effective oral communication. This skill to move from one mental frame to another is necessary for exchange of ideas, beliefs and feelings.

### Language Barrier

The language of communication should be simple and in a medium which is understood and spoken by both speaker and listener. The accent of the language in use should be clear and understandable.

### Lack of Interest

If an individual is not interested in the topic being discussed, no matter how hard he tries he would not able to concentrate on that topic.

### Ego

It is the biggest communication block which the individual erects as he is not willing to accept the viewpoint of the other person.

The reason could be a subordinate or in opposition which does not satisfy or match the ego of the receiver.

### Involved with the Self

If the listener is too busy with his own thoughts or is individual with himself there are bound to be discrepancies in understanding of the intention of the spoken word.

In this two-tier process, either the receiver is listening to his own self, or is trying to decipher the intention of the sender.

### Imperfect Past

Lack of self-confidence that may occur due to some uncontrolled factors in the present environment of the listener or, because of some past event.

A lot of time is wasted on thinking about the past which may have been problematic or imperfect.

### *Fear*

Developing fear or being scared of an individual/situation can close the mind to whatever is forthcoming.

The element of fear blocks the mind of the participant to the ongoing activities.

### *Preconceived Ideas and Notions*

To enter into any kind of interaction with the preconceived ideas, notions and thoughts can have negative impact on the listening process.

### *The Familiarity Trap*

Quite often our knowledge of a particular topic can close our mind to the ongoing communication. This is what is normally referred as the familiarity trap.

### *Stress – Double Connection*

Sometimes we can have both positive as well as negative impact on some listeners.

## IMPROVING THE LISTENING ABILITY

### Characterstics of Poor and Good Listeners

A good listener helps and encourages the speaker by his/her expression and body language. This makes the speaker feel that the listener is interested and can understand what is being discussed or spoken.

Poor listeners irritate and upset the speaker. They also show disinterest and interrupt what is being discussed by putting in 'yes', 'but' and 'ifs', while listening.

**Checklist to help us identify our behaviour and listening problem.**

Please tick mark those statements that you believe describe you as a listener. You can separately list down areas of your listening problem. There is no human behavioural problem, which cannot be overcome by consciously working on it.

### Exercise-1 Listening Problem Checklist

(*Source:* Michael Osborn and Suzanne Osborn, *Public Speaking,* Indian adaptation (Delhi: Bizterntra, R004), p. 61.)

1. I believe listening is automatic, not a learned behaviour.
2. I stop listening when the speech is uninteresting.
3. I find it hard to listen to ideas about which I feel strongly.
4. I react emotionally to some words.
5. I am easily distracted by noise when someone is speaking.
6. I don't like to listen to speakers who are not experts.
7. I find some people too objectionable to listen to.
8. I nod off when someone talks in a monotone.

9. I can be so dazzled by a glib presentation that I don't listen critically.
10. I don't like to listen to messages that contradict my values.
11. I think of counter-arguments during the speech when I disagree with a speaker.
12. I know so much on some topics that I don't need to hear more.
13. I believe a speaker and not the listener is responsible for effective communication.
14. I find it hard to listen when I have a lot on my mind.
15. I stop listening when a subject is difficult.
16. I can look like I'm listening when I am not.
17. I listen only for facts and ignore the rest of the message.
18. I try to write down everything a lecturer says.
19. I let a speaker's appearance determine how well I listen.
20. I often jump to conclusions before I have listened to all of a message.

## How to Listen

If as a friend, supervisor, or subordinate, you can do more than to be a good listener, you still will have done a lot.

1. Hearing is not listening
2. Listening must take place at two levels:
   - The level of words
   - The level of feeling
3. You can't listen to others unless you are listening to yourself
4. Exploration is one thing. Argumentation another
5. Just avoiding interrupting would be a great step forward
6. People need to listen to each other.

**Listening to another says:**

- "You are important too"
- "You are worthy of my time and my attention"
- " You are really an interesting person"
- " You are ok"

### *Listening Skills*

Something should be conscious of:

- Eye contact
- Affection and attention can be better expressed by eyes
- Posture

We speak with our bodies.

## Types of Listening

### 1. PASSIVE LISTENING

- The physical presence but mental absence of the listener can be defined as passive listening or hearing.
- Heard but not really absorbed.
- In passive listening there is no invasion on the thought process.
- This kind of listening is commonly found in classroom situations when the teacher is seen to reprimand the students for their physical presence but mental absence in the class.

### 2. MARGINAL LISTENING

- Provision of too much information can lead to information load. As a result of this listening again tends to get hampered.
- The most common factor which can be attributed to this kind of listening is fatigue or boredom.
- The respondent erects a barrier through which he allows information to seep only in bits and pieces.
- As a result partial or marginal information can be retrieved if the situation demands or the need so arises.

### 3. PROJECTIVE LISTENING

- In projective listening the responses of the receiver are in a state of "restful alertness".
- Each individual has within him a frame of reference in which he tries to adopt the perspective of the interactant.
- Projective listening is an attempt by the receiver at viewing the world.
- It is the combination of micro and macro. Where micro – would be narrow perspective of receiver, and macro – is the broader perspective presented by the sender.

### 4. SENSITIVE LISTENING

- It lies on the ability of the receiver to match his perception with those of the sender.
- It is a myth to presume that words always mean the same to everyone.

### 5. ACTIVE LISTENING

- The most important type of listening.
- The receiver absorbs all that is being said and also makes an attempt to verify all that he has been listening to.
- When combined with sensitive listening it can result in the best kind of listening.
- Active listening is not solely a product of capabilities of the listener. Part of the onus for making the receiver respond actively to the proceedings lies on the shoulders of the speaker.

## Essentials for Good Listening

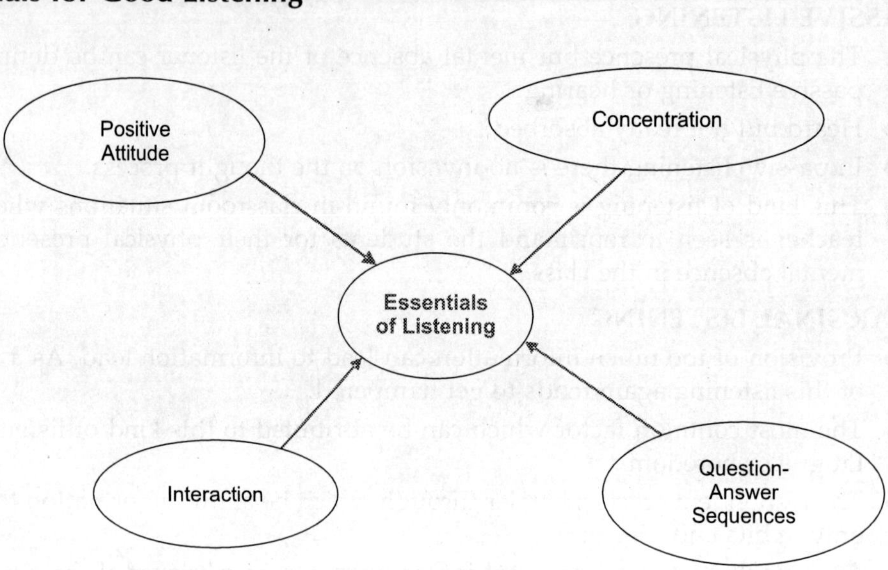


## Guidelines for Listening Improvement

Good listening is important for successful communication. The words spoken should be carefully heard, understood, interpreted and registered in the listener's memory.

Effective communication requires effective speaking and effective listening. Our words should be spoken correctly and clearly.

## Guidelines for Listeners

When someone is speaking, let him complete the dialogue then start your conversation Talking and listening is not possible at the same time. In a class if a teacher is giving a lecture, students are expected to stop talking so that he or she can be heard and understood.

### *Speak Less Listen More*

The purpose of listening is to know from others what they want to tell you or what you need to know from other sources. Listening is an act where knowledge and experience of others are taken advantage of. Listening encourages learning more than speaking.

### *Concentrate on Main Points*

Listen for the main points and concentrate on the main idea of conversation.

### *Examine the Body Language*

Listen to how things are being said by listening the feelings, attitudes and emotional reactions of the speaker from body clues.

### *Focus on the Speaker*

Make the speaker feel that you are interested in what he is saying. Face the speaker and make eye contact.

### *Do not be Part of the Speaker*

Personal impressions or prejudice of the listener should not be affected by the speaker's status, fame, charm or other physical and personal attributes. This will separate the person from his/her ideas.

### *Listen Attentively*

Give attention to what is not said, this will help to tell you a lot about the person's feelings and attitude regarding what is being talked.

Listen, without any disturbance in your mind or intervention of any thoughts. Enjoy the purity, the beauty and the magic of the sound.

### *Listen Intelligently*

Learn to listen intelligently, and try understanding the others' point of view. Understand the idea by concentrating what you are listening.

### *Avoid Emotional Contact*

Objectively express yourself and do not be emotionally charged, or excited by the speaker's words.

### *Understand and then Conclude*

Do not jump to hasty conclusions Let the speaker conclude his own point of view and then interpret.

### *Empathize with the Speaker*

Listen from the speaker's point-of-view by keeping in mind his/her situation, background constraints/limitations or special needs and emotional state.

### *Respect the Speaker as a Person*

Do not hurt, ignore or insult the speaker and listen to him and respect his self-esteem.

### *Listen with Open Mind*

New information can be absorbed by an open mind. A prejudiced mind to certain ideas affects the attitude of effective listening.

### *Develop a Rich Vocabulary*

The capability to listen and understand will be more if you develop a rich vocabulary. The more you know the better is your understanding and listening capacity.

These points will give great value to improving his/her effectiveness as a communicator.

### How to Become an Effective Listener

- Concentrate on what a person is saying rather than how he looks
- Repeat the key areas to yourself
- Try to relate the speaker's remarks to your personal background and experience.
- Do not let your mind wander away from what the speaker is saying
- Listen with positive attitude
- Listen to between the line messages – body language, expression, voice annotations
- Ask questions
- Go easy with arguments and criticism
- Stop talking
- Be patient
- Empathize with the speaker
- Hold your temper

### Factors that Help in Listening

1. **INTELLIGENCE:** Is an important factor that helps or hampers listening capabilities.
2. **VERBAL COMPETENCE:** It also plays a significant role, for there is a greater comprehension if one is familiar with the nuances of the language.
3. **MOTIVATION:** Boost the morale of the speaker, how well he motivates his listeners, arouses their interest and keeps them engrossed and alert.

## 10.3 PUBLIC SPEAKING

For an effective communicator etiquette also plays an important. Hierarchical communication is of utmost importance to all members involved.

Good speaker can earn a living by speaking to people in a public setting. Verbal communication is an essential part of business.

Speaking can be used as a tool to accomplish your objectives. Planning to manage the impression you create by consciously tailoring your remarks and delivery style to suit the situation. For effective communicator:

- Remember to become aware of what is being said.
- Think the purpose, main idea, and your audience.
- Organize thoughts in a logical way.
- Decide on a style that suits the occasion and then edit.
- While speaking watch the impression of the person communicating.
- Persuade speaking to inform, inspire and motivate.

The first step in making a speech is choosing a topic.

The second step is to define the purpose of your speech.

The third step is to get to know your audience.

The fourth step is to gather information for your speech. The sources of information, are interviews, the Internet, scholarly journals, government documents, newspapers, and magazines. Support your ideas with relevant examples.

The fifth step is to organize your speech. Start by identifying the main points, order them chronologically, problem-solution order if you are presenting a problem followed by a solution.

The sixth step is adding introduction to your speech. The introduction is aimed at getting the attention of your audience.

The seventh step is adding a conclusion to your speech. You can restate your main points, ending with a quotation that summarizes your main points, or by making a dramatic statement that emphasizes your main points.

## 10.4 DELIVERY OF SPEECH

### *The Audience*

It is desirable if the speaker has some knowledge of the people he is going to address. It is an advantage to know about the range of thoughts, likes and dislikes. He should also know something of the audience and the occasion, expectations from him, the duration of speech. Other speakers with him, the spirit of audience, the subject.

### *The Beginning*

The first impression made by a speaker may often determine his success or failure. A natural and easy posture should be assumed and the beginning should have a quite conversational voice. Modesty and confidence are required to make a successful start. A public speaker must be a leader. He should look into the eyes of his audience. This is an effective means of riveting their attention. This eye-to-eye communication will help to emphasize his words and estimate the effect of his words.

### *Progress*

There must be substantial progress by the speaker on his subject, for maintaining the interest. The tendency of the speech should be onward rising, with increase in volume of voice wherever needed, gravity of feeling, force of facial expression, and greater variety of gestures. For control over the audience, the prime importance for the speaker is to keep the flow of communication. One should not loosen his hold because sometimes it becomes doubtful if he could again gain control of them. Strong special points in the address should be prepared to lead up.

### *The Climax*

It is the duty of the speaker to lead his audience step by step because in every speech there is a point to be reached. The highest powers of vocal climax is reached by the speaker and is brought into play – voice, gesture, facial expression, and body movements, all are summoned to aid him in this final appeal.

### *The Close*

The climax should be concise, important and dignified. Close to the address a few words should be added in a quieter style if desirable. These words should be to the point. Speech should not falter towards the end, because that will be the final impression to be carried home by the listener.

### *Afterward*

After a speech is delivered the speaker should remain quiet to hear the response. He should give some consideration to the speech he has delivered, and understand the effect on his audience, to see how far it was successful and in what respects it failed. Honest criticism or praise voluntarily offered by others should be cheerfully accepted, but it is neither wise nor dignified to invite discussion of the merits of the speaker's address.

**General Suggestions**

1. Be simple.
2. Be clear
3. Speak with completeness of sentences, accurately and fluently.
4. Be natural.
5. Regulate the pitch and force of your voice
6. Do not speak fast, be clear with each word
7. Be yourself at your best.
8. Cultivate attentiveness.

## Necessity of Persistence and Secret of Good Delivery

Good delivery will make these matters go a long way.

Three things matter most in giving delivery:

1. Who says it.
2. How he says.
3. What he says.

First essential of a good talk is the sense of communication, your natural tone of eloquence matters a lot.

There is a single spark of individuality that makes one different – develop it – it's your only real claim to importance. Cling to your individuality. Cherish it and develop it.

Most famous debates of the world took place in 1858 between Senator Douglas and Abraham Lincoln.

**Lincoln:** Tall and humorous – rational, humble and forging low thinking.

**Douglas:** Quick flashes – rush of a whirlwind.

**Lincoln:** Quitter – deliberate and deeper. They were courageous and had good sense to themselves. Had they tried to imitate speech before an audience?

**Necessity of Persistence:** Keeping everlastingly to the job till it is achieved even after hundred defeats.

## Certainty of Reward

Keep yourself busy faithfully and with enthusiasm. Your success as a speaker and conversation depends on two things:

(a) Your native ability.

(b) Depth and strength of your desire, wish sincerely what you want to be.

Success in any thing depends on patience. Never despair.

**The will to win:** Confident walk, nice handshake complement an image of able, earnest and useful individual. Right mental attitude of courage, frankness and good cheer is necessary for a good delivery.

## How to Conquer your Nervousness of Speaking in Public

1. Don't expect to eliminate speakers fright simply to bring it under control. Being a little bit keyed up always makes for a better speech.
2. Being nervous about speaking in public is extremely common.
3. Prepare carefully. Knowing what to expect will reduce your nervousness.
4. Deep breathing and relaxation exercises are also helpful.
5. Aim for competence, nothing more.
6. Remember if you, in the end, perform badly, you will be no worse than many other speakers.
7. Concentrate on your topic, not on being in front of an audience.
8. If other techniques do not work, distract the attention of audience from yourself.
9. Think of giving out to the audience and (in a nice way) dominating them.

### *What Makes a Good Speaker?*

- The audience is your first concern, message second.
- Use comparisons and picture words.
- True speaking consists in saying all that should be said, not all that could be said.
- Use notes only if absolutely necessary.

- If you are asked to speak to a group, speak about your work or current interest
- Common shortcomings
    - Poor eye contact
    - Poor body language
    - No emphasis on keywords
    - No variety in tone

## Secrets of Good Conversation

- Be interested
- Be friendly
- Cheerful, good humoured
- Be animated yet relaxed
- Be flexible
- Be tactful
- Be courteous

### *8 Don'ts in Conversation*

- Don't be dogmatic
- Don't be condescending
- Don't be argumentative
- Don't be lifeless
- Don't be insincere
- Don't be egocentric
- Don't aim to be the life of the meeting; you may be the best speaker because you speak better than anyone else.
- Don't be a mumbler
- Speak clearly

## 10.5 BUSINESS ETIQUETTE

The forms, manners, and ceremonies established by convention as acceptable or required in social relations, in a profession, or in official life is business etiquette. Visual impact is the prime necessity in business etiquettes and it includes:

### *Visual Impact*

- Facial expression
- Body language
- Dress
- Grooming

*First Impression*

It is better *to be looked over* than overlooked:

- When you walk into a room, walk with a sense of purpose.
- You represent yourself and your organization.

An initial impression is made up of:

- Non-verbal perceptions (55%).
- Vocal quality (38%)
- Words (7%).
- First impressions are made within five seconds.
- Your eye contact, posture and smile say it all!

In today's competitive business environment, social skills and etiquette can mean the difference between finding and winning the job of your career and standing still in your career. To be successful in the business world, a person must use proper words. Following are some specific rules for addressing others in business settings:

- Superiors: Always address superiors with the appropriate gender-specific title, unless he/she gives express permission to do otherwise.
- Colleagues: It is a generally accepted procedure to address colleagues by the first name. Exceptions arise when the relationship is formal or unfamiliar.
- Subordinates: If the superior has established an informal relationship with the subordinate, use of the first names is appropriate. If the relationship is formal or unfamiliar, the appropriate gender-specific title is necessary.
- Clients and customers: Most relationships with clients or customers are formal, dictating appropriate gender-specific titles. Occasionally, though, an amiable relationship has been established and would allow the use of first names.

For proper business etiquette have a proper telephone procedure. Since much of today's business is done over the phone, using correct telephone etiquette is more important than ever. Lasting impressions may be formed during and after telephone conversations.

**Business Attire**

"What you wear speaks so loudly, I cannot hear what you say".

Dress makes a good impression in the business and corporate world. A cultured image factor in career advancement. A proper business attire represents the image you are presenting.

- A professional business attire reflects the personality of the person he wants to project.
- Wear dress in which you are comfortable and more at ease to attend a meeting or a business. Wear dress which suits your personality keeping in mind the professional standards. Be sure about the correct size.

- The clothes should be clean and well ironed.
- Avoid fashion fads in business. For girls/women do not wear gaudy jewellery.
- When attending business functions keep the business cards in a cardholder which is easily assessable.
- Give an organized look to your handbag or briefcase or carry files.

**Business** attire includes business suits, shirts, and ties for men. For women business-oriented suits for women, traditional dress- sari, suit or pant-shirt.

### *Five Rules of Personal Marketing*

- Exude confidence
- Create a powerful aura
- The art and science of impression management.
- Create a powerful verbal business introduction card.
- Develop a prosperity consciousness.

## Golden Rules of Good Manners

I–INTEGRITY: Act in an honest and truthful way
M–MANNERS: Never be selfish, undisciplined
P–PERSONALITY: Communicate your own values, attitudes and opinions
A–APPEARANCE: Always present yourself to the best advantage
C–CONSIDERATION: See yourself from the other person's standpoint
T–TACT: Think before you speak

### *Six P's of Personal Marketing*

- Persona
- Packaging
- Positioning
- Presentation
- Promotion
- Passion

## Successful Telephone Skills

Whenever you make a call or receive one at work, you are representing yourself and your department. The impression you make or create will be a lasting one. The voice in which you speak should reflect mannerism and show your alertness!

### *Answering the Phone*

Answer promptly when receiving the call

### *Identify Yourself*

Answer the call by giving the organization's/department's name and then your own name. The caller should also identify himself/herself and give reason for calling. Try to pronounce the caller's name distinctly. A person always likes the sound of his/her own name!

### *Try to be Helpful*

To avoid delays in the organization, handle as much of the business deal as you can yourself.

### *Leaving the Line*

If you need to obtain information by leaving the line, be courteous, give the caller the option of waiting or being called back. You might ask, "Would you prefer to hold?" or "Shall I call you back?" Let the caller know that he/she has not been disconnected or forgotten by giving the progress reports every 30 seconds or so. Thank the caller for waiting, when you return to the line.

## Your Telephone Voice

Volume while speaking should be loud enough to be heard. One can use different degrees of loudness for emphasis. Speak directly into the receiver for clarity.

- Normal rate of speech is 125 words per minute to keep the caller's interest.
- Focus on controlling the speech and avoid running words together.

### *Pitch and Voice Modulation*

Pitch is the highness and lowness of voice, changes in the pitch causes inflections.

- Identify key information you may want to emphasize and use appropriate inflections.
- Avoid talking in a one tone.

### *Fluency and Pronunciation*

- Articulate well and have proper pronunciation to one's credibility over the telephone.

### *Articulation*

It refers to the precision and clarity one uses in uttering sounds.

- Select the right words to communicate your message and plan an alternative way for presenting the information

### *Altitude and Enthusiasm*

- Altitudes, convictions, and emotions are conveyed through your voice; especially over the telephone.

- Do not use a voice that communicates indifference or irritation to the caller. This can lose your customer forever.

## Using the Telephone

- Speak at your natural volume
- Hold it around one inch from your lips
- Keep the receiver down gently
- Answer the phone with a "hello" or "who is calling please"?
- In office answer your name and dept.
- Be brief
- During long calls, write down the main points.

**Telephone Etiquette:** Before you answer be prepared with pens, pencils and notepaper handy.

*In answering the phone:*

- Answer calls promptly
- Greet the caller and identify yourself and your company/department/unit
- Smile while speaking it reflects on the phone.
- Controlling your volume and speed while talking.
- Be enthusiastic, natural, attentive and respectful with your tone.
- Ask, "To whom am I speaking?", or ask, "How may I help you?"

*In the course of the conversation:*

- Always speak calmly and choose your words naturally.
- Express clearly and distinctly.
- Use simple English and avoid unnecessary jargon and acronyms.
- Use active listening skills to clarify and check for understanding.
- Project a tone that is concerned, empathetic, and apologetic if there is a problem
- Avoid the phrase. "I don't know "Instead, use: "let me find out for you" or offer to connect.
- Be positive

**In concluding the call:**

- End the conversation with the agreement on what is to happen next.
- Thank the caller for calling; invite him to call again.

*In transferring calls:*

- Transfer ONLY when necessary; get the information yourself.
- Explain why you are "transferring" the call and say: "I am going to connect you with".

- Give the caller the person's name and direct number
- Stay on the line and introduce the caller.

*In taking messages:*

- Identify yourself and for whom you are answering the phone.
- Write down all the important information given: The name of the caller. Ask for spelling if unclear, telephone number, and message. Deliver the message timely.

### *Never*

- Eat, drink or chew while on the phone.
- Leave an open line.
- Place the caller on hold.
- Check back with the caller frequently: every 30-45 seconds.

### *Always*

- Put a smile in your telephone voice and let your personality shine!

## Conducting a Meeting

A well planned meeting requires proper attention in detail to accomplish its objectives. The organizer of the meeting is responsible for managing and maintaining the course of the meeting till its final result.

### *Planning Steps before Meeting*

- Seating arrangements: The guests of distinction should be seated in view of presenters, whiteboards, projection screens, or other points of visual interest. The important guests can be seated in a specified seat and others can choose their own. Latecomers can fill in empty places.

The defined purpose of your upcoming meeting should be known. The following steps should be taken:

1. Review the problem and determine the precise purpose.
   Take some time to write the central purpose of the meeting. Personal preparation adds to meeting effectiveness. Do your homework, collect information, check your data, and confirm your conclusions." I don't know" in response to the manager's question is harmful to your career. To put it mildly, be overprepared.
2. The Participants
   A small group (3 – 5 members) are usually a harmonious group for a regularly scheduled meetings. They may draft some preliminary information and lay out some options before going to a larger group.

3. Arrange for meeting date, time, place

   The time and date and venue should be intimated. E-mailing a reminder to participants.

   Be precise to location. If a change of venue is proposed inform both orally and by E-mail.

4. Create an agenda

   The roadmap for a meeting should be there with a proper agenda. Intimation in advance should be sent or distributed.

   Policy or procedure questions occupy most of your meeting: What should be done? What action should we take? Who should carry out a decision?

*Distribute the Notice for the Meeting*

The agenda for meeting should be decided on who, what, when, and where you are ready to send out the notice for the meeting. Some notices are simple and brief; others may be detailed.

*Check on Physical Arrangements*

- ☐ Select the seating pattern.
- ☐ Determine what kinds of materials are needed in the room.
- ☐ Have available the usual electronic visual aids.

## Procedures During the Meeting

Prepare an introductory remark and begin with an opening statement and introduce the guest. At the beginning, let the participants know the objectives to be accomplished in the allotted time. Even if the agenda is provided, to reaffirm the objective.

Encourage Discussion: If you act as the leader motivate all to participate, to give their views. Use a board or chart wherever necessary to write down the points. List the problems and the possible solutions. Then discuss. Keep the participants on the main path to keep the discussion moving. Set clear ground rules at the beginning so that the participants should understand whether they are expected to contribute to the conversation, or just listen, to keep the meeting on track. To avoid interruptions, switch off mobile phones or set on vibration mode.

An overview of the meeting has to be given to the new member by a competent team member or facilitator if he is asked to join a group, particularly a standing group that has already worked together.

Group task roles: Anyone may play these roles, even the chairperson.

Initiator-contributor
Information seeking
Opinion seeker
Opinion giver
Information giver

Elaborator
Coordinator
Orienter
Energizer
Recorder

Group building and maintenance roles: keeping the goals of the group in mind through group-centred attitudes characterize these roles.

Encourager
Harmonizer
Standard setter
Group observer
Compromiser
Follower

"Individual" roles: The emphasis here is self-oriented roles, often at odds with group building and maintenance roles.

Aggressor
Blocker
Help seeker
Dominator
Self-confessor

## Evaluation after Interpreting Data for Solution

Encourage and observe the advantages and disadvantages of the options given and then try to evaluate. Dot not impose opinions on the group.

Plan of action after the conclusion is made which should be clear for action. Conclude the meeting.

- ☐ Summarize.
- ☐ State individuals responsible for specific actions.
- ☐ Indicate the target time for the task to be completed.
- ☐ Extend thanks to the members for attending and completing the task.

## Follow-up after the Meeting

Final responsibilities of the leader: distribute the minutes of the meeting and responsible committees, departments or individuals are appointed to complete the decided upon actions. Minutes should include who and when a task is to be completed.

The minutes of the meeting should include the following:

- ☐ Name of the organization, department, or group.
- ☐ Date, time, place of meeting.
- ☐ Names of members present, including who chaired the meeting.

## Participants' Responsibilities in Meetings

### *Effective Participants' Roles in Meetings*

*Organizer:* Meetings should move with direction. As an organizer, steer the group back to main, central issues.

*Clarifier:* A clarifier tries to make the unclear ideas clear and point out misunderstandings.

*Questioner:* Questions raised need clarification and this has to fill in your knowledge gap. Be careful. When asking questions and know the difference between the critical or an insignificant question.

*Factual Contributor:* Substantial information can make a valuable contribution. Be positive in presenting factual information. Watch your tone and statements before giving information.

*Energizer:* Energy to the meeting is needed to keep the discussion moving, and stimulating members to reach their goal.

*Idea Creator:* The contributor risks the ideas that may be new, different, and even unusual. If you are an idea creator, you are willing to test an idea in the open forum of the meeting.

*Critical Tester:* Every meeting should have a person willing to challenge, tactfully, the validity and reasonableness of contributions. Focus on the idea, the consistent information, the clarity of language, the content, the evidence, the reasoning, whenever a misleading or inaccurate statement is made.

*Conciliator:* Deadlocks are common in meetings. Sometimes both sides refuse to shift; and violent disagreements occur. So a conciliators tries to convince the either party for a mutual agreement.

*Helper of Others:* A final role you can play is to invite other participants to join in. You do not wish to embarrass others, but try to help those who may feel inadequate or who are simply hesitant to speak up in the forum. Tact, sensitivity, and cooperativeness with the chairperson characterize this role.

### *Suggestions to the Participants in a Meeting*

- Be energetic, show honesty and integrity in the meeting.
- Use the agenda, for discussion so that the meeting leads in the right direction
- Listen to the discussion and then contribute. Also give opportunity to others to contribute, and encourage the non-contributors to share their views.
- When taking input from the group, limit the comments not to go beyond a specific time and let each person speak for a set period of time.
- The contradictions in the group should be resolved.
- Examine body language of the person for non-verbal disagreement.
- Do not interrupt when some other person is making a speech. Let his conversation finish then start your views.

- To show the speaker's point was heard ask follow-up questions.
- Acknowledge the valuable suggestion given by other participant.
- Arrive early to greet other attendees and get a sense of the mood.
- If presentation is to be made the slides should be systematically arranged.
- Put only a few words or one picture on a slide.
- Distribute handouts when the presentation is to be made.
- Use only as much time as you are given for your presentation.
- Practise answering in advance to handle questions from the audience.
- Thank the people who invited you to speak.

*Time Management in Conference/Meetings*

Whatever be one's style for conducting any important meeting, thorough planning is essential. Conference should not be allowed to be interrupted by visitors or telephone calls. New ideas and conflicting views are welcome, but no one should be allowed to digress from the main issue or switch over to unconnected routine issues or repeat what has been brought out earlier. These things are best left to brainstorming sessions.

Conferences are two-edged weapons. They should not make an excessive demand on participants' time and their frequency should not interfere with the normal routine of executives. Hence, the meeting must be well planned and the agenda and start/finish timings must be conveyed to members beforehand.

## Exercise-2 Effective Meetings

### QUESTIONNAIRE

Think of what is generally true of your group's meetings? If the statement expresses generally what happens at your meetings, check "Yes". If generally speaking, it is not true, check "No".

| | Yes | No |
|---|---|---|
| 1. Do your attend more than four meetings a week? | ___ | ___ |
| 2. Do you spend on an average 10-12 hrs on meetings a week? | ___ | ___ |
| 3. Are most of the meetings irrelevant as far as Your KRA's are concerned? | ___ | ___ |
| 4. Can you delegate some of these meetings to your subordinates? | ___ | ___ |
| 5. Do you find that you feel frustrated/angry at the end of most meetings? | ___ | ___ |
| 6. Do most meetings end without a sense of a accomplishment? | ___ | ___ |

7. Do most people attend meetings without being fully prepared? ____ ____
8. Do you find that the same few people talk most of the time? ____ ____
9. Do the same problems crop up at all meetings? ____ ____
10. Do most meetings extend beyond the stipulated time limits? ____ ____
11. Do most people seem indifferent to the meetings and are not really bothered about its outcome? ____ ____
12. The solutions and decisions are normally in accord with viewpoint of the chairman? ____ ____
13. Are people afraid to be frank and express their feelings? ____ ____
14. Do the meetings usually not begin and end on time? ____ ____

>10 Yes: You seem to be attending very unproductive meetings. You and your department could do well to examine your style of holding meetings.

>5-10 Yes: The chapter on effective meetings will help you have even more effective meetings.

>5 Yes: You can do well as a consultant on effective meetings!

## Guidelines for Effective Meetings

1. Circulate a clear written agenda to all the members at least two days before the meeting so that they can come prepared.
2. Start the meeting on time and end on time.
3. Start the meeting by defining the purpose and go systematically through each item on the agenda.
4. Listen actively.
5. Speak one person at a time.
6. Encourage active participation from all members.
7. Ensure that no one dominates the meetings.
8. Restate important points.
9. Make sure the meeting is not interrupted by telephone calls, etc.
10. Refrain from distracting behaviour like yawning, doodling, pencil rapping, etc.

11. Summarise the key points and decisions taken at the end.
12. After the meeting, question yourself: Did the meeting really contribute to my objective? How can I improve it in future?

## 10.6 INTERPERSONAL COMMUNICATION

The term "interpersonal skills" is used often in business contexts to refer to the measure of a person's ability to operate within business organizations through social communication and interactions.

Employers appreciate employees who get along with people at all levels; therefore, they seek employees who have good interpersonal skills, such as communication, problem solving, and teamwork abilities. Interpersonal skills enable you to work with others harmoniously and efficiently.

When our relationships with people are healthy, open, fulfilled and mutually rewarding, they enhance our lives and provide the cornerstone of future growth and development.

Interpersonal skills are all about working with other people. They include being able to support and encourage others, being able to give and receive constructive criticism as well as being able to negotiate. The key to healthy interpersonal relations lies in openness. The self-centred person would hardly be able to master excellence in human relations.

### Ten Ways to Improve Interpersonal Communication

- Smile.
- Be appreciative.
- Pay attention to others.

- Practise active listening.
- Bring people together.
- Resolves conflicts when they arise. Learn how to be an effective mediator.
- Communicate clearly. A clear and effective communicator avoids misunderstandings with coworkers, colleagues, and associates.
- See it from their side. Empathy means being able to put yourself in someone else's shoes and understand how they feel. Try to view situations and responses from another person's perspective.
- Don't complain.

## CASE STUDY

### The Case of Two Choices

Shyam was a manager of a restaurant. He was always in a good mood. When someone would ask him how he was doing, he would always reply, "If I were any better, I would be twins!" Many of the waiters at his restaurant quit their jobs when he changed jobs, so they could follow him around from restaurant to restaurant Why? Because Shyam was a natural motivator. If an employee was having a bad day, Shyam was always there, telling the employee how to look on the positive side of the situation.

Seeing this style really made me curious, so one day I went up to Shyam and asked him "I don't get it! No one can be a positive person all of the time. How do you do it?" Shyam replied, "Each morning I wake up and say to myself, I have two choices today. I can choose to be in a good mood or I can choose to be in a bad mood. I always choose to be in a good mood. Each time something bad happenes, I can choose to be victim or I can choose to learn from it. I always choose to learn from it. Every time someone comes to me complaining, I can choose to accept their complaining or I can point out the positive side of life.

I always choose the positive side of life." "But it's not always that easy," I protested. "Yes it is," Shyam said. "Life is all about choices. When you cut away all the junk every situation is a choice. You choose how you react to situations.

You choose how people will affect your mood.

Several years later,

I heard that Shyam accidentally did something you are never supposed to do in the restaurant business.

He left the back door of his restaurant open.

And then ??? In the morning, he was robbed by three armed men. They want?

While Shyam trying to open the safe box, his hand, shaking from nervousness, slipped off the combination. The robbers panicked and shot him. Luckily, Shyam was found quickly and rushed to the hospital. After 18 hours of surgery and weeks of intensive care, Shyam was released from the hospital with fragments of the bullets still in his body.... I saw Shyam about six months after the accident.

When I asked him how he was, he replied, "If I were any better, I'd be twins. Want to see my scars?" I declined to see his wounds, but did ask him what had gone through his mind as the robbery took place.

"The first thing that went through my mind was that I should have locked the back door," Shyam replied. "Then, after they shot me, as I lay on the floor, I remembered that I had two choices: I could choose to live or choose to die. I chose to live. Shyam continued, "The paramedics were great. They kept telling me I was going to be fine.

But when they wheeled me into the emergency room and I saw the expression on the faces of the doctors and nurses, I got really scared. I asked? In their eyes, I read 'He's a dead man.'

I knew I needed to take action.

"What did you do?" I asked "Well, there was a big nurse shouting questions at me," said Shyam. "She asked if I was allergic to anything 'Yes,' I replied."

The doctors and nurses stopped working as they waited for my reply. I took a deep breath and yelled, 'bullets!'

Over their laughter, I told them, "I am choosing to live. Please operate on me as if I am alive, not dead". Shyam lived. Thanks to the skill of his doctors, but also because of his amazing attitude.

I learnt from him that every day you have the choice to either enjoy your life or to hate it.

**The only thing that is truly yours — that no one can control or take from you — is your attitude, so if you can take care of that, everything else in life becomes much easier.**

### *Answer the following questions*

1. What was the idea of life according to Shyam? Do you agree the way he thought about two choices in life? If yes. Explain.
2. How does attitude play a big way in communication. Explain.

## SUMMARY

- Communication is always purposeful. The purpose of oral communication is to bring forth immediate and desired response. Written communication is to facilitate informed decisions and actions. Thus, while the objective of oral communication is to earn listeners, written is to earn a reader.
- Without proper communication nothing much would happen in an organization. Good communication oils the wheels of activity in an organization and facilitates action. The paperless office does not mean that oral communication is or will be more important than 'written'.

- Effective communication comprises the seven C's and four S's.
  Seven C's: Clarity, Completeness, Concreteness, Conciseness, Consideration, Correctness and Courtesy.
  Four S's: Shortness, Simplicity, Strength, and Sincerity.
- In an organisation, communication is a means:
- Internal communication is essential for every organisation, and is a tool for bonding the organization, improving the morale, counselling and promoting open-door policy and reducing grievances. The root cause of most of the problems ineffective communication within the organization.
- To engage and express fully as we communicate, we can keep in mind the following points, which will initiate a meaningful and pleasant conversation which are the positive attitude, being a good listener, to learn to master your emotions, ask effective questions, and maintain eye contact.
- Andrew Finlayson, author of *Questions That Work* advises seven elements to asking questions, which are awareness, ability, atmosphere, attitude, answer, appreciation and action. To listen is to pay attention to what someone is saying. It is a deliberate act of attentively hearing one person speak. Listening is a vital component of communication. It is determined by the extent to which listening and comprehension take place in the course of an interaction.
- Listening is an integrated process. It consists of the following phases: undivided attention, hearing, understanding, interpreting, evaluating, empathizing, and conceptualizing.
- Guidelines for listeners: Speak less listen more, concentrate on main points, examine the body language, focus on the speaker. Do not be part of the speaker, listen attentively, listen intelligently, avoid emotional contact, understand and then conclude, empathize with the speaker, respect the speaker as a person, listen with open mind, develop a rich vocabulary.
- Speaking can be used as a tool to accomplish your objectives. One must learn to manage the impression you create by consciously tailoring your remarks and delivery style to suit the situation. Some points which will make you an effective communicator are: remember to become aware of what you are saying; apply the same process you use in written communication when you are communicating orally; before you speak, think about your purpose, your main idea, and your audience; organize your thoughts in a logical way; decide on a style that suits the occasion and then edit your remarks mentally.
- In today's competitive business environment, social skills and proper etiquette can mean the difference between finding and winning the job of your career and standing still in your career. The key to proper business etiquette is: "Do unto others as they would want you to do unto them."
- Telephone etiquettes: Speak at your natural volume, hold it around one inch from your lips, keep the receiver down gently, answer the phone with a "hello" or "who is calling please"? In office answer your name and department, be brief, during long calls, and write down the main points.

- A well planned meeting requires proper attention in detail to accomplish its objectives. The following steps should be taken for planning a meeting: Review the problem and determine the precise purpose, determine the participants, arrange for meeting date, time, place, create an agenda, distribute the notice for the meeting.
- Interpersonal skills are used often in business contexts to refer to the measure of a person's ability to operate within business organizations through social communication and interactions. Employers appreciate employees who get along with people at all levels; therefore, they seek employees who have good interpersonal skills, such as communication, problem solving, and teamwork abilities. Interpersonal skills enable you to work with others harmoniously and efficiently.
- The seven techniques of improving relations runs as follows:
    - The six most important words – " I admit I made a mistake ".
    - The five most important words – " You did a good job ".
    - The four most important words – " What is your opinion ".
    - The three most important words – " If you please ".
    - The two most important words – " Thank you ".
    - The one most important words – " We ".
    - The least important word – "I".
- The components of interpersonal communication is leadership, networking and teamwork.
- Ten ways to improve interpersonal communication are: smile, be appreciative, pay attention to others, practise active listening, bring people together, resolve conflicts, communicate clearly, humour them, see it from their side, don't complain.

## QUESTIONS

### I. Explain in Brief

1. What are the seven C's and four S's of communication?
2. Mention five guidelines for listening improvement.
3. What is the need of communication in management?
4. What are the golden rules of good manners?
5. What are the eight don'ts of conversation?
6. Mention the seven techniques of improving relations.

### II. Answer the following questions.

1. Describe on completeness and courtesy the two C's of communication.
2. Write down the factors which are needed for listening. What is the difference between passive and active listening?

3. What are interpersonal relations? How can you maintain healthy interpersonal relations in an organization?
4. What etiquettes should a receiver keep in mind while answering a phone call?
5. Describe in detail, what an organizer of a meeting should keep in mind while conducting a meeting.

## ASSIGNMENTS

1. Visit a library. Read five articles and make a synopsis of the articles and present it before others.
2. Surf the first page of five multinational companies. Underline the seven C's of communication utilized by the company.
3. Listen to the TV advertisements and write down the slogans used by them.

## PROJECT

1. Divide into groups of 4-5 members each. Do brainstorming on the latest happening and make meetings for the above.
2. The class has to go for a industry interaction and visit a manufacturing industry. Make a communication plan for execution.

***Tips***

Short listing of industry: Visit to the industry, interaction with the concerned employee, written communication for visit, visiting the industry.

# 11 UNIT

# Work Life Success

## Learning Objectives

- Case Study – Enough Fish to Feed the Family
- Skills needed in the 21st Century
- Professionalism
- Steps Leading to Success
- Work Life Checklist
- Happiness in Life

### Enough Fish to Feed the Family

An investment banker was on the pier of a small coastal village when a small boat with just one fisherman docked. His boat was full of beautiful yellow tuna. The banker complimented the fisherman on his catch, asking how long it took to catch.

The fisherman replied, "Only a short time."

The banker asked why not stay out and catch more. The fisherman replied, "I've enough fish to feed my family."

The banker then asked what the fisherman did with the rest of his time. He replied, "I will sleep late, fish a little, play with my children, take a siesta with my wife, stroll into the village each evening, sip wine with my friends, play my guitar, I have a full and busy life."

The banker was not impressed. "I have a Harvard MBA and could help you. You should spend more time fishing and with the proceeds buy a bigger boat and from those increased proceeds you could buy several boats and soon have a fleet. Instead of selling your fish to a middleman, you could control production, processing and distribution by building your own cannery. You could leave this small coastal village and move to the city then to New York where you could run your expanding enterprise."

The fisherman asked, "How long will this take?"

The banker said, "Ten to twenty years."

"But what then?"

"Next you would announce an IPO and sell your stock to the public, making millions and millions. Then you could retire to a small coastal village where you could sleep late, fish a little, play with your kids, take a siesta with your wife, stroll in the village in the evenings, sip wine and play your guitar with your friends," said the banker smiling.

**Answer the Questions**

1. What according to you is meaning of life and work success?
2. What are the different approaches to life of the fisherman and banker? Which approach is agreeable to you and why?

## 11.1 SKILLS NEEDED IN THE 21ST CENTURY

On the threshold of change one has to chalk out the roadmap for growth and development in the 21st century.

- Communication
- Integrating knowledge from various disciplines
- Acquiring and processing information
- Synthesizing knowledge
- Research management
- Creative thinking, innovation
- Analytical skills
- Management skills
- Understanding of business environment
- Coping with conflicts
- Negotiation
- Interdisciplinary skills and knowledge
- Problem solving
- Entrepreneurship
- Ethics and values

- Social networking skills
- Computer science skills
- Language skills
- People and relationship managements skills
- Problem solving
- Art of persuasion

## 11.2 PROFESSIONALISM

Professionalism may be a virtue, what exactly is implied by being a professional is often found lacking in individuals and companies. The word 'professional' in the dictionary, means

1. One is something that is related to a job or profession.
2. The other means well-trained, or a person who is good at one's work.

A professional is dedicated to his/her job with an intention for fulfilment of targets assigned. Simply doing a job over and over again does not make us a professional.

### Qualities of Professionals

| | | |
|---|---|---|
| Dependability | : | The ability to be assigned a task and see it through despite all foreseen and unforeseen pitfalls. |
| Enterprising | : | The ability to put in one's 100% |
| Flexibility | : | The ability not to take on a rigid stance in case a situation demands a review or change in course of action |
| Integrity | : | The ability to ensure adherence to an ethical course of action |
| Knowledgeable | : | To be well informed abut the content of the job at hand |
| Inter-activity | : | To be able to create and maintain good rapport with one and all |
| Tolerate | : | To be able to view and accept and reject others' perceptions in an objective manner |
| Eagerness | : | The enthusiasm to learn. Assimilate and act creatively in a manner which benefits the organization optimally |

## How to be a Professional

1. Planning

   Planning for implementation is necessary. A proper goal should be targeted for this planning should be strategic.
2. Decision making

   Decision making shows how professional we are.
3. Communication

   How we communicate also shows how our professionalism. A doctor who explains a point to a worried patient is much better than one who simply writes out a prescription.
4. Doing our job

   Finally, our attitude gets reflected in the job that we do. Professionalism demands NO mistakes. It also means keeping an eye for details, however minute they may be.
5. Doing what is right

   A company which treats its workers well is professional. The moment we do something which we believe is wrong, we are not professional, no matter how many degrees we may have.

Professionalism is an attitude towards our work rather than anything else and it is acquired over a period of time. It is also the only way to survive in today's world.

Professionalism entails placing the interest while setting and maintaining clear standards of behaviour that emphasize compassion, competence, and integrity.

## CAREER IS A MARATHON: NOT A SPRINT, IT IS A JOURNEY

Success is to be measured not so much by the position one has reached in life, as by the obstacles which one has overcome while trying to succeed.

"Success depends on the ability to do better than good enough. One ought to shed the fear of the unknown and have the confidence to take risks, to experiment to think and act differently, and have belief in oneself."

### Think Positive

Say to yourself every morning:

- Today is going to be great day!
- I can handle more than I think I can!
- Things don't get better by worrying about them.
- I can be satisfied if I try to do my best!
- There is always something to be happy about!
- I'm going to make someone happy today!
- It's not good to be down!
- Life is great make the most of it!

## 11.3 STEPS LEADING YOU FOR SUCCESS

In an era of stiff competition, success can only be achieved if one makes the right kind of endeavour at the right time and in the right direction.

The following are the seven mantras for success:

1. Communication skills
2. Influencing abilities

3. Managing skills
4. Problem solving
5. Creative thinking
6. Social skills
7. Managing money: If in spite of possessing all the above-mentioned skills you fail to achieve success it may be because you are poor in the number game! You must have your figures, statistics and accounts in place. You must be shrewd in the money matters. As an old saying goes. "money begets money".

## EVERY JOURNEY STARTS WITH A SINGLE STEP

When you undertake a journey – you pack and take with you some essential items to take care of all possible eventualities.

Similarly, you are stepping out in a new world. You need to equip yourself with the right tools.

**Your own resolution to succeed is**
**More important than anything else**

### Butterfly's Struggle for Freedom

A boy was sitting in the garden of his house observing the wonders of nature. He saw the colourful flowers and the butterflies. His gaze suddenly went on a small opening of the tree where he saw a butterfly struggling to force its body out from the cocoon. After sometime he could not see any progress so he thought to help and removed the bit of the cocoon with the help of scissors.

The butterfly came out easily but with a swollen body, small withered wings.

The boy thought with his help the butterfly could avoid the struggle and help the butterfly enlarge and expand her wings and thus support the body.

Nothing of this sort happened. He felt sorry to see the butterfly crawl with its swollen body and wrinkled wings for rest of its life, never to be able to fly.

The impatience and hurriedness, usually spoils the work. The restricting cocoon and the struggle which the butterfly went through was to make her ready for the flight, after achieving freedom from the cocoon.

Struggles and obstacles help us to face the challenges and help us to be strong and determined so one should face them with a positive attitude.

## Achieveing Goals by Thinking

Once you've set realistic, measurable and time-bound goals, you've made a great start. Here are some guideposts:

1. Make a list of your goals where you can read them daily (next to your mirror, or on your wall or desk).
2. Regularly consider of your goals.
3. Use your imagination.
4. Be realistic and picture the obstacles you will have to face: obstacles within you and obstacles without.
5. Definite action steps will you take and when? Write them down. Remember that the longest journey starts with one small step.
6. The aids at hand for achieving your goal? What people and resources are needed?
7. Talk about your goals with others, especially with those who are skilled in the field.

**What you give is what you get.**

## Importance of Sense of Humour and Positive Thinking in One's Personality. How to Develop it

"God gave us sense of humour to prevent us from going mad". There are several problems in the present world and to overcome them, we must turn to the lighter side of life also.

Laughter: It saves from dwelling on things which lead to disasters, wise and humorous remarks can save several situations, human relations can be put on easier level.

Such remark should be natural and spontaneous and befitting to the occasion.

How to develop sense of humour:

1. Contemplate on things, which are happy and humorous, read funny stories and see funny films.
2. Cultivate an optimistic attitude in life, count your blessings, see good in everything.
3. Try to enjoy your work. Regard duties challenges, opportunities (do fast reading in the morning.)
4. Learn to take yourself less seriously.
5. Do not be self-centred.
6. Do not be too egoistic.

Have positive thinking: Stop lights – (red light) for one it is go ahead sign and others regard its frustration. Hard times either lead to failure or they prove as opportunities leading to success.

(a) I know what to do bust just I can't get to it.
(b) I could have done a lot better but I never had a chance.
(c) I am to old to try that.
(d) Clear the ground first.

You are the master of your mind, don't let bad intruders enter into it. Happiness, success, confidence, victory, goodwill can all be yours, in case you master the above-mentioned points. Living and growing is mainly to learn as to how you can solve the problems. Love and forgiveness be your watchwords.

Balloon seller and the boy.

Our attitude takes us up - ...........

Foundation of success is attitude or positive thinking.

They all can be good with their attitude – student, parents, teachers, salesman, employer, employees.

Benefits of positive thinking attitude: Better atmosphere, more productivity and profits, better relations, pleasing personality.

Negative attitude creates: 1. Bitterness 2. Resentment 3. Ill Health 4. Stress 5. Negative environment and becoming liability on society.

## MAPPING YOUR FUTURE

### *Ten Steps for Planning Your Career*

1. **Develop a career plan. Think about what you want to do and find out more about the kind of training, education, and skills you will need to achieve your career goal.**
2. **Assess your skills and interests. Think hard about what you enjoy, what you are good at.**
3. **Evaluate yourself**

   What are your greatest strengths?
   - What are your weaknesses (and what are you doing about them)?
   - Where do you want to be in five years? In ten?
   - What is your major and why did you choose it?
   - How did you choose to spend your summers while in university?
   - What courses in university did you most like and why?
   - What school activities did you get involved in?
   - What is your ideal job and why?
4. **Once you have found a career that matches your interests and skills, you are ready to set your career plan of personality you are, and the values you hold.**

   Steps to develop a career plan
   - Develop a career plan to determine your interests and skills.
   - Make a list of skills you have.
   - Once you have determined what career path you want to follow, assess what you need to do to prepare for that career.
5. **Research occupations. Find out more about the nature of the jobs that interest you, such as educational requirements, salary, working conditions, future outlook, and anything else that can help you narrow your focus.**
6. **Choose your career goal. Once you've decided what occupation matches up best with you, then you can begin developing a plan to reach your career goal.**
7. **Improve your communication skills**
   - Mind your language.
   - Follow through.
   - Deal with uncertainty.
   - Be an active listener.
   - Manage conflict.
   - Respond, don't "re-act."
   - Give feedback.
   - Invite participation.
   - Keep your team up-to-date.

- Connect personally with employees.
- Take advantage of communication resources.

8. **Learn about job hunting tips you prepare to graduate or move into the job market. Finding your first job can be both a rewarding or frustrating experience.**

   Here are some tips you may want to follow in your job search.

9. **Your resumé is critical to your job search. It is the first impression you give to an employer. If your resumé is poorly organized or presented, you'll have less chance of landing a job.**

   Include your name, address, phone number, education, and work experience on your resumé. You also may want to include the following:

   - Job objective: state what type of position you want
   - Awards and honours

   When you apply for a position, include a cover letter stating why your qualifications fit the particular position and why you want to work with the company. A good resumé and cover letter, perhaps with a follow-up letter, should lead to an interview.

10. **A job interview can make even the most self-confident person nervous. Preparation is the key to getting over those pre-interview jitters.**

    1. Make sure you understand your own accomplishments. If you were asked to talk about yourself or what you've done, what would you say?
    2. Find about the company interviewing you. Many companies have websites with valuable information. Why do you want to work there? You need to answer that question during the interview. Also, it gives you an opportunity to decide if the job is right for you. Does it suit your career plan.
    3. Think of some questions you may be asked in the interview and have some well thought-out answers. With this in mind, be ready for some curve balls — an interviewer may ask you some unexpected questions.
    4. Arrive on time. Don't schedule other appointments too close to your interview time. You don't want to be late, and you don't want to rush out of the interview to your next appointment.
    5. Following the interview, immediately send a "thank-you" letter to the interviewer. This is an opportunity to thank them for their time, to remind them of your qualifications, and to affirm your desire for the position.
    6. Some tips for handling the interview:
       - Dress appropriately.
       - Bring extra copies of your resume.
       - Treat everyone with courtesy.
       - Don't be nervous about being nervous.
       - Don't discuss money in the interview. Wait until you are offered the position.
       - Be yourself.

Getting ready for the interview is not so complex as it appears. You cannot fit yourself to a new personality just because you are appearing for a civil services interview. The most important thing to remember is that we should be what we are. Hence, one has to be relaxed and be at his best, which is possible by avoiding any anxiety or worries about one's performance. There are few dos and don'ts which you should remember while trying to project yourself as warm, sensitive, respectful, and attentive youngster. Remember it is important that you realize the significance of each of these adjectives.

## 11.4 WORK LIFE CHECKLIST

Essential requirements to make your personality felt include:

- Speak only the truth and nothing but the truth. This is not only to defend but also considered more convenient.
- You will be asked questions. Not the right word. The board makes "statements" and the candidates "respond". The board always searches the areas which you are familiar so that they can make you converse with them.
- Keenly follow what is asked to you. You must be extremely alert while listening to the board members.
- Never make any categorical statements or express strong views on any of the current happenings. You should always be preface or bring expressions such as: "far as my knowledge goes," "what have I understand from what I have read," etc.
- Always make an attempt to break the question into its constituent parts and then proceed analytically. If you are no table to tackle all the parts then you can frankly express your inability to justice to some part of the question.
- Be cool and calm as far as you can. You should look pleasant in appearance particularly when you are not able to tackle the question.

### What to Read?

- Read newspaper carefully.
- Every detail in the application form including the meaning of your surname.
- Today's issue of interest, primarily national and to some extent international themes.
- Good knowledge of one's own state and district.
- Whenever required you may have to bring into focus the knowledge of your own specialized field of study. Including the papers, which you have offered for the main examination.

## Some Dos and Don'ts

- Never distrust the board or any member of the board. Please remember that the board knows more than you.
- Do not get irritated when the board interrupts your talks. The board always keeps you in the twilight on confidence and nervousness. This is a tactic that every interviewing authority pursues.
- Show a feeling of nearness towards the members of the board, that is you are capable of joining the members of the administrators.
- Never judge the board or any individual members while you are with them. Reserve your judgment till the time you are out of the room.
- Avoid all the conversational clichés such as "as you know", "of course", "indeed", "obviously", etc.
- Never put a glum face during the interview. Now and then you can appear serious, but most of the time keep smiling.
- Show human concern for other people whenever possible in your answers.

**Dress**: The board would like to know how would you look like as an officer during formal official gatherings. It is also considered a mark of respect towards the board and your dress shows how seriously you have taken the occasion.

## 11.5 HAPPINESS IN LIFE

### Twenty-Five Ways to Live Happily

Positive thinking is a panacea for keeping many ailments at bay. Start your day in the morning in pleasant mood and retire to bed on a happy note and you will notice spectacular change in the personality. Observe regularly the 25 points given below and experience the improvement in yourself.

1. Smile, one smile makes two.
2. Listen more and talk less.
3. Learn to relax.
4. Practise meditation regularly.
5. Retreat into silence atleast one hour a day.
6. Put away a small sum everyday for charity.
7. Plan your day so that you have time for all the things you want to do.
8. Think positively, avoid negative thoughts.
9. Remember to think "can" instead of "can't", "misplaced" instead of "lost", "better" instead of "worse".
10. Do atleast one good deed everyday; build up the number gradually.
11. Look for the good in others, there is so much of it.
12. Share everything you have cheerfully; books, records, tapes, recipes and skills.
13. Remember birthdays and anniversaries with a phone call, a card, a visit or a gift. Everyone likes to be remembered.
14. Show appreciation to the smallest service by your loved ones or employees.
15. Believe in the organisation or association you work for.
16. Be courteous and respectful to elders.
17. Enjoy your work. Dispose of jobs in hand quickly and competently.
18. Be more courteous when driving or using public transport.
19. Open doors for people behind you instead of slamming them in their faces.
20. Pick up a stone or rubbish in your path, it may hurt somebody.
21. Keep the roads in front and at the back of your house clean.
22. Stop people cutting trees from doing so.
23. Treat public property as your own.
24. Keep the volume of voice, radio and television low.
25. Take warmth, sunshine and humour with your wherever you go.

## Tips to Healthy Happiness

- Some people worry because they do not have anything to worry about.
- If we think happy thoughts we will be happy, if we think miserable thoughts, we will be miserable, if we think of fearful thoughts we will be fearful.
- Allowing emotions to govern one's actions bring failure. Acting with restrain brings success.
- Happiness results from discipline. A regular life is essential for happiness.
- Nature gave you your face, but you have to provide the expression.
- Happy memories require preparation.

- Getters generally don't get happiness; givers get it.
- If you are patient in one moment of anger, you will escape a hundred days of sorrow.
- "What the mind of a man can conceive, and believe, it can achieve." Conceive HAPPINESS.
- One should be honest and also appear to be honest.
- One small deed accomplishes more than a thousand words.
- Some of our problems are self-inflicted.
- Staying calm is the best way to take the wind out of an angry person's sails.
- Practise abstinence, for riches will not last.
- Take time off to make yourself happy. Use your prosperity, SUBSTRACT your worries, MULTIPLY your happiness, and DIVIDE your problems with equal number of solutions!
- Don't worry, be happy!!

## Balance of Life

*Our Birth is our Opening Balance*
*Our Death is our Closing Balance*
*Our Prejudiced Views are our Liabilities*
*Our Creative Ideas are our Assets*
*Heart is our Current Asset*
*Soul is our Fixed Asset*
*Brain is our Fixed Deposit*
*Thinking is our Current Account*
*Achievements are our Capital*
*Character and Morals are our Stock-in-Trade*
*Friends are our General Reserves*
*Values and Behaviour are our Goodwill*
*Patience is our Interest Earned*
*Love is our Dividend*
*Children are our Bonus Issues*
*Education is Brands/Patents*
*Knowledge is our Investment*
*Experience is our Premium Account*
*The Aim is to Tally the Balance Sheet accurately.*
*The Goal is to get the Best Presented Accounts Award Our Birth is our Opening Balance*
*Our Death is our Closing Balance*

Let's learn to control the mind !!

**See Things Differently**

- You can't do things differently until you see things differently.
- Your mind is a bank account. Deposit in it good ideas, positive thoughts and pleasant experiences. For example, refuse to view sub-standard TV or video programmes. The result? You can draw good ideas.
- Your mind is a computer and therefore is programmable.
- Your mind is a "thought factory". You are the production manager. It can produce either positive or negative thoughts. Ideas of others are your raw material.
- Fight for a king, queen and bishops, but throw away the pawns, a habit of graceful surrender on trivial issues, will make your difficult to resist when you stand and fight on a major issue.
- Listen to others but see your own judgment.
- Mistakes are the best teachers.
- Never expect gratitude. In case you get it. Be pleasantly surprised.
- Never pay a compliment as if you expect a receipt.
- A lightning call is the result of a postcard not having been mailed when it should have been.
- Ninety-six per cent of the old records and letters are never referred to again.
- Banks are just like any business. They are out to make profits. Do not put all your business in one bank.
- A grain of sand or a grain of wheat, contains more knowledge than a library; all we have to do is to ask, ask, and ask.

- A budget is a challenge.
- Creativity is not a function of size. Small is beautiful, a smart chartered accountant may be more effective than the biggest accounting firm.
- Don't be afraid of your auditors, massage their egos and they will help you to improve your profits by telling you about avoidable activities.
- Before you kick the dog, find out the name of its master.
- Not even the most productive cow can be milked forever without investment.
- Be patient while analyzing and impatient while executing.

## To Achieve your Dreams Remember the ABC's

**A**void negative attitude, people and habits
**B**elieve in Self
**C**onsider things from every angle
**D**on't give up and don't give in
**E**njoy life today; yesterday is gone and tomorrow may never come
**F**amily and friends are hidden treasures; seek them and enjoy their riches
**G**ive more than you planned to
**H**ang on your vision/dreams
**I**gnore the ones who try to discourage you
**J**ust be on the right track
**K**eep trying till you achieve; things will get easier
**L**ove self first and most
**M**ake things happen to you
**N**ever cheat self and others
**O**pen your eyes and see things as they really are
**P**ractice makes life perfect
**Q**uitters never win; winners never quit
**R**ead, study and learn about everything important in life
**S**top procrastinating
**T**ake control of your task/identity
**U**nderstanding yourself in order to better understand others
**V**isualize your dreams
**W**ant more, exploit your potential
**X**cellerate your efforts
**Y**ou are God's creation; nothing can replace you
**Z**ero in on your target and go for it

### Quotes

Holding your head high, And being the best you know you can be
When life seems to fall apart at your feet,
Facing each difficulty with the confidence
That time will bring you better tomorrow
And never giving up,
............... means CONFIDENCE

To the question of your life,
You are the only answer.
To the problems of your life,
You are the only solution.

When you keep saying you are busy,
Then you are never free.
When you keep saying you have no time,
Then you will never have time.
When you keep saying you will do it tomorrow,
Then your tomorrow will never come.

Time is like a river.
You cannot touch the same river twice,
The flow which has passed will never pass again.
Enjoy every moment of life..................

Treasure every moment that you have because...
"Yesterday is history.
Tomorrow is a mystery. Today is a gift.
That's why it's called the present.'

Winning doesn't always mean being first,
Winning means you're
Doing better than you have done before.....

## CASE STUDY

### Struggle for Achievement

Prateek was showing his children an aquarium full of tadpoles. He had bought a whole bag full of them to show his children to watch them grow into frogs. The children enjoyed the whole day watching the tadpoles swim in the aquarium! The children noticed a big rock in the aquarium and asked their father about it, why he had put a rock right in the middle of the tadpoles' environment, Prateek told them an interesting story.

He said that he was instructed by the salesman to be sure to "put a big rock right in the middle of the aquarium." He explained that "there should be some incentive for the tadpoles to face the obstacle to climb up and thus split their little wiggly tails so that their legs can begin to develop. If there is no rock or obstacle to climb up, the tadpoles will never turn into frogs. They wouldn't be able to learn how to hop by just swimming around in water. There must be some resistance to give them the incentive to leap forward.

The salesman went on to tell Prateek that one school teacher had come back to the store and complained that the tadpoles she had taken did not turn into frogs. He asked her if she had put a big obstacle, like a rock, in the middle of the aquarium. She had not put an obstacle in the aquarium so the tadpole remained a tadpole because they did not face any obstacle or barrier that could have forced them to grow.

The children were amazed and delighted to hear that story. The father wanted them to know that life presents obstacles and barriers before us, but they are there to cause us to grow. Our attitude makes lot of difference and helps to realize that the obstacle we are facing is really a gift that has come our way to help us grow and mature, we will be much more likely to face it in a positive manner.

The children watched those tadpoles all night to see them convert into frogs by facing the obstacle of big rock in their aquarium. They now understood that obstacles are the stepping stones to help us leap forward in whatever situation we find themselves. They now knew that, the harder they study the result will be more fruitful.

Most of us have no idea of what our life will be. We don't understand that the barriers and obstacles, challenges, difficulties and hard times that come our way each day are actually there for a purpose. Hard work and struggle come our way and give us the incentive to grow, or to become better, or to strive harder.

So, when you see a frog hopping around, thank him for the lesson and smile at him, and remember the struggle he had gone through the wild somewhere, facing the barrier in his life and develop his personal strength to hop around.

### *Answer the Questions*

1. What do you signify by the story? What are the learnings?
2. Explain an incidence in your life and how did you come out of it.

## DID YOU KNOW?

Eagle senses when the storm is approaching before it breaks. The eagle flies to a high spot and waits for the storm to come by setting its wings. It believes that the wind will lift it up above the storm and it will be soaring high above while the storm will rage below.

The eagle does not escape the storm. But it uses the storm to lift it and rises on the winds that bring the storm.

Storms (sickness, tragedy, failure and disappointment) are like challenges of life – we all experience them – we all can rise above them by setting our goals and belief in self.

It is not the burdens of life that weigh us down, it is how we handle them.

## CHANAKYA QUOTES
## (INDIAN POLITICIAN, STRATEGIST AND WRITER, 350 BC – 75 BC)

1. "A person should not be too honest. Straight trees are cut first and honest people are cut down first."

*************************************************************************************

2. "Even if a snake is not poisonous, it should pretend to be venomous."

*************************************************************************************

3. "The biggest guru-mantra is: Never share your secrets with anybody! It will destroy you."

*************************************************************************************

4. "There is some self-interest behind every friendship. There is no friendship without self-interest. This is a bitter truth."

*************************************************************************************

5. "Before you start some work, always ask yourself three questions - Why am I doing it, What the results might be and Will I be successful. Only when you think deeply and find satisfactory answers to these questions, go ahead."

*************************************************************************************

6. "As soon as the fear approaches near, attack and destroy it."

*************************************************************************************

7. The world's biggest power is the youth and beauty of a woman."

*************************************************************************************

8. "Once you start working on something, don't be afraid of failure and don't abandon it. People who work sincerely are the happiest."

*************************************************************************************

9. "The fragrance of flowers spreads only in the direction of the wind. But the goodness of a person spreads in all directions."

*************************************************************************************

10. "A man is great by deeds, not by birth."

*************************************************************************************

11. "Never make friends with people who are above or below you in status. Such friendships will never give you any happiness."

*************************************************************************************

12. "Treat your kid like a darling for the first five years. For the next five years, scold them. By the time they turn sixteen, treat them like a friend. Your grown up children are your best friends."

*************************************************************************************

13. "Books are as useful to a stupid person as a mirror is useful to a blind person."

*************************************************************************************

14. "Education is the best friend. An educated person is respected everywhere. Education beats the beauty and the youth."

## A Few Points to Remember

1. To create your own thoughts, feelings and actions.
2. Situations do not affect us. It is the view we take of the situation which affects us.
3. There are always different possibilities of looking at situations. You have the power to change your perception. Remember that perceptual alternatives are open to you. You can tap the potential of the progressive power of positive perception.
4. Action ....... Choosing the active line, creating, doing, achieving through choice. Reaction ........ Prisoner of habit, passive, reacting, blaming, helpless.
5. Thoughts, beliefs, perceptions
   ↓
   Emotions, Feelings
   ↓
   Actions
6. You are beyond all conclusions about yourself. A growing process never concludes.
7. Everything in life will strengthen me. Everything will nourish me.

A
VISION WITHOUT ABILITY TO
EXECUTE
IS
**PROBABLY A**
***HALLUCINATION***

CONFIDENCE COMES FROM NOT
ALWAYS BEING RIGHT
BUT FROM NOT FEARING
TO BE WRONG

THOSE WHO MAKE THE WORST USE OF

**THEIR TIME**

ARE THE FIRST TO ***COMPLAIN***
OF **ITS SCARCITY**.

**WILL** IS THE ONLY DIFFERENCE BETWEEN THE IMPOSSIBLE
&
THE POSSIBLE

**P**ROPER
**P**RIOR **P**LANNING
**P**REVENTS
**P**OOR
**P**ERFORMANCE.

**THERE IS NO LIMIT TO WHAT A MAN CAN ACCOMPLISH, IF HE DOESN'T CARE WHO GETS THE CREDIT.**

**FIRST ORGANISE THE NEAR AT HAND,**
THEN *ORGANISE* THE FAR REMOVED.
**FIRST ORGANISE THE INNER,**
THEN *ORGANISE* THE OUTER.
**FIRST ORGANISE THE BASIC,**
THEN *ORGANISE* THE DERIVATIVE.
**FIRST ORGANISE THE STRONG,**
THEN *ORGANISE* THE WEAK.
**FIRST ORGANISE THE GREAT,**
THEN *ORGANISE* THE SMALL.
**FIRST ORGANISE YOURSELF,**
THEN *ORGANISE* OTHERS.

***HE WHO KNOWS NOT ,***
***AND KNOWS NOT THAT HE KNOWS NOT .***
***He is a Fool. SHUN him.***
***HE WHO KNOWS NOT,***
***AND KNOWS THAT HE KNOWS NOT***
***He is Ignorant. TEACH him.***
***HE WHO KNOWS ,***
***AND KNOWS NOT THAT HE KNOWS***
***He is Asleep, AWAKE him.***
***HE WHO KNOWS,***
***AND KNOWS THAT HE KNOWS***
***He is Wise, FOLLOW him.***
*- an Arabic Saying*

**MOST OF US HAVE A DESIRE**
**TO LOOK**
**AT THE EXCEPTION**
**INSTEAD OF THE DESIRE**
**TO BECOME**
**EXCEPTIONAL**

**EVERYONE IS AN EXPLORER. HOW COULD YOU POSSIBLY LIVE YOUR LIFE LOOKING AT A DOOR**

**AND NOT OPEN IT.**

## SUMMARY

- What exactly is implied by being a professional is often found lacking in individuals and companies.

   1. Ten Steps to Planning Your Career: 1. Develop a career plan. 2. Assess your skills and interest. Think hard about what you enjoy, what you are good at. 3. Evaluate yourself. Once you have found a career that matches your interests and skills, you are ready to set your career plan of personality you are, and the values you hold. 5. Research occupations. 6. Choose your career goal. Once you've decided what occupation matches up best with you, then you can begin developing a plan to reach your career goal. 7. Improve your communication skills 8. Learn about job hunting tips you prepare to graduate or move into the job market. 9. Prepare your resumé is critical to your job search. 10. A job interview can make even the most self-confident person nervous. Preparation is the key to getting over those pre-interview jitters.

- Positive thinking is a panacea for keeping many ailments at bay. Start your day in the morning in pleasant mood and retire to bed on a happy note and you will notice spectacular change in your personality.

## QUESTIONS

### I. Explain in brief

1. Mention ten skills which an individual should possess in the 21$^{st}$ century for his career growth.
2. List down five qualities which are essential for a professional.
3. Evaluate yourself and prepare a checklist of your personality.
4. Why is change essential in today's scenario?
5. Write down what do you mean by A, F, H in ABC of your dreams to be achieved.
6. Do you dream? Write down a list of your dreams.

### II. Answer the following questions

1. What is professionalism? Write down the tools for increasing individual professionalism.
2. Write down some guidelines for achievement of your goals by thinking.
3. Explain in detail each step leading you for success.
4. "What the mind of a man can conceive, and believe, it can achieve." Discuss.
5. Write down ten points required for living happily. List down five points which are required by you for your self improvement.
6. What do you understand by happiness ? Explain by giving examples.
7. Explain ten steps to planning your career. Outline your career plan.
8. "A man is great by deeds, not by birth." — Chanakya. Explain in detail and discuss in a group discussion.

# Index

## T



## U



## V



## W